9781849040891

JSCSC Library

Date: -4 MAY 2011

Class Mark: 1: 355 COK

5c

Hobson Library
302991

BARBAROUS PHILOSOPHERS

CHRISTOPHER COKER

Barbarous Philosophers

*Reflections on the Nature of War
from Heraclitus to Heisenberg*

HURST & COMPANY, LONDON

First published in the United Kingdom in 2010 by
C. Hurst & Co. (Publishers) Ltd.,
41 Great Russell Street, London, WC1B 3PL
© Christopher Coker 2010
All rights reserved.
Printed in India

The right of Christopher Coker to be identified as the author
of this publication is asserted by him in accordance with
the Copyright, Designs and Patents Act, 1988.

A Cataloguing-in-Publication data record for this book
is available from the British Library.

ISBN 978-1-84904-089-1 (*hardback*)

This book is printed using paper from registered sustainable
and managed sources.

www.hurstpub.co.uk

CONTENTS

Part One
War and Philosophy

1. Rousseau's Complaint — 3
2. The Dialectics of Warfare: War and Peace — 11
3. Pascal's Rules — 37

Part Two
The Nature of War

4. Why War? Why war changes the world and is itself transformed by the changes it promotes (Heraclitus of Ephesus c.540–480 BC) — 47
5. War and Human Ambition: Why the rules of war are paradoxical (Thucydides c.460–400 BC) — 63
6. War and the Soul: Why war is Trinitarian (Plato (1) c.427–347 BC) — 77
7. War and Art: Why war encourages imitation (Plato (2)) — 89
8. War and Politics: Why war is a continuation of politics by other means, and not its negation (Aristotle 384–322 BC) — 107
9. War as Pacification: Why war can be seen as policing (Tacitus AD 54–120) — 117
10. War and Peace: Why peace is a contested concept (St Augustine AD 354–430) — 129
11. War and Social Norms: Why we still distrust mercenaries (Machiavelli 1469–1527) — 139
12. War and Human Nature: Why war (unlike warfare) encourages competitiveness, not competition (Thomas Hobbes 1588–1679) — 153

CONTENTS

13. War and Battle: Why battles are rarely 'decisive' (Montesquieu 1689–1755)   169
14. War and Ethics: Why we should respect our enemies even if they don't respect us (Immanuel Kant 1724–1804)   179
15. War and History: Why war is often 'ethical' (or progressive) (Hegel 1770–1831)   193
16. War and Technology: Why weapons have a social history (Marx 1818–83)   207
17. War and Culture: Why war has its own 'cultural grammar' (Engels 1820–95)   221
18. War and the Warrior: Why the warrior is a human type (Nietzsche 1844–1900)   233
19. War and the Future: Why war is not a science (Heisenberg 1901–76)   245

Bibliography   259
Index   273

'In war genius is thought in action.'

(Honoré de Balzac (ed.), *Napoleon: Aphorisms and Thoughts*, No. 116)

'Isn't war just another way of writing and speaking their [the peoples'] and the government's] thoughts?'

(Clausewitz, *On War*, Book 8, Chapter 6)

Part One

War and Philosophy

1
ROUSSEAU'S COMPLAINT

I open books on law and ethics and listen to the scholars and legal experts. Permeated with their persuasive talk ... I admire the peace and justice established by the civil order, bless the wisdom of public institutions ... well versed in my duties and happiness, I shut my book, leave the classroom and look around me. I see unfortunate nations groaning under yokes of iron, the human race crushed by a handful of oppressors, a starving crowd overwhelmed with pain and hunger ... and everywhere the strong armed against the weak with the power of law ... I raise my eyes and look into the distance. I see fires and flames, the countryside deserted, towns pillaged ... I hear a terrible sound: what an uproar. I draw near; I see a scene of murder, 10,000 butchered men, the dead piled in heaps, the dying trampled under horses' hooves, everywhere the face of death and agony ... so this is the fruit of those peaceful institutions. Barbarous philosopher! Come and read us your book on the field of battle.

(Rousseau, 2002, pp. 422–3)

Rousseau set out with two purposes in his short essay on war, written at the height of the Enlightenment's confidence in the future. One was to contrast the so-called civility of the European way of war with the true state of affairs, to contrast the philosophical with the real. The other was to show why it was foolish to think that war could be rule-bound, or humanized, that it could be constrained by ethical protocols, laws and conventions. It was wrong of the philosophers—it was simply 'barbarous' (a better and more apt word would be 'unthinking')—to try to philosophize war, to do anything that made it possible.

How could men ever be happy when a state could find itself at war with its neighbour at any time? True neighbours should live at peace—hence the invention of diplomacy, but the attempt to avoid war did not lessen its frequency. Instead, by 'civilizing' the practice it had made collective organized violence possible for humanity (Hinsley, 1967, pp. 49–50). No institution, he insisted, could be justified unless it promoted the happiness of mankind.

Rousseau's critique can be faulted on many counts, one of which was his reading of human nature. He believed that human beings were, by nature, sociable and peaceful. Only states made them, in his felicitous if misleading phrase, 'accidental soldiers'. Only when in uniform were they willing to kill each other with a good conscience. In giving a soldier the right to take the life of another soldier, the state effectively absolved him of his own humanity: the respect he should show another man as a member of the human race.

He only arrived at this conclusion, of course, by denying that warfare was as endemic in man's original state as Hobbes and many others supposed. Hobbes' state of nature is one of *zero-sum* game survival; it is a world in which conflict is powered by negative emotions such as anxiety, anger and sadness. Rousseau's world is driven by sexual selection—it is a *positive-sum* game process that favours virtue and is governed by positive emotions. In reality, most of us accept that life is driven by both.

But the point Rousseau is making is that it is only when man contracts out of the state of nature into a 'state' that negative *zero-sum* conflict tends to prevail. It is for this reason that we need to ground our actions on moral codes. Morality does not inhere in our nature, but our attempts on leaving the state of nature to rediscover it in society. Once we leave the state of nature we are no longer creatures of instinct, but creatures of history, and we can only re-affirm our commitment to our common nature through the medium of a community of citizens. It is our own humanity that makes us so anxious to secure the good of others. It is those moments of compassion for others which make us civilized. It is this 'becoming' which fuels the process of self-creation. We are united through our common alienation from the world. 'It is man's weakness which makes him sociable; it is our common misery which turns our hearts to humanity.' Through compassion we are united with our fellow sufferers and, at the same time, reunited with ourselves—we are no longer the divided selves which we have been since leaving the state of nature (Froese, 2001, p. 73). Our humanity, in a word, is the product of an historical process; it evolves over time. It just happened to have evolved (in Rousseau's view, of course) furthest in Europe, at a particular historical moment: the eighteenth century.

It is worth remembering here that Rousseau might have been critical of life outside the state of nature, but the picture he paints of it was not one that he himself found especially attractive. It is a world without violence, of course, because there is no private property; everything is held in common. But it is also lifeless. Men are happy only because they are not yet moral beings. Only civilized men can realize their potentialities. Rousseau's contention was that the civilization they had forged on leaving the state of nature was imperfect and unrealized (not least because war was one of its prevailing features). He did not want humanity to return to its earlier state (as Voltaire believed—or rather chose to when he wrote to Rousseau that his *Discourse on Inequality* would encourage men once again to walk on all fours). He wanted instead to improve human behaviour which meant, of course, forging a world without war. His case against the philosophers was that in the attempt to try to fine-tune (or humanize it) they had merely perpetuated it as a social institution.

He was objecting, unfortunately, to the paradoxical nature of life. He regretted that the alternative to the state of nature was not a perfect society but an imperfectly conceived one; he regretted that the attempt to limit war (to give it rules) had indeed made it possible for humanity. Like all essentializers he disliked complexity (which is in turn why the French revolutionaries took him to heart and canonized him as St Jacques). He also did not foresee a further paradoxical outcome partly of his own making: once you identify yourself with suffering humanity you may choose to fight in its name. Modern history furnishes many examples of fraternity—Garibaldi enlisting in the French war effort in 1870; the central European Jewish communists who fought and died in the French Resistance, the Spanish Republicans who were among the first to liberate Paris in August 1944. Ironically, he did not foresee that for the next two centuries the Europeans (followed by the Americans) would go to war for mankind—to make the world safe for democracy or in the case of Kosovo (1999) to fight the very first (and possibly last) 'humanitarian war'.

Rousseau was not alone in his criticism of philosophy. In expressing these views he was speaking for an age. Philosophy, Hegel reminds us, is thought frozen in time. We are all creatures of the times; our thoughts are historical through and through. In his *Philosophical Dic-*

tionary (1764) Voltaire mounted a similar attack. The *Dictionary* is a product of his later years (it appeared a few years after *Candide*). As one would expect of the self-professed great atheist of the age, Voltaire's main target was religion but he was also bitterly critical of war, the most devastating of what he called ironically 'the fine arts'. And for him the most extraordinary part of the 'infernal enterprise' was that the states who engaged in war had their flags blessed by the priests and their principles justified by philosophers. 'Moral philosophers! Burn all your books ... humanity, beneficence, modesty, temperance, mildness, wisdom and piety: what do they .... matter to me while half a pound of lead, shot from the distance of six hundred steps, shatters my body...' (Voltaire, 2006, p. 231). If the philosophers had spent half as much time condemning war as they had in drawing up 'laws of war' and norms of good practice, humanity would be in their debt much more.

Both philosophers attacked their own profession on two counts. First, in talking up 'peace' they had ignored the extent to which they had also insisted that it was a product of war. Had not Aristotle insisted that the only purpose of war was peace—it followed that peace had to be fought for; war and peace were two sides of the same coin. And as peace is a 'contested concept'—one person's peace is unlikely to appeal to another for that reason—war tends to be endless. At the same time the great writers of the Enlightenment had legitimated war by hedging it in with conventions and rules (derived in large part from philosophical observations). In humanizing it they had made it into a fine art. Eighteenth-century Europe's conflicts were bloody but regulated, and rarely allowed to get out of hand. Lord Chesterfield, in a private letter written shortly after the outbreak of the Seven Years War (1757), commented ironically that 'every war is pusillanimously carried out in this degenerate age, quarter is given, towns are taken and the people spared'. One French writer put it very well: 'Wars are like games of chance in which no-one risks his all; what was once a wild rage is now just a folly' (Bell, 2007, p. 41).

All this was to change with the French Revolution, which ushered in a quarter century of conflict. Although states strive to keep conflict within bounds, there is never any guarantee that the rule will always hold. Other writers who did see the reality at close hand were often moved to anger too by the knowledge that the general public believed only what they read. One of the most faithful of the memorialists of the battle of Albuera (1809), one of the bloodier encounters of the Napoleonic wars, noting the headless bodies cut down by cannon shot, wrote of the danger of 'philosophical indifference' when reading accounts of the scene (Haythornewaite, 1996, p. 17). One hundred and fifty years later, in a preface to his novel *Brave New World*, Aldous Huxley castigated the philosophers in even harsher terms. By then they had retreated from the salon to the classroom; they had become professors. If you wanted a memorial to philosophy—he wrote bitterly in 1946—visit the bombed-out cities of Germany and Japan where he suggested that a sign should be erected that read: 'Sacred to the memory of the World's Great Educators' (Huxley, 1998, p. ix).

Unfortunately, all three critics were mistaken about the purpose of philosophy itself. Philosophy is a critique of the world and of life; it is an implicit reproach to the world that is, and an invitation to think what it might become. 'Become what you are' was Nietzsche's challenge to humanity. But philosophy has two other tasks to perform. One is to address universal concerns (it is an enquiry into the human condition). It accepts that what human beings share in common (whatever the inequalities and injustices which divide them from each other) is the capacity to think and to reason out their own condition. Philosophy does not discriminate between cultures or races; it is inclusive. It privileges no language, not even the one in which it is written. Its natural element is language, but within that natural element it institutes a universal address (Badiou, 2006, p. 38).

Its second task is to mobilize the power of argument and reason to understand the logic of life. The philosophers' task is to reason out life's complexities: to find the 'regularities' that drive or underpin it, which allow us to reason out good practice. Plato's gift to philosophy and us is the concept of praxis—we enquire into the reality of things not out of mere curiosity but because we want to make a difference. Philosophers devise rules of conduct because life would be far more dangerous if we did not have them, and the rules that have been devised to keep war within bounds provide some safeguards, however minimal. It is when there are no 'rules' that the real threats often emerge. On leaving the internment camp in China in which he had spent much of the war, the young J.G. Ballard found that the Japanese surrender did not mean he or his family were safe. On the contrary, as he roamed the countryside and saw the peasants turning on their former conquerors, as well as each other, he realized that peace was more threatening because the rules that sustained war had been suspended (Ballard, 2008, p. 107). In the absence of war we may find, instead of peace, a state of warfare. It was one of the formative episodes of his childhood and may account for the dark view of human nature which pervades many of his later novels. It is surely the first duty of philosophy to make sense of the world. Wittgenstein was wrong when in the final sentence of the *Tractatus* he wrote, 'Whereof one cannot speak, thereof one must be silent.' Philosophy justifies itself precisely in endeavouring to say what cannot be said, or what may be too painful for us to hear.

Philosophy cannot tell us how to live our lives since it has no grasp of the 'meaning' of history (though it can spin a tale of its meaning: as a species we need to know what is meaningful and what is not). The sort of thing philosophers know and the sort of changes they can help make in the way people think may eventually do some good, but usually only in the long run and only indirectly. There is no 'science of Man' (as the Enlightenment *philosophes* used to call it) which can help argue us out of anything including war—or for that matter crime or terrorism, or unemployment. Religion—revealed truth may do so for those who believe in the truth of revelation but faith does not provide arguments, only marching orders and imperatives concealed in some grand intelligent design. Philosophers can only do one thing if we conclude that war is a social evil. It is to tell us that, all things being equal, there are rules that allow war to be pursued to a useful end, but one day even knowing the rules may not help because war may have yielded all it has to offer, from a creative point of view (always accepting that even this re-description is not a 'truer' version than the old)—there are no intrinsic features of the 'real' to grasp—only the world in its bizarre and invigorating (and also frightening) complexity.

The philosopher Richard Rorty put it very well in an essay that is to be found in his collection *Philosophy and Social Hope* (1999). The context, he tells us, is all important. The context that philosophers found themselves working in for the last two thousand years or more was one in which conflict, not cooperation, seemed to be the best way of effecting change, whatever the collateral damage. This is why Rousseau thought them 'barbarous'—he criticized them for trying to understand war instead of condemning it. War, as I shall claim (and it is a big claim), is as much an invention as peace, and the early philosophers invented it—it was their great contribution to the civilizing process.

ROUSSEAU'S COMPLAINT

Today the context has changed again: war is becoming increasingly ineffective as a political instrument. The world is simply too complex for it to deliver its traditional pay-offs; it no longer pays the same dividends on belief.

The philosophers could probably have told us this some time ago if they had not retreated into language games. It was Wittgenstein who once said that philosophy is 'a battle against the bewitchment of our intelligence by means of language' (Wittgenstein, 1974, Section 109). And indeed language does cast a spell; it can deceive. But one can't help questioning whether in exploring its mysteries philosophy hasn't taken its eye off the main script. Even many philosophers complain that as taught in the academy it has become what Alain Badiou calls sophistry (though to be fair one must add that he claims Rorty too was a minor sophist) (Badiou, 2008, p. 21). What Badiou is really saying is that philosophy used to tell stories, or 'narrative fictions', which centred us in the world and gave us a sense of our purposiveness. It no longer does. Or the stories it does tell are marginal to our lives, usually cast in a language inaccessible even to a relatively educated person. Science and religion still may vie with each other, but they still tell stories. Natural selection, adds Mary Midgley, is the latest 'myth'—almost a religious creed—for some biologists.

On this occasion, however, Rorty was surely correct: 'contexts provided by theories are tools for effecting change. The theories which provide new contexts are to be evaluated by their efficiency in effecting change.' Philosophy cannot, as Marx and many others claimed, reveal some deeper truth of existence—such as the 'meaning' of History (in the upper case), or the mystery of Being, or even in the case of Rousseau, the immorality of war (Rorty, 1999, p. 221). We will have to discover that for ourselves.

2

THE DIALECTICS OF WARFARE

WAR AND PEACE

'Here and elsewhere we shall not obtain the best insight into things until we actually see them growing from the beginning.'

(Aristotle, *The Politics*)

Our starting point must be Clausewitz and his seminal work, *On War*. In the book he argued that despite war's evolving character its nature is universal and timeless. And the latter should not be confused with the way war looks at a particular time. That it alters its appearance is unimportant—what really matters, writes W.B. Gallie, is war itself—it is the true subject of his life's work, as are 'the different qualities, relationships and dependencies which ... are connected to a single aim: to make clear what this terrible and tragic aspect of human life is about and how it operates' (Gallie, 1976, p. 61).

From Clausewitz we derive two received ideas which still dominate military thinking. Not only does war have a nature which never changes over time; it also has a character which changes over time (and which he illustrated at length in his book). War changes, as we change—in that sense we can say it 'mutates'—though I much prefer the word 'evolves' as we do. Clausewitz tells us that its character changes from era to era: the Tartars waged war differently from the Romans, and Rousseau's age of Enlightenment more differently still. The idea has great appeal, for it makes sense, and it is the stuff of military history. But it is also a heuristic device. It helps us understand that war is protean—it adapts to its external environment: it changes culture by culture, and over time. Hence the wisdom of the pre-Socratic philosophers and especially Heraclitus. 'Men awake have one common world, but in sleep they turn aside each into a world of their own.' Or take another of his fragments: 'One must follow what is common, but though the world (the *logos*) is held in common, most men live as if they had a private understanding of their own' (Murdoch, 1992, pp. 348–9).

Heraclitus is merely saying here that language is common to all of us. Grammar is public or social, as well as an instrument of socialization. Without it, we would not be able to communicate with one another. But each of us has our own private insights, thoughts and dreams. We have a common nature, but we all live different historical lives, and forge different historical experiences. In other words, there is a cultural grammar of war which is distinctive to different societies. There is also a general grammar of war from which we derive rules or regularities that transcend time and space. As Nietzsche argued, 'nothing is definable unless it has no history' (Hayman, 1995, p. 1). War certainly has a history. It evolves, mutates, metastasises—our use of metaphors is revealing for what they reveal about us. But the nature of war never changes.

Clausewitz too encouraged us to draw a distinction between the nature of war and its character, partly because of his own philosophical frame of reference. German Idealists like Kant and Hegel set out to invest traditional kinds of knowledge such as religion and history with an essential 'core' or 'nature'. Behind every phenomenon there is an 'essence'—a conceptual poetry. Long before that, however, metaphysics in revealing (to its own satisfaction) the relativity of the world as experienced had also reasoned out an unconditional reality thanks to which the conditioned reality becomes intelligible for the first time. The distinction between the nature and character of war is central to Clausewitz's understanding of the phenomenon he was studying. And, in part, because of him, we now take it for granted. We tend to believe that, unlike the character of war which is indefinable because it is always changing, the nature of war can be defined because it does not.

War has a nature which is eternal but which at the same time takes a finite form (it has a character which is particular because it is a different expression of the same phenomenon). It is in the nature of war to specify itself in a variety of different forms (Bronze Age, Iron Age, Age of Steel); in different epochs (pre-modern/modern) and in different

THE DIALECTICS OF WARFARE: WAR AND PEACE

cultures (western/non-western). In describing philosophy itself in similar terms, Hegel borrowed metaphors from anthropology and nature. Different philosophies (such as his own) are different expressions of an eternal truth, in the same way that 'the man, the youth and the child are all at one and the same time the same individual', or the way that different branches are branches of the same tree (Ferrarin, 2007, p. 35). Every war in changing in character transforms its past and appropriates it at the same time. The nature of war is not transformed through history, its nature is made manifest in time, but time does not substantially affect the eternal; the character of war is the actualization of its nature.

It is the definitions we come up with that make possible common thoughts; history too requires that we distinguish and discriminate between 'uncommon' practices. This study is concerned with the nature of war. It is a 'philosophical take' on war, informed by the western philosophical canon, beginning with Heraclitus, the pre-Socratic philosopher who has fascinated so many thinkers from Plato to Heidegger.

I shall start with the most important contribution philosophers have made to our understanding of war—the way they have encouraged us to distinguish between warfare, war and peace. Such distinctions historians may find unhelpful, but it is what philosophers do; it is their *métier*. Nor do they see this task as inimical to the study of history itself, or indeed the work of historians. The distinctions were not always intended to be taken literally: they were idealized representations, or what Max Weber calls 'ideal types'. Those familiar with his work will know that it is a key term in his methodology. When he used the word 'ideal' he did not intend it in the normative sense of desirable or preferable. What he meant was a pure form of a particular phenomenon which enables us to tease out its historical complexity, which is what interested him most. Ideal types, in other words, are merely conceptual tools which enable us to engage much better in comparative analysis, not to ignore or override the complex pattern of history. But Weber did insist that one cannot approach any phenomenon without a conceptual language: it is the concepts that allow us to understand it, not merely describe it.

Let me add a second rider. An ideal type is also not a typology in the conventional sociological sense, nor a dichotomous list of contrasting elements. Weber himself wrote that they help analysts arrive at 'an analytical accentuation' of certain aspects of historical reality by allowing them to isolate the inessential from the essential, and thus render more explicit the general and individual characteristics of empirical reality. It is only by postulating that war has a *nature* that allows us to distinguish it from warfare. And philosophers want us to make the distinctions because they want us to stay out of the state of nature. The categories they identify are intended to help us not only understand the phenomenon, but to change our lives. It is only by understanding warfare that we can devise rules for war that may make the practice a little less horrific for the rest of us. And it is only by understanding war that we can employ it as an instrument for peace.

In his *History of Warfare* John Keegan takes issue with Clausewitz for 'struggling with all the considerable philosophical force at his disposal to advance a universal theory of what war *ought* to be' (Keegan, 1996, p. 6). But that is the point: philosophers produce conceptions and trade in categories to get us to think how we might do things differently. What they wanted us to do in the twenty-six centuries in which they have been thinking about the phenomenon is how much warfare and war differ; they also wanted us to recognize that 'perpetual peace' (if it exists) will arise only when we conclude that war has finally exhausted its possibilities.

Warfare

Let me begin by turning to Nietzsche and an early essay, 'Homer's Contest', which was written in 1872, the year which saw the publication of his first major work, *The Birth of Tragedy*. It opens with a salvo that would have shocked a contemporary audience that was trained to think of the Greeks as representing all that was most noble in life. Shelley famously said, 'we are all Greeks now'. Fifty years later the Europeans still believed it. The classics were at the heart of a gentleman's education, and they preached that civility was at the heart of civilized life.

That is why one of the opening paragraphs of Nietzsche's youthful essay was so provocative.

When we speak of *humanity* the idea is fundamental that there is something that distinguishes man from nature—In reality man is wholly nature ... those of abilities which are terrifying and considered inhuman may even be the fertile soil out of which alone all humanity can grow in impulse, deed and work. (Kaufmann, 1968)

THE DIALECTICS OF WARFARE: WAR AND PEACE

Years later, in *Human, All Too Human*, he specifically took Rousseau to task for what he referred to as his 'superstition'—his belief in 'a miraculous primeval but as it were *buried* goodness of human nature'. History revealed instead the 'dreadfulness and excesses of the most distant ages' (Nietzsche, 1986, p. 169). What he most admired about the Greeks was that they had managed to combine a belief in humanity with an unerring willingness to see human nature for what it was. Of all people, he insisted, the Greeks were the most humane of the ancient world (by which he meant they were the most interested in what makes us human; they had even invented the concept of free will which was grounded, in turn, on a theological need: 'the right to the idea that the interest of the gods in Man could never be exhausted'. But then no other society glorified so much in war or rendered it so artistic. War is central to Greek culture: they practised it with a single-mindedness to such an extent that it became a defining quality of the culture as a whole. They celebrated war in fiction (*The Iliad*), in fact (Herodotus' *Histories*), in the first tragedies (*The Persians*), in the epigrams of Simonides. Without war they would have had no identity. The Greek word for courage, *andreia*, meant literally manliness. War was the exclusive business of men, just as it was the exclusive business of citizens, as Plato tells us in *The Laws*. War really did father everything, just as philosophers later fathered war.

Homer's world, as Nietzsche points out, however is one of unremitting violence; it is a world of darkness tinged with few shades of light. Only the poetry allows the archetypal heroes who still inspire us to shine out, to be luminous in our imagination. The purity of Homer's lines, Nietzsche claimed, raise the reader above the actual content of the poem. 'Through an artistic deception, the colour seems lighter, milder, warmer, and it is in this colourful warm light that men appear better and are more sympathetic' (Kaufmann, 1968). Strip away the poetry, however, and we find ourselves soon enough in the pre-Homeric world about which he is writing—for Homer's poem describes a conflict that had taken place centuries before in a world ruled only by the children of night: strife, lust, deceit, old age and death. And then we find a striking phrase in the essay: 'In this brooding atmosphere, combat *is* salvation. The cruelty of victory is the pinnacle of life's joy.'

The Greeks had turned warfare into war, a contest with rules but one that was still fought for real:

Not only Aristotle, but the whole of Greek antiquity, thinks differently from us about hatred and envy and judges with Hesiod, who in one place calls *Eris* (strife) evil—namely the one that leads men into hostile fights of annihilation against one another—while praising another *Eris*—good—the one that is jealousy, hatred and envy which spurs men to activity: not the activity of fights of annihilation, but to the activity of fights which are *contests*. (Kaufmann, 1968, p. 35)

It is this second *Eris* that gives war its shape, a beginning and an end, and which also produces a victor too, who can be admired for his human excellence (*arete*). The hero, like an athlete, is honoured, whether he wins or loses. But like an athlete he is honoured because he observes certain rules. It is this which makes possible our escape from the dark night into the light of eternal glory. In other words, there is the *Eris* of warfare and the *Eris* of war. One leads to annihilation, the others to contests with rules. The escape from the world of warfare into that of war transforms zero-sum competition into non zero-sum competitiveness (a distinction that is central to the nature of war, as I shall explain in my discussion of Thomas Hobbes).

In short, 'war' emerged from warfare through the contest, just as it was from murder and the expiation of the act that the conception of Greek law emerged too. In a surviving fragment of his lost play *Sisyphus*, Euripides whisks us through the development of civilization up to the point where lawlessness has been brought under control by the invention of law (Waterfield, p. 37). The first challenge the city faced was to transform vendetta by clans into contests within the law courts. The problem of vengeance is central to all the tragic literature of the fifth century—all the plays that concern the fate of Orestes address the problem of revenge, none more so than the last play in Aeschylus' trilogy, the *Oresteia*. At the end of the play the Furies who have pursued Orestes for killing his mother are transformed into the *Eumenides*, the Kindly-Ones, their job now no longer to punish anyone who has committed a crime within the family but to watch over weddings and births. Their larger role is to guard over the harmony of social life by encouraging people to seek vengeance through the law—in the contest of course for the Greeks invented a highly competitive system of law: cases were won and verdicts delivered on the basis of argument (or proof)—the ultimate product of a rational, agonistic society.

Nietzsche is spinning a myth, of course. It is what philosophers do. But it is a powerful one because it has more than a ring of historical

THE DIALECTICS OF WARFARE: WAR AND PEACE

authenticity. By the sixth-century post-Homeric world, the Greek cities were aware that they had tamed the heroes of *The Iliad*. The wars which they unleashed were not for the personal glory of the warrior but the collective fame of the city—not that this made the Greek world any more peaceful. It is nice, writes Frederick Raphael, to read high-minded lamentations about violence, especially in the great tragedies at the heart of the western literary canon. We read, for example, in Aeschylus' *Prometheus Bound* that brute force is a 'loutish enforcer'; time and again in the tragedies even war is reviled. But in practice violence was rarely renounced, still less tempered by chivalry (Raphael, 2003, p. 205). War is not distinguished by warfare in terms of its humanity, but the funnelling of lethal values into a contest with a distinct set of rules. The trick once everything is disputed and individuals are antagonistic to each other is to translate conflict into *agon* (or competition). And it is only in the city that conflict with others as well as conflict with other cities can take the form of a contest, just as lawlessness can only be tamed by law. This is why, Plato tells us in T*he Laws*, the city-states were in an almost permanent state of war against each other. In the words of Hans van Vees, they fought one another 'to demonstrate their "excellence" (*arete*)' which entitled them to a place at the top of the tree. At the same time they fought to stop inferiors from acting like equals, equals from acting like superiors, and superiors from demanding more deference than they deserved (Lebow, 2009, p. 187).

Nietzsche's essay also reminds us that in Homer's day the Greeks were much nearer to the state of nature than we are: their tribal memories were much stronger than our own. They actually remembered not so much the primal age before the emergence of the state but the return to that state of existence with the 'dark age' that had followed the collapse of the Mycenaean age whose ruins they saw around them every day, an age when even writing disappeared for reasons that historians are still not agreed. But when they emerged from the night they woke to an outside world, not as an object of knowledge separate from themselves, but to knowledge itself. In that world-making transition the two keys were the *re*birth of the city and the *re*discovery of writing.

Writing had vanished together with the collapsing Mycenaean kingdoms. When it returned to current use it was no longer subordinate to scribes or servants of the state. It was open to everyone. It was no longer employed to order society but to entertain: to expand the mind, to write down the Homeric epics. Philosophy emerged not from the invention but *reinvention* of writing, and it is our capacity to philosophize (to reason things out for ourselves) that allows us to build an increasingly complex world. The Mycenaean cities had also been palace-based. The Ionian cities were quite different: they were smaller but more dynamic and dialogic (citizens encountered each other and interacted with one another in a more open society way). This allowed for cooperation but it also promoted conflict, including the social revolutions which prompted the revolt against the Persians (just as Heraclitus had predicted).

In his autobiography, *Conjectures and Refutations*, Karl Popper tells us that he was 'compelled to philosophy by problems which arose outside philosophy' (Popper, 2002, p. 95). He was referring to the time in which he wrote his flawed but brilliant masterpiece, *The Open Society and its Enemies*, which he completed in 1944, towards the end of the Second World War, safely sequestered from the war zones in Christchurch, New Zealand. The great problem of his age was the rise of totalitarianism and the prevalence of total war. For Heraclitus it was the civil wars which plagued the Greek city-state system and which eventually drove him out of Ephesus. The worst fate for a citizen was exile, or ostracism, in effect exile from one's own humanity. The worst fate was to become an outlaw (outside the law, that is, of the Polis). As Heraclitus tells us, inside the city walls there is light; outside there is nothing but darkness, the war of all against all.

Nietzsche gives us a wonderful picture of Heraclitus living in exile in the temple of Artemis, trying to escape from 'the noise and democratic tittle-tattle of the Ephesians, their politics, news of the Empire (Persia, naturally), their market affairs of "today"' (Nietzsche, *The Genealogy of Morals*, 3.8). But this engaging picture is not necessarily historically true. Heraclitus, one imagines, was one of those born exiles even if they never leave home. But the civil strife which drove him out of Ephesus may have been in some ways the objective correlative of his own inner turbulence. And we have no real reason to doubt that his natural misanthropy was probably reinforced by the fact that he found himself living outside the political realm. For Heraclitus was a political animal, through and through.

The cosmological principles whose existence Heraclitus postulates are actually political in nature. Heraclitus was challenging his fellow

THE DIALECTICS OF WARFARE: WAR AND PEACE

citizens to rethink their political situation. He was a practical writer who was interested not in metaphysics or the cosmos so much as the human built world. His work, adds Hans Gadamer, is intensely *political* for that reason (Gadamer, 2001, p. 43). When Aristotle defines man as a political animal three centuries later it was because reason itself was in essence political—for the Greeks the individual could not be separated from the citizen, reflection was the privilege of free men (Vernant, 1984, p. 131). And though conflict (or the contest) is central to civic life, political conflict has rules. It is the underlying threat to civic life and its propensity to degenerate into class war that requires us to be virtuous. Because there is no natural or social bond on which one can rely on, there is a constant struggle to shape it. Primitive communities have no need to legislate for themselves for they know no social discord. Only a community which is fragile needs to continually legislate itself into existence.

It was to drum this point home: to make its young men good citizens that the Athenians enlisted those who had reached the age of eighteen in the *ephebia*: a two-year military training period. After the first year of training, they served in the frontier fortresses of Attica. This period of service was a more civilized version of the Spartan method of turning young initiates out into the wild hills to live off the land by ruse, robbery and the murder of helots (slaves). The institution was called *krupteia*, based on the verb *kruptein*, 'to hide, to conceal oneself, to dissimulate' which also includes trickery and lies (Sartre, 2009, p. 123). Plutarch later saw the ritual as one of the cruellest practices of Spartan training but today it reminds us of the initiation rites of hunter-gatherer societies. For it offered the Greeks a quite deliberate re-immersion in the primal night by highlighting the differences between warfare and war—the organizational differences between lightly armed men versus the heavily armed citizen-army of the hoplites; between separate, small group operations as opposed to heavily armoured phalanxes; between all-year operations as opposed to regular summer campaigns; between young men fighting at night, as opposed to grown men fighting during the day. This inversion of military norms was a rite of passage into citizenship (Knox, 1989, p. 86).

The system was also meant to drum home in young, adolescent minds what Homer himself reminded them time and time again in his poem: men can turn into beasts soon enough. Achilles' clansmen, the Myrmidons, are described as wolves who eat raw flesh as they are unleashed into battle. Men and beasts are not that different. Indeed, writes Jonathan Gottschall, Homeric man is an unrealized ideal, a work in progress (Gottschall, 2008, p. 163). Even the noblest warriors who haunt the pages of *The Iliad* are 'killer apes' who have applied the superior intelligence of human beings to robbing their fellow men of all they hold dear: their wealth, their women and ultimately their lives. With Plato the philosophers set out to 'domesticate' the warrior—to tame him by specifically linking his existential being to instrumental ends. It doesn't really matter if we employ the concepts of another era—if we claim, for example, that they tried to curb ferocity by 'reason' or by 'civilizing' desires. The attempt involved re-configuring the conception of courage, separating it from the crude will-to-power. Courage becomes fortitude, the kind of dogged resistance the Spartans had shown at Thermopylae when they had fought to the death, not as wild animals but as citizens inspiring their fellow citizens to fight on.

Indeed, by the time of Plato, the animal imagery which Homer had employed to describe his warrior-heroes had largely disappeared. The use of the word animal now excluded one from the moral community (i.e. to behave like an animal was to behave badly). This long break with our animal origins thus began, only to be arrested (not reversed) through the work of Darwin. 'He who understands baboon would do more towards metaphysics than Locke' (Midgley, 2006). It is Darwin who marks the great breach with the de-animalization of man that had begun with the tragedians, in particular with Sophocles' great speech in *Oedipus* where man is seen as the measure of all things.

From the perspective of evolutionary theory, a perspective which was not available, of course, to the Greeks, one can see the biological imperatives in war as a return to a primal darkness. Homer himself, writes Gottschall, probably would not have been particularly scandalized by *The Descent of Man* because he was interested in much the same question: what are we? It is our animal nature that we cannot escape; any more than we can emancipate ourselves from our evolved biology (Gottschall, 2008, p. 160). Evolutionary psychologists are pessimistic about the human condition for that reason—they recognize that we are what we are and there may be limits to how much we can change. There may be a limit in other words to what we might yet 'become'.

THE DIALECTICS OF WARFARE: WAR AND PEACE

War

Aristotle insisted that systematic thinking starts with making distinctions. The Greeks were great philosophers because they were the first to make the distinctions we take for granted today: between time and space; quality and quantity; cause and effect; form and matter. We still employ them to help us think systematically. There were also other distinctions that we don't use today but should: the most important being the difference between warfare and war.

There is a passage in Thucydides' *History of the Peloponnesian War* which tells us that women joined in the fighting in Corfu, hurling tiles from rooftops, 'with a courage beyond their sex' (Thucydides, *History*, 3.74.2). The word Thucydides used, *paraphusin*, means beyond their nature (Cartledge, 2002, p. 86). For the Greeks true bravery is reserved for the battlefield and displayed exclusively by men, immortalized by epic poetry. We remember Achilles and Hector because Homer wrote about them, and he wrote about them because he thought they were worth remembering. What we are remembering, of course, are acts of men in a realm exclusive to themselves. Their courage comes naturally to them: it invokes intelligence, judgement and justice. The bravery of women may be real but is like that of animals: it is emotional and passionate. Those very passions, of course, are brought out in civil wars which Thucydides described as well, like the conflict in Corfu.

Thucydides makes the same point about barbarians whom the Greeks thought to be warlike by nature. Take the passage in his *History* in which he describes the actions of a band of Thracian mercenaries hired by the Athenians in 413 BC. They were raised to fight in Sicily but arrived too late to affect the final outcome. So they returned and conducted instead a scorched earth policy in Boeotia. At one time they went completely berserk, killing old men and women, and even animals. Thucydides says they showed 'boldness' (*tharsos*) but he uses the word ironically. It is an example of the famous irony which is such a feature of the great work which he left to posterity. For the barbarians are certainly bold enough against women and children and animals, in other words those who cannot fight back. They are brave enough to slaughter them indiscriminately. And he singles out for condemnation one notorious incident (the 'Beslan' tragedy of the Greek age), when the Thracians descended on a school and killed every child. This was not only tragic, it was a real disaster. In robbing the city of the generation of successors, it really did threaten to foreclose its future.

BARBAROUS PHILOSOPHERS

The contrast the Greeks drew between themselves and the barbarians is revealing. Plato acknowledged that barbarians could show great courage—bravery was often their defining characteristic. The Athenians, by contrast, had no defining characteristic; they exhibited all the emotions. In one of the dialogues in the *Timaeus* the origins of the city-state are traced back to a goddess who loved both war and wisdom, and Athenian life was considered to embody both. Courage was tempered by intelligence; that was the mark of civilization (a word of course the Greeks did not use). Returning to Thucydides' account, we can see how it engages with all the polarities that were central to the Greek imagination: the distinctions between human beings and animals, Greeks and barbarians, and of course men and women. Polarizing is what we humans tend to favour, and of the many binomial distinctions none is more important than one implicit in their writing: the difference between warfare and war.

The most extensive categorization can be found in Aristotle's logic of opposites, which he derived in part from the Pythagorean school of philosophy (Aristotle, *Metaphysics*, 986a).

Pythagorean Principles

Unlimited	*Limited*
Even	Odd
Plurality	One
Female	Male
Crooked	Straight
Darkness	Light
Evil	Good

We could draw up a similar logic of opposites for the two categories under discussion in this book.

Warfare	*War*
Unlimited	Limited
Asymmetrical	Symmetrical
Non-State	State
Regular	Irregular

For Aristotle this was largely a theoretical construct. He was the first to recognize that reality is far more complex. Classifications of any kind tend to be overly reductive and often arbitrary. War, after all, can regress to warfare easily enough (the essential theme of Thucydides'

THE DIALECTICS OF WARFARE: WAR AND PEACE

History is how *polemos* (war) turned into *stasis* (warfare); this is more likely to happen the longer a conflict continues, and the conflict Thucydides narrated lasted thirty years. Even war (practised against those like ourselves) can be brutal. There is little that Homer spares us in his depiction of conflict between two people who spoke the same language and worshipped the same gods. And 148 forms of wound are to be found in *The Iliad* (three-quarters of them lethal).

Contrary to popular opinion, the Greeks did not draw an ontological distinction between themselves and the 'other'. They always recognized that, in one sense, the distinctions were Weberian ideal types, at least in the sense that there were always exceptions (they invented history to chronicle them). They rarely made the mistake of confusing an ideal type for absolute reality. For many Athenians, the Spartans were the great 'other'—sometimes they asked themselves were they really Greek at all. Barbarians, too, could come in many forms. Some like the Persians achieved so much that Herodotus thought it well worthwhile to record their 'great and marvellous deeds'. His admiration was real. In his description of the battle of Thermopylae, he mentions some of the Persian dead by name (a touch of humanity entirely absent from the recent film *300*). Even Thucydides who is much more judgemental of barbarians (precisely because he was of the generation that could look back with pride on the Athenian success against the Persians) conceded that 'Greekness' was also a relative term. Some Greeks could act like women, beasts or barbarians (he singled out the Thebans who had dishonoured everything the Greeks held dear by leaving the Athenian dead unburied on the battlefield for seventeen days).

But what we find in Aristotle is a clue to the nature of war—it is rational: it is the integration of intellectual and practical life that distinguishes it from warfare. It was the Greeks who defined humanity in terms of language, just as the Christian Church would later define it in terms of reason. It is language that allows us to reason what is good for us, and what is not. The idea that man is an animal distinguished by language goes back to the pre-Socratics. The first to enunciate it formally is Parmenides who celebrated the unity of thought and being which makes it impossible to think nothing. People in the state of nature clearly think something: hunter-gatherers have an instinctive tactical acumen, but they do not think far ahead, and they do not think through—they live in a world without consequences.

What condemned mankind to live in a state of darkness was not the absence of reason so much as the use to which it was put. In a world

23

in which reason was not institutionalized there were no consequences to anticipate—little was demanded of the warrior except native cunning. For it is a great mistake to assume that hunter-gatherer societies always know why they are fighting. Anthropologists find that tribes do not always grasp the systemic causes and consequences of battle. They tend to refer back to their own personal experiences and motivations, prior to the outbreak of hostilities. They tend to think in terms of immediate results, not causes and consequences. They tend to be preoccupied with the glory of 'blooding' themselves in battle; or the status that will accrue to a warrior who has proved his worth in killing others. A warrior about to set off on a head-hunting expedition welcomes the opportunity to capture his enemy's soul. He gives little thought to 'redeeming' the community.

These motivations certainly explain why people fight. All collective violence, however primitive, has a rational basis, and it is also possible for anthropologists to identify larger forces which drive conflict, such as population pressure, or the need for women. But usually hunter-gatherers don't think about conflict at all—each round of fighting provides sufficient motivation for the next. They cannot imagine alternative solutions that would involve less suffering, or fewer casualties in any future encounter. They cannot even imagine peace as anything other than a truce, or a brief cessation of hostilities. And because they cannot think in terms of causation, they cannot think systematically: they tend to explain their going to war in terms of the need to avenge violent actions.

There is a passage in *The Republic* (435a-435c) where Plato writes that bravery is not unique to the civilized world. 'It would be ridiculous to claim that bravery has not passed from the individual in which it is found to those states as in the case of the inhabitants of Thrace, or of Scythia'—two barbaric peoples. But he then goes on to add that the desire to learn might be considered peculiar to the Greek (civilized) world, because it is only through education that we learn the prudent use of bravery—we are taught that courage should be a matter of practical intelligence, not passion. As Machiavelli writes in *The Discourses* (1, 52, 203), 'Before deciding upon any course ... men should well consider the objectives and the dangers which it presents, and if its perils exceed its advantages they should avoid it, even though it has been in accordance with their previous determination.'

In describing the *stasis* that arose in Corfu, Thucydides writes that people were no longer able to practise moderation because they were unable to exercise 'practical intelligence' (3.82.4). And his understanding of 'practical reason' gives us an insight into another factor which makes war rule-bound. The application of reason does not make us any more reasonable, and it certainly does not make us any nicer—but it does get us to reflect on the consequences of our actions. Aristotle makes a similar distinction in the *Nichomachean Ethics* (1139 A29–30; 1139 A29–1142A). War is a product of reason, and in this case reading too, because we can only anticipate the consequences of our actions by discovering precedents in history, or literature which even more than history stimulates our imagination. As Machiavelli writes, the prudent prince reads history to observe the actions of 'excellent men'. He reads how they conducted themselves in war, observes the causes of their victories and defeats in order to escape the latter and copy the former (Machiavelli, *The Prince*, p. 99). We can only *reason out* the consequences of our own acts through reflection.

Only in the course of the eighteenth century did the Europeans begin to think they had marketed war largely themselves—that they were the only ones that really knew the rules. Influenced by thinkers such as Adam Smith and Adam Ferguson, they contrasted their own rule-bound world of competitiveness with 'quarrelling that had no rules'. And they found examples of the latter in the history of non-western peoples whom they had begun to encounter in their own expansion overseas. In the past cities had been razed, captives sold, mutilated or condemned to die, wrote Ferguson. His own age, by contrast, had made war more 'civil'. 'We have mingled politeness with the use of the sword; we have learned to make war under the stipulation of treaties and cartels and trust to the faith of an enemy whose ruin we meditate' (Ferguson, Part 1, Section 4). The Europeans, in a word, had introduced over time a set of rules or etiquettes that every state was expected to observe. The victory of reason over emotion was evidence of their own humanity gained through education.

But Ferguson went one step further. Not only did he insist that the western nations were less cruel, he also insisted that it was a mark of their civility that they only went to war for humanity. Paradoxically they were able to identify more readily with suffering humanity because they thought they could speak on its behalf and wield power in its name. They were guided by what he called the principle of 'employing force only for the obtaining of justice and for the preservation of natural rights'. Natural rights soon became human rights, another direct consequence of the Enlightenment understanding of civilization as an ongoing historical process which transformed uncivil into civil behaviour. In this civilizing process, the Europeans believed they were a Kantian, liberal avant-garde.

What they were actually observing was another periodic change in the *character* of war; they mistook their own cultural grammar of war for its nature. In this particular case they had embraced a very modern idea first formulated by Ferguson's fellow Scotsman, Adam Smith: the idea of breaking down tasks into separate pieces, allowing those parties with particular advantages to apply their skills where they fitted in best. This found expression in Ferguson's work where civil society was distinguished by the very fact that (contra Rousseau) soldiers were only 'accidental' (i.e. put to a temporary instrumental use). In illustrating this point he cited a New World example, that of an American 'redskin chief' addressing the governor of Jamaica at the beginning of a war with Spain. The chief was astonished that the civilians in the colony had escaped enlistment. The governor explained to him that in the civilized world merchants took no part in war. 'When I go to war I leave no one behind but the women,' the chief had replied. At this point, Ferguson added, with the condescension of a man who clearly knows better, that the chief did not understand that in the modern world the merchants financed wars. Different tasks, the same end, and the key was specialization. In civilized societies 'the character of the warlike and the commercial are variously combined; they are formed in different degrees by the influence of circumstances' (Ferguson, 1969, p. 267).

By the late eighteenth century battle too had become central to the mythology of war. Warfare does not have battles; wars by contrast, are remembered because of them. They still cast a spell over historians. The great commanders are still celebrated for battles lost or won. Battle was seen as the deciding factor that made war a reasonable or rational activity. It is embodied in the idea of Nietzsche's 'contest': a day's fighting brings the enemy to see reason, to behave more reasonably, to accept peace on one's own terms. It also demonstrates the usefulness of military training: courage as rational calculation. In his *History*, Thucydides has a Spartan general dismiss the barbarian tribes as men who tend to avoid battle because they cannot withstand shock assault on the battlefield.

This line of thinking dominated western thinking (and still does). Even Hobbes, though acknowledging that 'war existeth not in battle only or the act of fighting', also insisted that the interval between battles was important only 'as a track of time wherein the will to contend in battle is sufficiently known'. Indeed, the main attraction of battle is that it is taken to be the supreme expression of the will to win. There is an inherent truth in battle. It is hard to disguise the verdict of the battlefield and nearly always impossible to explain away the dead. The verdict of the battlefield is cathartic: it keeps war within bounds. Both sides are expected to abide by the verdict, or they are meant to. Hannibal was lost when the Romans continued fighting after Cannae, Napoleon when the Russians simply ignored the outcome at Borodino, the bloodiest battle of the Napoleonic wars. The point is that if war continues despite the verdict of the battlefield, we tend to think that there has been an inversion of the natural order. It is particular frustrating when the enemy refuses to admit defeat. When Clausewitz saw Cossacks for the first time attached to the Tsar's army in the 1812 campaign he realized this would be a different kind of conflict. As William Hazlitt wrote, when Napoleon saw the domes of Moscow, he must have realized that he was dealing with a 'different species of war' (Hazlitt, 1991). In the Cossacks both writers saw a glimpse of the primal night.

Peace

War for many people today is as anachronistic as religion is for others. Its appeal is much diminished. Even our generals have become agnostic about the virtues of their own profession. Some prefer to see themselves as humanitarians, not soldiers ('I didn't join the military to kill people', General Wesley Clark told an audience in Keene, New Hampshire during the 2004 Presidential campaign; 'I came into the army because I believe in public service' (O'Rourke, 2005, p. xvii). But we still sanction killing, which is why even if we ourselves are conflicted about war we should show it the same respect that some atheists show religion. To quote Bernard Williams, 'granted that its transcendental claim is at fault, human beings must have dreamed it, and we need an understanding of why this was the content of their dream. Humanism—in the contemporary sense of a secularist and anti–religious movement—seems seldom to have faced fully a very immediate consequence of its own view—that this terrible thing, religion, is a *human* creation' (Midgley, 2004, pp. 41–2).

The same is true of war. We are the only species that practise it. It is there for a reason which can be explained by anthropologists, evolutionists, psychologists, even economists, who have delighted in telling us that we are conditioned to fight it. Conditioned or not, we have to understand it. The outright condemnation of war, i.e. pacifism, is an ideology which, like all ideologies, simplifies the truth. It is ahistorical in ignoring the positive role that war has played in human history. And pacifism (like militarism) also has a history. Both are nineteenth-century products of a particular social and historical environment. Peace, writes Michael Howard, is a very recent invention (Howard, 2000). War is a very old one, but like peace it is also the invention of philosophers. Both were conceived in the minds of men.

Few philosophers before Kant had imagined a world without war. From Plato onwards the point of philosophical enquiry was to come to terms with the fact that it seemed to be a permanent feature of the human condition. This being so, they have to come to terms with the world as it is. Not one of the philosophers discussed in this book thought war was an absolute value. But they have also refused to accept that it was an absolute evil either, for in the end it was the only means to peace. Even Hobbes wrote, 'every man ought to endeavour peace as far as he has hope of attaining it; and when he cannot attain it, that he may seek, and use all help and advantage of war'. War, in other words, is merely a means to a good greater than itself.

But one of the main reasons why we have not secured a permanent peace is that peace has not always offered the source of meaning provided by war. Or to put it another way, it has not been valued as highly. To argue this case is not to devalue peace, it is merely to appreciate that everything we consider valuable is historically conditioned. What we find valuable, others have not, and may not in the years to come. We must never dishonour our ancestors for not being ourselves.

Now, when philosophers discuss value they tend to identify three kinds. The first is *instrumental*: the value derived from the way in which a particular practice serves to promote some other value. Aristotle tells us that war has no value in itself. It serves only one purpose: to secure a better kind of peace. The state trains its citizens, he writes in *The Politics*, to exercise their reason from which they will be able to reason out that their best interest is peace. But the state is sometimes forced to train them for war. 'It will do the things that are not themselves the things of reason for the sake of things which are; it will choose things necessary and useful as means towards things beautiful and good' (Barber, p. 429).

But as Aristotle also tells us, war serves more limited instrumental ends. In particular it is 'a form of acquisitive activity' (Shipley, 1993). It can enrich the victor. War in his day was self-financing; it had to pay for itself, often in the currency of human suffering: slavery. Aristotle discusses five main ways by which men live by their labour—the usual ones are there, such as trade and farming, but so are piracy and hunting, and it is the last category that is of most interest. For he also adds several significant subcategories—game hunting (wild animals and birds), the hunting of people (slave raiding), the hunting of movable objects (plundering) and the hunting of people and possessions together (war) (Shipley, 1993, p. 83). The Trojan War can be seen as a great manhunt on which the kinsmen of Menelaus embarked not only to avenge his dishonour (and by association their own) but because they knew that they would be immeasurably richer if Troy fell. We must always ask *cui bono*—who benefits? War usually always serves an instrumental purpose in terms of power, wealth or status. All three can be found in Thucydides' account of the Peloponnesian War.

Instrumental arguments are not confined to economic advantage, but we tend, given our present obsession with the 'dismal science', to seek an economic explanation for everything. Clearly, many ends or values can be served other than economics, but the economic motive is most in fashion because it is so utilitarian. None of these are examples of what Marxists would call 'false consciousness'. The economic benefits of war at times have been real enough. But we have often not always appreciated the hidden costs; on a strict cost-benefit analysis, it might have been better to live in peace. Not that an instrumental value is to be measured only in terms of instrumental rationality. This too has a history which is recent enough. It is an example of what Nietzsche called 'historical philosophizing'. We think different thoughts at different times. What is true to say is that war has become increasingly instrumentalized, and that utilitarian philosophers from Bentham (who hated it) to the Free Trade supporters (Cobden, Bright, and pragmatists such as John Dewey) have increasingly cast into doubt its instrumental worth. Dewey was always talking of the 'cash value' of ideas—if an idea turns a profit it is worth holding; it if does not it is worth cashing it in for another idea. What has happened more recently is that we have discovered that there are easier ways of acquiring wealth, or retaining status, or maximizing power. War, as a result, has lost much of its instrumental appeal.

But the argument does not end there. For philosophers identify the *existential* values that constitute our humanity. We cannot understand ethical preferences (such as justice) on the level of animal desires, because all human cultures throughout history have given central place to the distinction between the lower appetites and higher goals by which our appetites can be judged and regulated. Indeed, we live in a world in which there is less and less material need and therefore even greater desire.

The two most important desires, writes Montesquieu in *The Spirit of Laws* (1, 2), are freedom and justice. He also adds that 'peace [is] the first law of nature'. Like Vico and Montaigne the French philosopher put all he knew into one book, and he never reached a more appropriate conclusion. If he is right about peace (as I believe he is) it follows that the highest principle of government is security. All states have a general aim which is to secure themselves and their citizens, but this end is not conceived merely negatively as the preservation of life. It is the preservation of liberty. 'The love of liberty is natural to mankind' (Montesquieu, *Spirit of the Laws*, 5.14).

Montesquieu, of course, was writing from the vantage point of the Enlightenment, but his argument transcends the time in which it was written. We must recognize (as he did not) that the freedom for which so many people over the centuries have been willing to fight is not necessarily one that fits our own understanding of the term: the freedom of the autonomous individual. Most people have not fought to realize what Isaiah Berlin called 'a negative area', in which a man is not obliged to account for his activities to any other man in so far as they are compatible with the coexistence of all in an organized society. Nor is freedom necessarily rooted in the idea that we cannot be truly human without it, either in the sense of 'being' (i.e. rooted in self-worth), or in the sense of 'becoming'—a freedom that pulls us towards a future in which we will behave better or even become better people. There is no Hegelian teleology here—history, unfortunately, is not as Hegel told us, the story of freedom becoming conscious of itself.

What does seem true is that people since time immemorial have fought against tyranny. One of the most striking statements about freedom to be found in the ancient world is invented by Tacitus (that most patrician of historians). He gets the British leader Caractacus to say: 'if

THE DIALECTICS OF WARFARE: WAR AND PEACE

you want to rule, does it follow that everyone else welcomes enslavement?' (Tacitus, *Histories*, xii.36). In the course of narrating one of the many military campaigns against the Germans he puts in the mouth of another warrior the words 'we may have nowhere to live, but we can find somewhere to die' (Tacitus, *Histories*, xiii.56). The empires that have persisted the longest, such as the Roman, have been the most tolerant of local rights, local traditions and local gods. The wish to be valued is embedded in human culture though we have wished to be valued over the centuries for different things. If Nietzsche is right and there is no essence of humanity except what is biological, as social beings we seem to have hard-wired into our DNA a need to value ourselves, our gods, and our customs.

And then there is justice. From infancy most people insist on fairness as if it were instinctual; its absence is a ready source of resentment. Injustice is felt as an injury, which is why it is a powerful spur to action. In Book 4 of *The Republic* Plato remarks that justice is not something that the community invents, or philosophers debate amongst themselves: it is not even a matter of codes or social customs though it is often codified, and societies do develop ideas of what is just and what is not. Ultimately, Plato insists, it is something that touches on our own being: it is found within ourselves (*The Republic*, Book 4). Justice is a big word, so perhaps we need to turn to an older one—*thymos*, which means many things including the confidence to be oneself. It is something like an innate human sense of justice (Fukuyama, 1992, p. 165). People believe they have a certain worth and do not appreciate other people acting as though they are worthless. The matter was put best by the German aphorist, Lichtenberg: 'I believe that man is in the last resort so free a being that his right to be what he believes himself to be cannot be contested' (*Aphorisms*, Book L, Number 98). We are all value-esteemers, and war has been one of the principal ways through which (often by default) people have asserted the right to be what they are, or to aspire to what they would like to become. The great problem, of course, is that what we wish to be or to become is often achieved at the expense of other people. The trick has been to find a way of asserting one's freedom without reducing the freedom of others.

In other words, when our worth is not accorded its correct value or estimation, then we tend to become angry. War, in that sense, can be seen as a *thymotic* assertion of self-worth. Plato understood the dynamic very well. We can only think of justice, he adds, when an injustice has arisen. Justice arises from the (irreconcilable) divisions which all societies establish (which is part of the complexity of civilization) in states where there are lords and servants, rich and poor, where there is the beautiful and noble and where there is the desire to invade the sphere of others—in other words where there is war. The just state is one that reconciles differences, not abolishes them (for difference as complexity is what defines a civilization). Justice constitutes what has been brought back (often through war) to moderation from a state of historical excess (injustice). It is human discontent that gives us the insight into what justice is, and why we demand it for ourselves (*The Republic*, 372d).

The great western philosophers have all written at length about justice and the happiness that it is deemed to confer. War makes many of us unhappy, of course; it robs us of the best (the youngest). As the old Greek adage goes, 'In peace sons bury their fathers; in war fathers bury their sons.' War also reduces many of us to the level of our circumstances. As Thucydides warned, it is inherently cruel for that reason. But would the world be any better without it? War can offer a sense of one's place in a whole greater than oneself, one for which sacrifice may be entirely proper. Many societies fight wars not because they think they may become richer or more secure or more powerful, but because on some occasions they conclude that is the right thing to do. They fight, in other words, because they think they have to. George Orwell discovered this for himself while serving in the Spanish Civil War. 'There was much in it that I did not understand,' he wrote later in *Homage to Catalonia* (1938). 'In some ways I did not even like it, but I recognized it immediately as a state of affairs worth *fighting for*' (White, 2007, pp. 1–2).

In the modern age we have fought for universal principles—the universal values that bind us together rather than the individual or tribal attachments which tend to divide. It is those universal values that have become both a legitimizing factor and reason for war. In the course of the eighteenth century war became differentiated from warfare by a new philosophical discovery: transcendental humanism. The idea of finding oneself involved in something larger than life, in a cause, or crusade, has enduring appeal because justice does too. It can be found in the work of André Gide, who confided in his journals in April 1932 that he would be willing to die for the Soviet Union. 'If my life were necessary to ensure the success of the USSR, I should give it at once ... as will do so many others, and without distinguishing myself from them' (Sontag, 2007, p. 68). Gide later fell out of love with the Soviet Union when he recognized the Soviet experiment for what it was, a denial of human freedom. For this he was never forgiven by many on the Left, including the philosopher Jean-Paul Sartre.

Unfortunately, in recent years we have tended to elide two concepts: justice and human rights. It would be more sensible, suggests Mary Midgley, to talk instead of human 'wrongs'. Human beings know instinctively right from wrong, and are quick to wish to revenge themselves for the wrongs done to them (Midgley). Only recently have they been willing to die (and also kill) to advance 'rights'—both those owed to them, and those owed other people. The idea of fighting for a right (or an entitlement) is not only modern, it is largely western. For a peasant to proclaim himself a member of humanity is to efface and subordinate himself; for a European intellectual (post 1789) it is to exalt himself. Indeed, to go to war for humanity is to give war an existential appeal that it has never had before.

We moderns tend to define injustice in terms of natural human rights that are derived from another modern myth, the social contract. Our social imaginaries are modern because they are theorized—could we imagine a democratic society without social contract theory? Injustice for pre-modern societies was conceived of very differently, and more narrowly as any event or practice that challenged routine, or what was taken to be the norm. In pre-modern societies, and many non-western cultures today, the demand for justice is frequently a demand for the restitution of a traditional way of life. In the past societies have preferred to haul in their own history to shore up the future: they have invoked an earlier age of political and social harmony, or invoked an ancient way of life as the only sure way of 'restoring' justice. Most rebellions against injustice in the last four centuries were directed against modernization—the revolts against enclosures in sixteenth-century England; or against the reform of Church practices in the century that followed; or the Luddite smashing of machines in the early years of industrialization. In his *Second Tract on Government* (*c*.1662) Locke told the story of a city of Tartars who had surrendered their persons, wives, families, liberty and wealth ('in short all things sacred and profane') to their Chinese conquerors. But when they were ordered to cut off the plait of hair which by national custom they wore on their heads, they had taken up arms again and were slaughtered to a man. For Locke this demonstrated that men will often be willing to fight for 'the general esteem and the custom of their race'. The story which he probably borrowed from a contemporary history of China that had been published a few years before was taken to show that the Chinese had provoked the revolt by challenging custom—by inflicting one injustice too many (Locke, 1997, p. 60). Marx and Engels were later to refer to such incidents as examples of 'the idiocy of rural life': what can you expect from peasants who have no true consciousness of their own predicament. We tend to be less dismissive, but we can agree that modernity makes all the difference. It is only we moderns who accept that justice can only be achieved through the new, and that often the new has to be fought for. We consider that the reform of institutions is desirable in itself, in part because some traditions are not worth defending, but, in larger part still, because modernity requires constant renewal (Bauman, 2008).

What makes our own intervention today often unjust in the eyes of many is its challenge to tradition. B52 pilots who bomb backward-thinking Mullahs have become something of a western tradition too. It is the unfamiliar: the departure from the norm which is taken to be both abnormal and unjust. It is the unfamiliar that is the problem. We shouldn't be surprised. The wish to reform, renew, change and modernize is good in itself: the idea that we should change things, not restore them; our belief that our quest for justice should be cast in universal terms (what is good for us must by definition be good for other people) is the triumph of the modern and it is the last fallback position—the last existential value that we still attach to war (the defence of what George W. Bush called 'the non-negotiable demands of human dignity' (State of the Union Address, 2002).

A third value which philosophers debate is one that is considered *absolute*, independent of any evaluation at any historical moment or in any particular culture. One is knowledge. No society has ever espoused ignorance, though it is common enough. And only one has championed war as the supreme value: Nazi Germany. Fascism preached that war was the only viable state of being because of the imperatives of Social Darwinism—it was deemed necessary for the survival of the race. For Fascism, war was both cause and effect, the condition and consequence of its own existence. And it was, of course, the essence of the Nazi project. Even with defeat looming, it fought on

THE DIALECTICS OF WARFARE: WAR AND PEACE

to the bitter end. The German army lost 300,000 soldiers a month between February and April 1945. A further 100,000 German citizens chose to take their own lives rather than wait for the arrival of the Red Army.

But liberal societies tended to reify war in their own fashion. In pursuit of Kant's 'permanent peace' they went to war (or at least claimed to). Woodrow Wilson was the first President to promise the world a New World Order. So did George H. Bush after the Gulf War (1991). Addressing a joint session of Congress eleven years to the day before the attack on the World Trade Center, he proclaimed, 'a hundred generations have searched for this elusive path to peace while a thousand wars raged across the span of human endeavour. Today the new world is struggling to be born' (Mead, 2007, p. 10). On the understanding that democracies do not go to war against each other (in part because they do not support terrorists who are at war with everyone else), Bush's son took his country to war for a second time in 2003. The trouble with calling every war the United States has fought a 'crusade for peace' (the term Woodrow Wilson invoked in 1917) is that it is not clear where war ends and peace begins. If peace is contained in the act of war, then war will always be with us until such time as a permanent peace has been secured.

Marxism too reified war by holding out peace as the 'end of history' which would witness the final victory of the proletariat. It rejected the western version of a democratic peace—Trotsky thought this Kantian dream to be a 'canting imbecility' (Keynes, 1951, pp. 72–7). Life and the life force existed only in the struggle against capitalism, which, ending as it must in the victory of socialism, would produce real peace for the first time (not the conspiracy of the rich against the poor). For Marxists, democracy was a conspiracy too. The world could never be at peace until the collapse of capitalism.

The argument took an even more bizarre turn after 1945. In Orwell's dystopian novel, *1984*, the slogan 'War is Peace' is one of the more blatant examples of Doublespeak, by which the regime traduces its own citizenry. Doublespeak was not coined by Orwell, but it is associated with him: it is a mixture of the novel's Newspeak and Doublethink—the ability to believe in two opposing ideas at the same time. It describes the phenomenon of saying one thing while meaning another. It is usually an example of lying, except in this case it is quite literally true, because the three totalitarian powers find themselves in a permanent state of war with each other. But it is a war that none of them aspires to win, for war is a condition of Big Brother remaining in power indefinitely. War is indeed the supreme value of the Orwellian state, as it was of the nuclear peace that held—just—more by luck than by foresight throughout the Cold War. With the atomic bomb there was no more interval between war/peace, only an interface. As the bomb implodes, so does time. An atomic conflict would have been over in hours; the mobilization for war was everything—the distinction between wartime and peacetime was effectively erased.

A somewhat baffled Henry Kissinger was moved to write at the very height of the Cold War, 'today we face the most profound problem of defining what we mean by peace'. This would have surprised Aristotle, who had no difficulty recognizing peace when he saw it. But the point is that although we no longer live in quite such desperate times, we still have difficulty defining peace—until we can we won't secure it. For no one can 'declare' peace until war has exhausted its possibilities; until that time, none of us can have peace of mind.

3

PASCAL'S RULES

St Augustine has seen that one labours uncertainly at sea and in battle and in all the rest, but he has not seen the rules of the game.

(Blaise Pascal, *Pensées*, 234)

In his book *The Invention of Peace* Michael Howard quotes the nineteenth-century English jurist, Sir Henry Maine. 'It is not peace which was natural and primitive and old, but rather war. War appears to be as old as mankind but peace is a modern invention... Not only is war to be seen everywhere but it is war more atrocious than we, with our ideas, can easily conceive' (Howard, 2000). In fact, as I have argued, war is quite recent, and it is an invention too, and it is just (contra Howard) as complex as peace; it took the philosophers to discern its true 'nature'. Of course, peace was dreamed of long before Kant wrote his masterwork *Perpetual Peace*, but it was not conceptualized. Kant supplied the categories we still apply today (including most importantly the democratic peace theory—the contention that democracies do not go to war against each other). Later Cobden and Bright offered us an insight into other factors, such as the triumph of sociability over sovereignty—the idea many of us still share that the aggregated interests of men acting freely in the marketplace produces an acute 'peace interest' (the words are Karl Polanyi's). Without the categories and schemes that philosophers provide us with, we can never hope to grasp the features of any phenomenon, and without an understanding of what the game is actually about, we cannot hope to grasp those 'regularities' which, as the quote at the top of this section shows, Pascal preferred to call 'rules'.

BARBAROUS PHILOSOPHERS

The composition of thoughts or reflections formulated as briefly as possible is a distinctively French tradition (think of La Rochefoucauld, a contemporary of Pascal's, and later Vauvenargues, Chamfort and Valery). In Pascal the aphoristic strategy extends to the higher reaches of theology and metaphysics. My own introduction to him came rather later in life. For many years a copy of his famous Thoughts (or *Pensées*) sat in splendid isolation on my bookshelf. I rarely bothered to consult it. I was aware, of course, of his famous wager—that since we do not know conclusively whether God exists or not, and we will never know for certain until it is too late, what harm is there in betting on his existence in this life so as to obtain a place in the next, and living as much as one can a good Christian life. Pascal's bet involved an 'as if'. He was modern enough to doubt the numinous; he advised us, therefore, to act in accordance with the wager 'as if' Christianity was in some way valid, and by so acting we could be helped in our belief in its validity. Each of us has to stake his destiny upon some world outlook. Reason cannot help us reason out the truth of Christianity. It is on this agnostic assumption that Pascal argues that the sane and prudent person would bet on the truth of Christianity: if God turns out to exist, we have won a life of bliss; if he does not exist and there is no life after death, what has been lost?

Of course, the answer is perhaps a great deal. Voltaire later took Pascal's wager to be a product of his declining health. Nietzsche thought it a sign of the declining health of western civilisation. For both, life was to be lived, not mortgaged to an unknown future. The other objection is that there are a wealth of alternative world views just as there are many different religions and Gods to worship. So if we are to take the bet seriously we had better make the right choice.

It was only later in life that I became aware of how the wager could be applied to the Cold War—for wasn't nuclear deterrence as a theory an existential bet on life? We did not know whether it would hold, and we could not afford to put it to the test. For those of us who thought unilateral nuclear disarmament dangerous, and therefore did not march against the bomb, the bet seemed reasonable enough. MAD— the acronym for Mutual Assured Destruction—was Pascalian *tout court*. For Pascal had found himself (and therein lies his greatness) in the paradoxical position of appealing to reason in order to communicate truths which are outside its province. The paradox is that only reason can persuade reason of its own inadequacy. Deterrence was at

PASCAL'S RULES

best a deferred suicide pact, and the two superpowers that had entered into it recognized its madness from the beginning. There could be no peace without the threat of war, and as long as there was no war, there was peace—the only one possible at the time. In the Cold War there were only two rational positions to adopt: deterrence or disarmament. Peace, as St Augustine tells us (and contrary to Pascal's claim, he did know the rules), is a contested concept—it is largely what we believe it to be. One country's peace can be another's purgatory.

In claiming that war is an invention too, I am claiming that its cultural grammar is an intellectual invention. Philosophy begins with the desire to understand the structure of the world. One of the first philosophers, Heraclitus, was also the first to insist that we try to see everything in accordance with its true nature (*kata phusis*)—the nature of everything shows itself in particular forms; it reveals itself in the world of appearances. Democritus was later to formulate this further—he created the concept of philosophy as a science, as a system of scientific explanations; philosophers show us the structures of life, and from the structures come the idea of *apaxa*i (principles). Like Heraclitus, however, he also argued that the truth of any phenomenon is hidden; as human beings we are separated from reality; philosophers have to tease out the nature of everything, to penetrate beyond appearance to reality itself. A third philosopher, Anaxagoras, was to write that 'appearances are a glimpse of the obscure' (Patočka, 2002, p. 67); why things are obscure is because we ourselves have difficulty understanding what is real: we get insights from time to time, but we always have to work at it.

Progress of Cognition—a Platonic view

	Objects	States of Mind
Intelligible World	The Good	Intelligence (*noesia*)
	Forms	Knowledge (*episteme*)
	Mathematical Objects	Thinking
	Visible Things	Belief
World of Appearance	Images	Imagining

(Plato, *The Republic*, 1971, Chapter XIV, p. 222)

Paradoxes, as Plato instructs us, inhere in the difference between appearance and reality, and philosophers employ them to test the limits

39

of their own knowledge: they may understand some of the rules—they have insights that others do not (which they share with us through their writing)—but they don't know the whole picture. For that reason fire was Heraclitus' chief constitutive agent of life—it flares up suddenly but then sinks back into darkness. We can only seize upon part of the truth. That is why life is not a science—the gift of philosophy is not to find scientific rules but to discover the *problematicity* of existence: we are part of the world we try to describe; because of this all truth tends to be paradoxical.

Indeed, the rules are not really rules—they are regularities, and knowing them won't necessarily help you to win. Most are actually paradoxes, which is why Rousseau disliked them. Indeed, the nature of war is paradoxical—that is the supreme insight that philosophy has given us. Although there are rules they are often traps—because knowing the rules will merely give you a better chance of success (all things being equal, which they often are not). War is paradoxical for that reason.

All the questions I shall pose in Part two are paradoxes: why are war and peace so difficult to distinguish? (Heraclitus); why is war not the suspension of politics, but its continuation in a different form? (Aristotle) Why are mercenaries, many of whom are often professional fighters, so distrusted? (Machiavelli) Why is competitiveness positive, and competition not? (Hobbes) Why should we do nothing in war that compromises peace? (Kant) Why is the essence of military technology not 'technological'? (Marx) And why, despite the rules, is war still an art, not a science? (Heisenberg)

Roy Sorensen takes the paradox to be a species of riddle—the oldest philosophical questions evolved from folklore and show vestiges of the semantic games that first generated them. Anaximander was the first philosopher we know of to pose a paradox when he asked himself whether everything has an origin? He was also the first philosopher to recount the riddle of the Sphinx. The creature asks every traveller a riddle she learned from the Muses: 'What goes on four legs in the morning, two legs in the afternoon and three legs in the evening?' Oedipus manages to find the answer by *decoding* the question: a baby goes on all fours before it learns to walk; it then walks on two legs, before becoming an old man who spends his twilight years hobbling about with a cane. The answer, as it happens, is so obvious that we may well ask why Oedipus was the only man to solve it. But this is not the point of the tale Sophocles subsequently spun in his play. Oedipus is remarkable not for his wisdom in answering the riddle but his courage in daring to come up with the answer. As a member of the Chorus remarks, perhaps the riddle was not meant to be answered. Indeed, we might well conclude that the punishment for not answering it (death) would have been better than the outcome: to kill one's own father and marry one's mother (Sorensen, 2005, pp. 3–5). As the Chorus remarks in Anthony Burgess' fine adaptation of the play: 'It is dangerous to answer riddles/ But some men are born to answer them/ It is the gods' doing. They hide themselves in riddles/ We must not try to understand too much' (Burgess, 1972, p. 80).

Perhaps Rousseau was right after all—it might have been better for all of us if the philosophers had not reasoned out war's 'rules'; perhaps the paradoxes of war might have been better left unaddressed. But then again would we really have wanted to have remained in the state of nature as we know it to have been, not as Rousseau would have us imagine it? In the introduction to his free translation of Sophocles' play, Burgess tells us that we pay a price when we leave the natural order behind. We always hear a voice: 'Don't try to disturb the mystery of order.' For order has both to be and not to be challenged—such is the paradoxical condition of the dynamic that keeps the cosmos going. What Sophocles tells us in his play is that exogamy means disruption and also stability: incest means stability and also disruption. The anomaly or paradox means that Oedipus is the cause of the state's disease, but also, through his discovery of and expiation for sin, the cause of its recovered health. He is a criminal and also a saint. In other words, he is a tragic hero. This is what makes tragic heroes of philosophers too, as Rousseau perhaps should have grasped.

It is to explain why we must grasp the nature of war to prevent another such outcome that I have written this book, conscious of the fact that I am a political scientist with an interest in philosophy, not a professional philosopher with an interest in war. The problem with Rousseau's case against the philosophers was that he imagined the historical existence of a prelapsarian state of nature whose inhabitants had lived with each other in perfect harmony—they had not yet become social animals. We know that Hobbes was more of a realist in painting a very different picture, that of a world in a state of almost endemic warfare. The great contribution of the philosophers has been to explain how we escaped that state, not by forging peace, but by translating warfare into war—and it was their great concern to explain how easily war can be translated back into warfare if we don't observe the 'rules', or what I call the regularities or general principles which constitute its 'nature'. What Rousseau saw as 'barbarous' (the fact that we want to make rules) most have seen as a mark of 'civilization' (the wish to create a life that is rule-bound). It is the mark of our intellectual curiosity that we try to understand the 'rules of the game' whatever the game may be—we want to do better next time, we want to learn from our mistakes and those of others. It is also the mark of our humanity that we constantly call into question the games we play.

Philosophers have been interested in war because war is interested in us. Even those who prefer a life of contemplation have to be aware of the storms raging in the outside world. It is striking that in Plato's most famous work, *The Republic*, the elite—the guardians, those whose job it is to think—are advised to be both 'strong' and 'quick on their feet' (material values which will help them survive in the competitive environment, not the values we traditionally associate with philosophy). Indeed, some philosophers in those harsh unremitting times were often judged in terms of their fortitude in battle. In his own day Socrates was more admired for his bravery than he was for his wisdom.

The need to regulate war has been an urgent demand of history from the time we first emerged from the hunter-gatherer stage of evolution. The great philosophers of the day could not afford to cater to wishful thinking, and they have a hard enough job because human psychology has a near universal tendency to let belief be coloured by desire ('thy wish was father, Harry, to thy thought', the world-weary Henry IV tells his son). For philosophers it is the thought that comes first, and in this book we will be looking at some twenty-six centuries of war and philosophical reflection.

In advancing the claim that philosophers invented war, let me make very clear what I am actually claiming. First, Pascal's Rules are dialogues with the nature of war. They are not scientific laws (though these too can be seen as dialogues with nature, as Ilya Prigogine holds). For Einstein the laws were 'fiction', but he thought the objective correlative to be some kind of underlying harmony. This, the main feature of which, as regards war, I have tried to identify in this book.

Secondly, in claiming that philosophers invented war, I also have to acknowledge that the claim that the Greeks invented philosophy does these days go undisputed. Does philosophy begin with the pre-Socratics? Were all of them Greek? Historians and philosophy have contended, for example, that the Ionian philosophers were the product of a specific multicultural environment: they benefited from living at the interface between two cultures, one Persian, the other Greek. What I am referring to is a tradition that one man, Aristotle, essentially created by deciding on a canon of works which went back to Plato and beyond to what we (but certainly not the Greeks) call the pre-Socratics, men such as Heraclitus who lived in the sixth century BC, and to whom Plato acknowledged an enormous debt. Greek philosophy may be an invented tradition, but it is a tradition nonetheless, and it happens to be the one that has influenced western thinking about war.

Thirdly, and most importantly, I am not claiming that the philosophers 'invented' war in the way that scientists invented the computer or the atomic bomb. Rather they discovered and clarified war's nature. Part of the meaning of 'discovery' is that to be discovered something has to exist prior to its discovery. Clearly, war existed before the Greeks—we can date it back to conflict between the empires of the ancient world a thousand years before the pre-Socratics. For much of my life I have always taken seriously Pascal's profound insight that we understand much more than we know—I have no doubt the ancient Egyptians understood many of Pascal's' 'rules of war'. Nonetheless, the fact that so few wars seem to have brought about any significant change (empires rose and fell with depressing regularity) suggests that war was not especially complex. Knowledge counts—it makes all the difference. The Greeks may have taken an independently existing reality but they transformed it by translating understanding into knowledge. As people become more reflective about their own practices, writes Daniel Dennett, they become more and more inventive in their exploration of the space of possibilities. The human capacity for reflection yields an ability to notice and evaluate patterns in our own behaviour (Dennett, 2006, p. 155).

Or to put it another way, how you wage war will depend to a large extent on how you think you should—the two are not identical but they are inseparable. There is an inescapable connection between the knower and the known. Instead of bringing war into being, therefore, philosophers discovered it in the sense that no one else had thought out its general principles or 'rules' (certainly not the warriors whose stock in trade was violence, who were not much given to reasoning out their own trade). They discovered that war has a nature which, unlike its character, was also a fit subject for philosophical reflection. They clarified its nature by engaging in careful investigation of how human beings could limit the damage they inflict on each other, and they did so outside any religious or mythological system that would have translated rules into rituals. They did this to war much earlier than they did to ethics, for even as late as Kant philosophers were dealing with the conundrum—how can there be an ethical system without an ultimate authority, or the categorical imperative of an *ought* (in short without God)? Only at the end of the eighteenth century did they cut through the problem by recognizing that ethical axioms are found and tested not very differently from the axioms of science—truth is what stands the test of experience.

In other words, philosophers clarified the nature of war very early in human history using all the resources at their disposal—from history (Thucydides) to poetry (Hesiod), the cultural tools which help us to make sense of the human experience. And in representing the nature of war they also influenced how it was conducted—their ideas penetrated the military consciousness, usually indirectly. As reflective creatures we respond to the representations we find in history or the answers we absorb from the philosophical canon. To the extent that generals allowed their minds to be shaped over time by the work of philosophy, they were the progeny of Heraclitus, the very first philosopher to ask: what is the nature of war?

At the risk of anachronism, I would call Heraclitus the first complexity theorist—the first writer we know of to echo the contemporary complexity theorist Herbert Simon in arguing that the purpose of philosophy is to understand the 'meaningful simplicity in the midst of disorderly complexity...' (Buchanan, 2002, p. 214). Behind the flux of everyday life, he saw an intelligent structure that had 'ordered' existence, one which it was the task of philosophy to uncover if it could. Behind daily experience lie deeper structures—truth. Behind the ever-changing character of war lies its 'nature' that needs to be grasped if it is to be waged successfully.

Part 2

The Nature of War

4

WHY WAR?

WHY WAR CHANGES THE WORLD AND IS ITSELF TRANSFORMED BY THE CHANGES IT PROMOTES (HERACLITUS OF EPHESUS C.540–480 BC)

War is father of all, king of all: some it has shown as gods, some as men; some it has made slaves, some free. (B 53)

Heraclitus was the first of the pre-Socratic philosophers (as far as we know) to ask the question: why war? And hence what was its beginning? The question begged an answer: it never assumed, of course, an end either to war let alone the enquiry. How could it? The contemporary Slovenian philosopher Slovoj Zizek claims that melancholy is in fact the beginning of philosophy—the interrogation into the human condition and its discontents. Heraclitus (in whom, in Hegel's vivid phrase, the history of philosophy struck dry land) was called the 'weeping philosopher' because of the sadness induced in him by the follies of the human race.

What precipitates our categorization of the world around us, which Aristotle taught is central to all philosophical questioning, is our purposive relationship with it, our need to make sense of it. What makes the categorization possible is our ability to see the analogy between one thing and another—like Heraclitus, to see war as the father of everything. The answer to his question, however, did require him to distinguish war from warfare, and to become the first philosopher to make the distinction which is at the very core of this enquiry. 'To found, to begin is to act essentially' writes Steiner (Steiner, 2001, p. 42). In asking the question 'why war?' Heraclitus was also enquiring into its essence—or nature. For him this also meant asking what was the essence of life, and he had no doubt of the answer—it was change; everything is in flux. The metaphor of strife was his way of explaining that change inheres in everything—'war is the father of everything' is still his most famous saying.

Heraclitus lived in Ephesus on the Ionian coast at the turn of the fifth-sixth century BC. There is a lot of allegory, mystery and magic mixed up in early pre-Socratic writing. His work survives as a collection of some 120 fragments, many of only one or two sentences in length. He left no school behind him and seemed to have little interest in the dissemination of his ideas. Unlike many of the other pre-Socratics, his works were never read publicly. Instead, he deposited them in the temple at Ephesus in the hope that they might be consulted by the curious, but then again they might not. Even the ancients found his sayings puzzling, if not often downright obscure. Socrates claimed to understand only half of his work. The rest, he added rather archly, would take a Delian master diver to bring to the light (Gadamer, 2002, p. 22).

It used to be thought that they were culled from a larger work, but it is now widely thought that he intended his work to be aphoristic and deliberately obscure. In other words he was ambiguous by design (it is a mark of his genius). There is a fragment of his that has survived: 'The Lord whose oracle is at Delphi neither asserts nor hides but gives a sign' (Warren, 2007, p. 59). He wanted his readers to tease out the real meaning of his words. They could only be understood by those who were willing and able to think and see the world in the right way (Warren, 2007, p. 62). You can see why this approach commended itself to many in the twentieth century when the idea that truth could be grasped in its entirety was challenged by many, including quantum physicists.

Heraclitus' claim that war fathers everything is of course a metaphor, and metaphors are important because they encourage us to think things through. Philosophy needs metaphors and metaphor is basic; how basic is the most basic philosophical question. As Aristotle points out in the *Poetics*, a skill for metaphor cannot be taught because it depends on genius: an individual's ability to perceive similarities in dissimilarities, the likeness in unlike things (Aristotle, *Poetics*, 57). Heraclitus' metaphorical style of writing sets him apart. Metaphors, of course, are part of the universal language we speak—they are a consequence, writes E.O. Wilson in *Consilience* (1998), of the spreading activation in the brain during learning, and therefore are 'the building blocks of creative thought' (Watson, 2002, p. 771). Through complex juxtapositions, metaphors fuse feeling, thought and images in ways that expand the experiences of the language. As Aristotle maintained, metaphors make things vivid in a way that the non-metaphorical use of language may not—they are arresting and often poetic; they get us to think, which is what every philosopher wants us to do. They also get us to see—to use our imagination, to picture a likeness we have not appreciated before.

What is the chief purpose of philosophy, asked Aristotle, if not to astonish us that the world is what it is in all its bewildering and magnificent complexity. The patterns that mathematicians and philosophers tease out reveal just how complex the world is—for that reason, to quote the eighteenth-century writer Giambattista Vico, at their best they allow us to experience the world anew (Beer/Landtscheer, 2004, pp. 24–5).

So, the use of metaphor as the basis of communication allows any number of interpretations of Heraclitus' message. Does this matter? In this case it does because it is important for us to understand what he is saying and to examine it closely to see whether we agree. Even Plato, despite his declaration of war on the poets whom he notoriously banned from his ideal republic, appreciated that it is often only through metaphors and myths—through the poetry of language—that the truth can be absorbed. We are an inveterately poetic species. For poetry moves us and astonishes us—so do mathematical proofs for those of a mathematical bent. Like philosophers, mathematicians find beauty in patterns (Euclid's infinity of prime numbers); that the patterns may eventually have a practical application is only a 'contingent bonus' for the pure mathematician (Steiner, 2001, p. 148). But war is not a 'contingent' phenomenon—it matters because it kills; those caught up in it cannot escape its influence.

A metaphor is not a correspondence, it is an analogy. It translates the strange into the familiar by transforming the experience into an idea. It helps us make sense of a world where phenomena have various degrees of significance according to the associations we make. As Steven Mithen writes, what makes us different from all other species is our ability to 'break down' separate mental compartments. Young chimps, for example, can identify objects. If taught by us they can learn to point out things such as a car, a cat or a house (Greenfield, 2008, p. 137). But only we can make connections between things; only we can think metaphorically, to see one thing in terms of something else, i.e. to see life in terms of war.

Metaphors, in short, do much of our thinking for us. They communicate complex ideas with extraordinary efficiency and channel our thoughts along certain predetermined axes. The most powerful metaphors express one thing in terms of something else with which we are familiar. The human mind, writes Steven Pinker, can only think in terms of concrete experiences—objects and forces, sights and sounds, and above all habits of behaviour in the culture in which we grow up (Pinker, 2008, p. 238). In claiming that life is war, Heraclitus reached for a metaphor with which his readers would have found an everyday resonance. For war was a condition of life for the ancient Greeks, as it was for most other peoples until recently, which is why Heraclitus' metaphor still has great appeal.

We are so conflicted that we still tend to identify our own minds with the battlefields of history—we still talk of winning rather than earning respect, of 'fighting' for our principles, or 'going over the top'. The answer to Heraclitus' question 'why war?' is that it is part of our humanity. Unlike his predecessors, who were too busy with the world to look for one within, he says 'I went in search of myself'. It is our ever-changing nature—our mood swings, our joy one moment and melancholy the next—that led him to his inevitable conclusion that we ourselves are constantly in a state of flux. We are always discovering our own humanity.

War is the great leveller: it finds each of us out. It 'proves some to be gods and others human beings'. The brave man is already brave, of course, but it is war that sometimes brings his bravery out, that transforms the memory of a man into a hero. War is indeed the father of everything because no one can escape it. It finds some equal to the demands they are asked to face, and others not. The coward will reveal his cowardice in trying to escape the battlefield; the brave man will also 'out' himself in his own fashion.

War has also been so central to the human story that it would be remarkable if philosophers had not spent a great deal of time coming to terms with it. If you do not believe me, imagine history without its crusades, or fights for liberty, or its revolutions with their revolutionary wars. Imagine no heroes fighting for justice, whatever they might mean by the term, no national liberation figures in the twentieth century, or no subject peoples fighting against imperial rule. If you try to think of human achievement without war you would conjure up a strange world indeed, one that would be less real than Daniel F. Golouye's *Counterfeit World* in which we all live in a computer simulation devised by some superhuman civilization. The point is that the absence of peace is not due to lack of imagination, it is the product of imagination. It arises from the belief that the world can be other than it is, better, fairer, or more just. War inspires us because it is based on our own potential to become what we are.

Now let us remember that the metaphor Heraclitus uses is war—do not confuse it for warfare, or elide the two. War fathers change—it generates it (it is generative—like a father it gives birth). Warfare doesn't; there is no change in the state of nature where people find themselves stuck in a permanent present where there is no flux, only chaos. It is the ordering principle of change that he wants to get us to confront; war is ordered, and change is possible only because it takes place within an ordered world.

Heraclitus was referring back to a myth shared by most civilizations—the primal night from which we have all emerged. Every civilization has such myths, including our own. The myth of original sin still has an especially tenacious hold on the imagination. Max Horkheimer called the concept of the Fall of Man as developed in the Old Testament the most seminal instinct ever fostered by man (Steiner, 2008, p. 198). Pascal argued that, wretched as we are, we would not attempt to seek happiness unless somewhere within us there remained a glimmer of past happiness, a remembrance of life before the Fall. In *The World as Will and Representation* Schopenhauer commended the tale for describing the human condition so accurately. For him man was a being whose existence is punishment and expiation. In that sense the myth of the Fall was metaphysically (and allegorically) true. 'Our existence resembles nothing so much as the consequence of a false step and a guilty desire' (Murdoch, 1992, p. 361). Steiner concludes that this absurd story—one that is outrageous and unfair at the same time in visiting the sins of the fathers upon the children—must have the force it does because of what lies buried in our unconscious: the remembrance of some disaster or dark catastrophe, some return to the night which the ancients recognized because they were much nearer to the night than we are.

To call it a myth does not mean it is a false story. It means that it is given symbolic power which is independent of its possible or proclaimed truth (Midgley, 1985, p. 33). A myth is merely a story we tell ourselves in order to understand the world and our place in it. Philosophy is useful in part, because it spins myths which provide the concepts through which we understand and act on the world. It is a natural extension of our interest in truth, and a very specific understanding of truth at that: not scientific truth or an objective reality that can be tested and demonstrated again and again in laboratory conditions, but something that is true for us (Scruton, 1996, p. 9). It is our experience of the world that constitutes the world. In a word, reality is often not what obtains but what we imagine it to be (and what we imagine is what we want to be true) (Vattimo, 2005, p. 10).

In claiming that war, not warfare, is the father of everything, Heraclitus drew upon a theogony that was handed to the Greeks by Hesiod writing in the seventh century. In his book *Did The Greeks Believe Their Myths?* Paul Veyne tells us that Hesiod knows that we will take him at his word: we will believe the myths he spins, and he treats himself as he expected to be treated: he believes everything that entered his head (Lane-Fox, 2008, p. 360). The reason why Hesiod believed this mythic revelation of the distant past to be true was that he believed he had been inspired to write it down by the Muses. George Steiner again:

> With uneasy tact, Hesiod twice relates the birth of the Muses. It is only through their gifts of remembrance and narration that moral men can know something of the birth of the world. But how can the Muses have been witness to their own creation? Hence Hesiod's far-reaching intimation that cosmological narratives deal with appearance, even if that appearance is held to be a truthful reflection of the facts. One cannot go back any further than inspiration. Creation and the poetic telling of the story are in some ultimate sense identical. (Steiner, 2001, p. 30)

Hesiod considered that the Muses were the authors of his whole work, so awed was he by the mystery of his own creative process. The Muses, he tells us, get us to remember what is buried away in our minds—though memory is valuable, of course, only if inferences can be drawn from what is remembered. And the inference the Muses want us to draw from remembering the primal night is that we have escaped from the state of warfare, not into a world at peace but into a world of war (if we want peace we will have to fight for it, but the fact that war has 'rules' allows us, at least, to strive for it for the first time).

WHY WAR?

Aristotle grasped that language was the essence of both humanity and order. *Logos*—the Word—gives rise to logic, an ordering of the world through naming and categorization. 'In the beginning was the word' is John's insight into how God created order out of chaos. Thus there is a connection between language and order. Language enables us to impose an order on things that are constantly in flux, just as war has its own language or cultural grammar which makes it transformative, not sterile. The first writers to use language to order the world were the poets—poetry, added the pre-Socratic philosopher Xenophanes, allowed the world of the gods to take shape (Sandywell, 1996, p. 161). The first philosophers like Parmenides were poets too. They made use of the Homeric hexameter to present their arguments. They followed the poets in asking questions. In short, the breakthrough from warfare to war required the poets and then the philosophers to make sense of the world (and thus ensure there was no return to the primal night).

Hesiod's theogony 'reveals' that even the gods too experienced the war of all against all—fathers fought sons, and sons formed alliances with their mothers against their own fathers. Incest and cannibalism were commonplace. Zeus' will-to-power (the violent path to his kingship of the gods) was unmediated by any claims of justice. We also read in Hesiod of the war against the Titans. Zeus held Olympus. The struggle for a long time wavered in the balance. And it did not end with the Titans' defeat. The Giants, the offspring of the blood from the wounded Uranus, staged a revolt against Zeus. Even after the defeat of the Giants, the gods continued to visit violence on others, in this case Man. Zeus exterminates humanity twice—once because it is ridiculously weak, and the second time because following Prometheus' theft of fire, it has become dangerously strong. No one in Heraclitus' world believed the gods would exterminate man again—men would do this themselves if they ever allowed war to degenerate into warfare

In short, Hesiod claims, what men know of the cosmos they *remember* (i.e. creation and poetic telling of the story are identical). What we know (through language) is appearance; war appears to be the father of everything; the appearance is held to be a truthful reflection of the fact (Steiner, 2001, p. 30). And once humans interpret reality—once they speak it or write about it, and attempt to understand it—they impose their own order. They order and re-order the world through the use of language with the result that it becomes more complex still.

BARBAROUS PHILOSOPHERS

In Euripides' play *Ion* the chorus of women at Apollo's temple in Delphi comment on a relief that shows the defeat of the giants by the gods. Athena fights one, Zeus another. These battles celebrated the victory of order over lawlessness—the victory of war over warfare. The tale of the battle against the giants had a special appeal to philosophers. [In the *Sophists*, Plato divides the world into two types of people: 'Giants' who only believe what is revealed by their senses (materialists) and (by implication) the gods (including philosophers), who can penetrate beyond the real to Forms or essences (Lane-Fox, 2008, p. 321).] What is central to the break out of the primal night is the violence of differentiation (the polarities of 'before' and 'after'). The emergence of difference is a result of flux, and the identification of difference is made possible through violence. Violence is the 'splitting' and ground of manifestation (Sandywell, 1996, p. 182). Every subsequent mode of existence owes everything to this violent break out from the night: the world of mortals and immortals, the earth and heaven. All 'being' (or questioning about being) arises from the break. Anaximander noted that all finite beings had committed an injustice against the infinite and must recompense by returning to that unbounded source: by *reflecting* upon it and the difference between the two (Sandywell, 1996, p. 185). But philosophers too, of course, have thoughts that they are often too fearful to express. For once you postulate the existence of gods, you next ask their origins: what is their nature, and where did they come from? And then you begin to ask some disturbing questions: who came before them? Why do they exist? And most disturbing of all, perhaps, what would the world be like if they did not exist?

It is also at this point in the story that we begin to ask what is the nature of war. Heraclitus was the first philosopher we know to ask that question and the first to proffer an answer: it promotes change. We must recognize that for the Greeks change itself was the problem. We must always remember how much we differ from them. They are sufficiently alike that we can understand them, but sufficiently different that the challenge of understanding them is worth meeting. And the Greeks found change disturbing because it can happen without warning. They called it *metabole*: abrupt change (Gadamer, 2001, p. 39). We think we know what peace is, but it can give rise to war very quickly. Peace, in other words, cannot be understood without war, or vice versa. But on another, deeper level of meaning, change is problematic too—for Heraclitus change is of no value in itself (as it is for us). On the contrary it is a symptom of the world's lack of perfection. A perfect world would be a changeless world. Things change because through movement they are always seeking repose, hence movement is both the consequence of imperfection and the means to overcome it at the same time. Heraclitus, in that respect, can be seen as the father of complexity theory. For we escape the state of nature into a world of change; we move from pre-history where change is painfully slow, and life relatively un-complex, into history where change begins to accelerate and complexity is the rule. In many cases war brings about those changes. Indeed, before the industrial revolution war was the primary engine of change. Historians may continue to debate whether in fact there was just as much cooperation as there was conflict in history, but of course cooperation and conflict are cut from the same cloth; or to mix metaphors they are joined at the hip. What's important is to study all the related patterns of conduct in order to understand the context, for it is the context which is important. It is the context which makes us aggressive or peaceful, which sanctions war or results in peace. It just so happens that the context of life for much of history gave competitive societies an edge, or a margin of error that less bellicose societies did not always enjoy.

We mustn't import Hegelian assumptions into this process of complexity: there is no 'cunning of reason' that can be detected; and there is no end to which the process is taking us; and there is certainly no promise that the eventual outcome will be an end to contradiction. Complexity multiplies contradictions, it doesn't resolve them. Nor is history the story of rapid, accumulating change which we call Progress. 'Progress' itself is something of a cultural construction, in its present form an Enlightenment concept which over the last two centuries has been translated into an ideology of life. It found particularly strong expression in Kant's 'hidden plan' and even Adam Smith's championship of the middle class as the vanguard of a superior economic and moral order.

It is more appropriate to incorporate into history a different concept—'development', and we can do so without smuggling in normative assumptions if by development we mean nothing more than increasing complexity. Indeed, it is far more credible to claim not that history is progressive, but rather that it is *directional*. And what is directional is our capacity to learn, to adapt to our environments and to learn increasingly quickly. If modern societies become complex at a faster rate, that is because they are much more receptive than premodern societies to new information—they tend to embrace it, and do so collectively (Wright, 2001, p. 248). In a word, they learn faster. Cultural evolution can be said to be Lamarckian in the sense that acquired traits and skills can be passed on over generations at ever faster rates.

History, of course, is full of fits and starts (or 'punctuated equilibriums' in the language of evolutionary biology), but the direction is clear enough to most historians. It is a direction away from simple sameness to diversity, towards complex sameness which we call, today, globalization (McNeill, J.R./McNeill, William, 2003, p. 320). For much of history war has been the main engine of social and political change; only very recently have we identified the market as more dynamic still (and it is its threat to market stability that has rendered recourse to war increasingly unattractive to the larger powers).

Heraclitus' metaphor is important for another reason: it raises fundamental questions about war too. If war is indeed transformative it is also subject to the very change it promotes; it has a protean character for that very reason, one which historians spend their time analyzing and/or describing. Heraclitus' whole thinking encourages us to think along these lines; everything is change. The fire is extinguished but then flares up again and next time it is not the same; everything flows but in flowing it undergoes transformation. You can't step into the same river twice. One of the best and most recent elaborations of this view is to be found in Philip Bobbitt's magisterial work, *Terror and Consent* (2008), which offers a sweeping *tour d'horizon* of the history of war, one similar in scope and ambition to his earlier work, *The Shield of Achilles*. Stated rather reductively, his argument is that war and the state order exist in a mutually affecting relationship. Not only do fundamental innovations in war bring about fundamental transformations in the constitutional order of states, transformations in the constitutional order bring about fundamental changes in the conduct of war (Bobbitt, 2008). In other words, it is in the nature of war that war itself is in constant flux. The very changes in social complexity that it engineers feed back into the way it is conducted. The Hoplite war of the Greek city-states gave way to the mass armies of the Hellenistic age; cavalry gave the feudal levies of Europe a decisive advantage; the gunpowder armies of Europe and western

WHY WAR?

Asia trounced the nomads once and for all; the mass conscript armies of the last century mimicked the assembly line production of late capitalism, and in so doing produced the industrial battlefields of the Western Front. The state of nature/warfare, by contrast, is unchanging. The battlefield melees photographed by anthropologists in New Guinea in the 1950s had been unchanging for thousands of years. If H.G. Wells' time traveller had travelled back through two thousand years of the island's pre-history, his trajectory would have been his own point of departure.

And, of course, as war changes so does our view of Heraclitus too—all metaphors lend themselves to interpretation as new challenges continue to arise. In the twentieth century the philosopher Emmanuel Levinas reformulated the phrase 'War is the father of everything' in terms that appealed to an age of Total War: 'Being reveals itself *as* war' (Hillsman, 2004, p. 28). Social Darwinism was one of the age's prevailing myths and it presented mankind with a world in which hope was a lottery. There was no God, and no recourse to prayer. Blind evolution determined the survival of the species, and those fortunate enough to survive lorded it over others. Life was a permanent state of nature, or warfare. Nazism preached a peculiar twentieth-century world view that war was peace. War became a metaphor for peace, and peace a metaphor for war. What was the Nazi will to power but in Freudian terms the satisfaction of the ego; indeed, all the ego-transcending conventions and taboos (including rules or laws of war) that made war so complex were repudiated or renounced.

The Nazis couldn't cope with the complexity of life, with its displacement, disenchantment and alienation. They were the great simplifiers and essentializers; they even sought to subtract a whole race from the genetic diversity of mankind. They couldn't deal with the ambivalent and paradoxical, which is why ultimately they couldn't understand the rules of war. The ego frustration of fulfilment turned them towards unadulterated violence. And because they believed it possible to attempt the impossible, their eventual defeat was predictable and predicted by some: the rules that reflected the complex world were torn up in favour of a world of fantasy. This fantasy was driven by only one urge: to push war to its absolute limits (Booker, 2004, p. 481). There was an inevitable price to be paid, a final reckoning: the Nazi fantasy could only be sustained by regressing into a primal state, and that meant ignoring all the things philosophers had told us about war and how best to wage it. Whenever fantasy ventures down the path of violence it runs into a dead-end.

Heraclitus was also championed by a number of other philosophers, many of whom were influenced by Heidegger, among them Jan Patočka who came to prominence in his native Czechoslovakia as a spokesman of a human rights movement called Charter 77 (he died in circumstances still unknown under intensive police interrogation just before his 70th birthday). Patočka liked Heraclitus most because he tells us that history (i.e. our humanity) is evolution from a state of being where life is to be survived to one in which it is to be lived. 'Thus *polemos* is at the same time that which constitutes the *polis* and the primordial insight that makes philosophy possible' (Patočka, 1996, p. 43).

The Greek city has always been special in western philosophy because it has been taken to be the birthplace of the political as we understand the term today. We can take one of the first cities, Jericho, which also happens to have the oldest massive fortifications in the world—stone walls that are twelve feet high and six feet thick. But Jericho wasn't a city as Aristotle would have understood the term—an entity which begins from need and continues for the sake of the good life. Jericho was a nomadic settlement behind walls. Its walls surrounded a central oasis around which two thousand people congregated for security who had no concept of citizenship, and conducted no political debates; they did not even share the concept of the 'political'. City life offered no opportunity 'to change what it was possible to do; it simply made doing it safer' (Allen, 2004, p. 230).

Philosophy, adds Barry Allen, whom I have just quoted, has always been an interrogation of the society that embeds it; there is no occasion for philosophical reflection before the city. It is the city which offers urbanity and civility, and everything it secures behind its walls sets the topics for every enduringly interesting work of philosophy, one of the topics being war. For as Patočka grasped, what is important about the *polis* is that it promotes contests—it nourishes the wish to excel. The fact that even the dead can spur us to consuming jealousy shows that reputation is everything. Plato would have banished Homer if he had had the power; Thucydides openly took on Herodotus. Ostracism—the banishment from the city into a realm of non-being—is the punishment, Nietzsche tells us, originally meted out not to the worst citizen, but the best, because if one claims to be the best the contest would come to an end. There would be no strife because there would be noth-

WHY WAR?

ing to strive against. There would be no politics. (In one of the surviving fragments Heraclitus wishes his countrymen nothing but bad luck for they had expelled the best of them, Hermodorus, saying, 'Let no one of us be best; if there is such a man, let him be elsewhere and with others.' B 121)

And for Patočka, like Heraclitus, it is conflict (the contest) that institutes change: the 'flash of being out of the night of the world'. Patočka was a student of Heidegger who had carved into a piece of wood above the front door of his hut in the Black Forest (to which he would retreat every summer) the Heraclitean aphorism, 'lightning strikes all'. Adversaries meet in conflict and create a new way of being human. History is life that no longer takes itself for granted. War is risk taking, and it is the courage to risk all on the battlefield that produces change. War, in a word, is the medium of history.

Here life does not stand on the firm ground of generative continuity: it is not blackened by the dark earth, but only by darkness that is, it is *ever confronted* by its finitude and the permanent precariousness of life. And only by coming to terms with this threat, confronting it undaunted, can free life as such unfold; its freedom is its innermost foundation, the freedom of the undaunted. (Patočka, 1996, p. xiii)

Philosophers don't write like this today, and metaphysical speculations have fallen out of fashion in the west. But the sentiment if not its quasi–Hegelian tone was quite common until quite recently. At a conference on her own work in the 1960s, Hannah Arendt's old friend Mary McCarthy questioned her love of the Greeks—after all what *did* they talk about in the Assembly since they excluded everything we debate in our Parliaments today, such as social and material suffering, or the rights we accord one another. If the Assembly only debated politics but excluded from discussion everything we consider to be political, then surely all that was left was war. Arendt acknowledged that her friend was right in many respects. Of course, the Greeks had created a body of philosophy and literature that was incomparable, but for good or ill, war was the most profound *political* phenomenon to have shaped the Greek consciousness. And living as they did in the second half of the twentieth century, both Patočka and Arendt accepted that war was still the determining theme of political life (Bernstein, 1986, p. 250).

It is no longer. Looking back from our vantage point of economic crises and environmental concerns, the importance attached to war may appear to be puzzling. In that sense we may have crossed a threshold—we may need to change our metaphors as a result. Human intelligence, writes Steven Pinker, does indeed have the capacity for Heraclitean thinking (Pinker, 2007, p. 238). It has an unlimited capacity to think cosmologically, in abstractions, and grasp the universal in the particular. But this human capacity has evolved out of primary circuitry for coping with the physical and social world. And since people think in metaphors, the key to understanding human thought is to deconstruct those metaphors which explain why people find themselves in conflict with each other. It is precisely because we frame our problems with particular metaphors that we find ourselves in conflict with others. 'The language of argument is not poetic, fanciful or rhetorical; it is literal.' We talk about arguments that way because we conceive them that way—and we act according to the way we conceive the world (Lakoff and Johnson, 2003, p. 5). To see war as the father of all things is of course to encourage us to go to war in order to change the world.

Heraclitus' metaphor just happened to be life-affirming precisely because warfare is so life-denying. For much of history it offered a uniquely optimistic cultural grammar. Let me invoke George Steiner's definition of grammar—the articulate organization of perception, reflection and experience (Steiner, 2001, p. 5). Warfare presents us only with the present tense (a perpetual bleak and uncompromising presence). War offers us for the first time the promise of a different future. It allows us to strive for peace, or at the very least to imagine it. It is this 'incommensurate grammatology' of verb futures, with its subjunctives and optatives, adds Steiner, that has proved indispensable to the survival of the species. It is the 'what if'—what if we have peace and not war (after all it is our choice); or what if by resorting to war we can secure a more long lasting peace? These questions are philosophical. Hope is one of 'the supreme fictions empowered by syntax'. But hope and fear, of course, are frequently conjoined. You cannot have one without the other, any more than you can have peace without war, or war without peace. For hope is always beset by the fear of not realizing one's dreams, and fear includes the seed of hope: the possibility of overcoming what makes us fearful (Steiner, 2001, p. 5).

We are the only species that entertains the knowledge of our own contingency, the indifference of the world to our existence. Perversely, that consciousness does not mean we put survival first. Some of us must find meaning in death. Our awareness of our own being transcends being in the world (Kolakowski, 1989, p. 166). We look back in fear to the primal night, or in hope of a future not yet attained. The consciousness of being in the world makes consciousness inexplicable by reference to the world that constitutes the present. This is why we invent myths; why we insist on inscribing meaning to the unmeant. Lezek Kolakowski postulates two kinds—those which contain obligations to a pre-historical state of Being older than the primal night itself, such as the 'essence' of our own humanity or some Kantian law, or some transcendent value such as obligation to God. In this myth the real world is a place of exile and we should honour what came before or what is outside it (Kolakowski, 1989, p. 95). We are indebted to Being (a debt that must sometimes be paid off with our lives). But a myth can also make other demands on us. It can be a destiny to be fulfilled or a destiny as yet unfulfilled. And the myths of the last century were often that. Both inspired their adepts to hurry off to their death.

'The conviction reigns,' wrote Nietzsche in *The Genealogy of Morals*, 'that it is only through the sacrifices and accomplishments of the ancestors that the tribe exists. One has to pay them back with sacrifices ... one must recognize (that) it is a debt that grows greater every year' (Nietzsche, 1995, p. 66). As he prepared for his last mission one kamikaze pilot in 1945 wrote a letter to his father explaining his commitment to die. 'The Japanese way of life is indeed beautiful and I am proud of it as I am of Japanese history and mythology which reflect the purity of our ancestors and their belief in the past. Whether or not those beliefs are true, it is an honour to give up my life for [them]' (Delgado, 2009, p. 9). With such sentiments on their lips many young men went into battle; by the end of the war Japan had sacrificed 1,228 planes and their crews.

The Second World War is a testament to getting the past into proportion. Germany also sent off its soldiers to die in the name of a primal Aryan essence—central to which, Hitler told the German people, was a primordial capacity for sacrifice, which was greater than that of any other race. The imagery of national socialism looked back quite self-consciously to the past—it traded in the stories of the Teutonic Knights and, further back still, German mythology with its references to Wotan and Valhalla.

Other myths, including the socialist dream of heaven on earth, hurried millions more to an early death in the killing fields of the Third

World. The Soviet dream was of a world without conflict, a conditioned world in which people were condemned to be happy. The American dream was of a world made safe for democracy, and through democracy permanent peace. That was the problem with the twentieth century. Hope, writes Steiner, is a transcendental inference, it is underwritten by theological–metaphysical presuppositions, a futures market. Hoping is a speech act which presumes a listener (God or History, or one's own conscience) 'in the hope' of support or at least understanding from something or Someone. As Kafka wrote:

> The 20th century has put in doubt the theological, the philosophical and the political–material insurance for hope. It queries the rationale and credibility of future tenses. It makes understandable the statement that 'there is abundance of hope but none for us'. (Steiner, 2001, p. 6)

And what of today? As Steven Pinker writes, we are not condemned to follow the metaphors of the past. We can change our myths in order to adapt to changing realities, which is the way in which serious changes are essentially brought about. But changing a myth is difficult (Midgley, 2004, p. 175). We cannot always jettison it or replace it with a new one. 'The habits of thought that express them are deeply woven into our lives' (Midgley, 2004, p. 152). The Heraclitean myth still holds because it still describes reality for most of us. We are not in a position to jettison Heraclitus just yet, even though war is unlikely ever again to provide the role models or archetypal heroes or axiomatic events by which nations define their destiny. War has been displaced from the forefront of our imagination; our generation is more sceptical about it than any other. Even so, we have not done with it yet, which is why we must continue to understand its 'rules'.

5

WAR AND HUMAN AMBITION
WHY THE RULES OF WAR ARE PARADOXICAL
(THUCYDIDES C.460–400 BC)

The best way for us to make ourselves feared by the Greeks in Sicily is not to go there at all; and the next best thing is to make a demonstration of our power and then, after a short time, go away again. We all know that what is most admired is what is farthest off and least liable to have its reputation put to the test.

(*The History of the Peloponnesian War*, 6.11)

It is said that when he was Chairman of the Joint Chiefs of Staff Colin Powell used to display a quote on his desk from Thucydides' *History*: 'of all exercises of power, restraint is the greatest'. It was at the heart of what came to be known as the Powell Doctrine. Thucydides never said it, as it happens, but the man who is quoted, Nicias, came nearest to saying it in the speech from which I have quoted. If Heraclitus informs us that war is transformative, it is Thucydides, the first strategist, who informs us that it is also paradoxical: once it is used, military power can diminish quite rapidly.

We know remarkably little about Thucydides (he himself does not tell us much). The best guess is that he was born around 460 BC and died in the first decade of the following century. He was a generation younger than Pericles, who is the great hero of his history. The quote above comes from one of Thucydides' 'problematic speeches', the great addresses he gave some of the principal characters of his story—historians continue to debate how much they represent what he heard them actually say, and how much was a product of his own imagination.

Thucydides actually tells us that, though he tried to keep as closely as possible to the general sense of the words that were actually used, he also tried to make the speakers say what in his opinion was called for by each situation (*History*, 1.22). The two requirements may have little to do with each other, and the second gives a wide license to authorial interpretation

The passage above comes from a speech by Nicias in the winter of 416–415, early into the second act of the long Peloponnesian War when the Athenians debated whether to despatch an army to help their allies in Sicily. Thucydides tells us that his fellow citizens had no idea how big Sicily was—they didn't know that it took a ship eight days to sail around the island. Nicias, who had negotiated a peace treaty with Sparta (the treaty was named after him), was opposed to the expedition from the first. 'What I fear is not the enemy's strategy but our own mistakes,' Pericles had lamented years earlier (*History*, 1.144). He had told the Athenians that there were many reasons why they should feel confident in ultimate victory provided that they did not go out of their way to court new perils. He had warned them against adventurism. Success, however, bred overconfidence and overconfidence bred recklessness, in turn. The outcome was a tragedy of Sophoclean proportions.

Nicias reminded his fellow citizens why they had grown overly ambitious. They had come to despise the Spartans because they had been more successful in the war than they had ever imagined. Hence their renewed determination to extend their empire by conquering Sicily, though they officially were only coming to the aid of a friend. The debate in the Assembly also exposed a dangerous inter-generational rift between the old (Nicias) and the young (Alcibiades): the former had grave misgiving about the wisdom of the venture, the latter had all the confidence of youth; they wouldn't allow lack of experience to hold them back. We come across this in a much later work, Plato's dialogue *Laches*, in which Socrates debates the meaning of courage with, among others, Nikias. We simply don't know whether the arguments Plato gives his protagonists are invented or whether they ever made them in real life. But there is an interesting historical footnote to the dialogue. We know exactly when it takes place, shortly before 415 BC, just before Plato's fellow citizens took the fatal decision to despatch an expeditionary force to Sicily. In the course of the dialogue the sons of Aristides and of Thucydides of Melesias remark that though their fathers were great generals they had passed on none of their skills to their sons—they had neglected to educate them properly. In the famous debate in the Assembly the young, including Socrates' pupil Alcibiades, were all for action, and the old, especially Nicias, for prudence; and in the end the young won out (Maier, 1993, p. 516). The expeditionary force sailed off to its doom. Plato records the helplessness of a generation that had not been educated enough. There is also an element of irony in the two young men's intentions to have their own sons trained first in the art of fencing. Plato insisted that the young should first be taught philosophy: what is the point of knowing how to use a sword if in this instance you don't know the true nature of courage. Philosophy is not an optional extra: it is deadly serious because the consequences of not philosophising can be just that—deadly.

This conflict between the generations had also been foreshadowed in Euripides' *Supplicants*. In the play Theseus (the founder of Athens) accuses the king of Argos of giving in to ambitious young men who are all for prolonging war so that they can pursue their own personal glory. Theseus' mother counters that cities grow through struggle and that those who live in peace are also condemned to live in obscurity. Theseus retorts that neither the rich youngsters who favour war for their own reputation nor the poor who find employment in the ranks benefit a city: the real democrats are to be found in the middle. Unfortunately, Athens had outgrown not its physical but its intellectual strength. As much as men like Alcibiades were needed, they were also intolerable. Pericles had led a different society. His nephew lacked his uncle's moral authority. When, swayed by the impassioned speeches of its young men, the Athenians voted to dispatch a force to Sicily, they unknowingly instigated the slow countdown to their city's eclipse.

It was Nicias' personal misfortune to have to command the expedition after the Assembly voted in favour of dispatching it, just as it was Colin Powell's to have to showcase the Iraq War (2003). More ironical still was the fact that Nicias, and not Alcibiades, was given the command of the expedition. For it was his strategy which proved fatal. He never followed up the early victories. He procrastinated, and then when defeat loomed, he fell back on false hopes. Historians are not agreed that Alcibiades' strategy might have succeeded had he been given the command, but there are some who are willing to make out such a case.

By now you may want to ask: what is Thucydides doing in a book on philosophy? In my defence let me add that, of all historians in the ancient world, he was recognized by philosophers as one of their own. The same respect was accorded to him by others—Hobbes' very first work was a translation of his *History*. He called him 'the most politic historiographer that ever writ', not only because his theme was war (the most visible expression of relations between the Greek city-states) but also because of his explicit concern that his readers should be able to extract from his work some general lessons about war itself. Those passages in which, to quote Hobbes again, he intervenes 'to read a lecture moral and political upon his own text' were the ones that are still of most interest to philosophers (Cartledge, 2002).

One of his earliest twentieth-century commentators called him an 'artist who could define the larger outline of suffering we call the Peloponnesian War and turn it into an instructive work: a tragedy' (Woodruff, 1993, p. ix). Tragedy deals in moral themes, and Thucydides is just as much a moral philosopher as he is a historian. Indeed, his history of the war is largely a morality tale writ large. Plato drew solace from postulating that moral ideals have a separate existence in Forms or Ideas, and the only way to close the gap between the two is to live a virtuous life. Thucydides was more of a realist. Nietzsche praised him for his moral courage. Unlike Plato, he had not fled into the Ideal, but had confronted reality unflinchingly. 'One must turn over line by line and read his hidden thoughts as clearly as his words; there are so few thinkers so rich in hidden thoughts.' The historian embodies all the qualities that Nietzsche most admired and which, alas, he did not always manage to embody in his own work.

There is another reason for claiming that Thucydides' great history is a work of philosophy. Historians have a narrower frame of reference; they are more interested in the character of war than they are in its nature, which they tend to leave to philosophers. But sometimes a historian can become a philosopher too. According to Aristotle, philosophy deals with the necessary, history with the actual. History makes static and thus comprehensible in the highest moments of the ephemeral what is essential or eternal in human life. That is not to say that the Greeks thought the eternal and actual were the same, but there are moments when actuality approaches eternity, when eternity appears in and through the actual, and one of those for Thucydides was the Peloponnesian War. Thus when he claimed that it was the greatest war of all time, he did not mean that there had not been greater conflicts in the past, or that there would not be others in the future. He meant that the war was so long, so calamitous and so diverse in form (in the degeneration of war into warfare) that it exposed to light every feature of the human condition: brutality, stupidity, guile, treachery, ambition, the heroism of individual soldiers, the greatness of vision of some (Pericles) and the smallness of mind of others (Cleon). And sometimes it revealed noble attributes (the willingness of the Athenians—from time to time—to be just both to allies and enemies alike).

This is the point of Thucydides' famous speeches—they bring out the eternal (Gillespie, 1984, p. 4). Like all ancient philosophers, he wanted to bring truth to the light (remember, Heraclitus tells us, nature conceals). Thucydides is anxious to reveal the real motivations (or what he took to be real). In that sense the philosopher and historian are one and the same, and Thucydides is much more a philosopher in this regard than Herodotus, whom he was trying quite self-consciously to outdo. War is a violent teacher, he tells us. It encourages people not only to be vicious, but to mask their vices with fine-sounding names. The speeches are what Thucydides thinks politicians would have said had they been speaking their mind and not trying to mislead their audiences. And that is why his speakers seem to persuade themselves of the truth even when, like poor Nicias, they fail to persuade their audiences.

Now, if we are willing to think of Thucydides not only as a historian describing the character of war—in his description of the naval defeat he paints a picture of naval warfare in this period: the special rams fitted to the Syracusan ships; the ships on the defensive forming themselves into a circle, a kind of floating stockade; the ships fouling each other in a confined space (*History*, 7.36)—but also as a philosopher describing the nature of war, then what we have in his work is the first written account of its *paradoxical* nature. History is to be found in the text, the philosophy in the subtext of the work, specifically in what we now call Thucydidean irony (*Twilight of the Idols*, Kaufmann, 'Selected Words', p. 558). He seems to have set out to write a tragedy in prose. He is too great an historian, writes Victor Davis Hanson (a very fine historian himself), to reduce strife down to perceptions about power and its manifestation. War is not a science, it is a human endeavour, subject as much to chance events and miscalculations as to reason. Thucydides' book is not a mere primer for staff colleges, nor did he encourage his readers to believe that might is right. 'Tragedy, not melodrama is his message' (Hanson, 2006, p. 312).

And tragedy is paradoxical by nature. It raises disturbing questions about the fairness of the gods, and the justice of one's own cause. In the theatre, tragedy allows all kinds of displacements and ironic inversions. Male actors play women who act with more than male aggression (*Medea*, 'Now that I have become a mother, greater crimes are expected of me'). The Gods appear side by side with mortals. The citizen could tolerate debate about everything they took for granted, including their own superiority as Athenians, precisely because it was theatre. The actors wore masks and their plays were performed in the precinct of Dionysus, the god of the dissolution of boundaries. But in the Peloponnesian War, the boundaries dissolved for real. Slaves and women took part in war, a previously all-male endeavour. Words were inverted in meaning, challenging reason, on which the Athenians prided themselves so much. Greeks behaved to other Greeks like barbarians, and sometimes worse, thus dissolving the binomial distinctions between themselves and others that were so important to their own sense of self.

The theme of the Peloponnesian War was tragic in many ways that conform to the classic Aristotelian norms, and what Aristotle found most interesting about a genre wholly unique to the Greeks was that it dealt in the paradoxes that interested philosophers like him most. Let me identify three that run through Thucydides' history.

Paradox 1: The Peloponnesian War had the complexity Aristotle called for in tragedy because the end result was a surprise. In tragedy the fate of the chief protagonist (Oedipus for example) is not what the audience expects at the beginning of the play. In the case of Thucydides' story, most contemporary Greeks would have expected the Athenians to have won the war (as they did themselves).

After all, they had shown a capacity to astonish the world. At Salamis they had defied the odds and won a battle, more, Thucydides is the first to admit, 'by decisiveness than luck, and more by daring than by power' (Meir, 2003, p. 305). That was the problem. Let us return to the quote at the head of this chapter. In the Athenians' speech to the Spartans in Book 1, the delegates remind the Spartans that power is best left untested. War, as the most unpredictable of human activities, should only be used only as a last resort. 'Action comes first, and it is only when they have clearly suffered that they begin to think' (*History*, 1.78). It is likely that Thucydides' readers would have recalled this speech when reading later of the great debate in the Assembly which led to the Sicilian venture.

A willingness to hazard all is always a risk. To be daring beyond one's power is to invite danger. Is there anything the Athenians cannot accomplish, asks a character in a play by a fifth-century comic poet, a contemporary of Aristophanes. According to Aristophanes, even the older generation of Athenians (and therefore presumably the wiser) used to say, 'what we decide foolishly and against all reason will in the end work to our advantage' (Meir, 2003, p. 305). Nikias is not one of them. He knows that every war has consequences. His caution is couched in the language of risk. His first set of arguments (which Alcibiades never directly challenges) is that they should not risk what they have for an advantage, which is dubious in itself and which may not be attainable in the end. When Alcibiades' emotional appeal wins over the Assembly, Nikias plays his second card: he tries to insist on dispatching a much larger force than originally planned in the hope the Assembly will rein in its ambition, or baulk at paying the price. But to his surprise, the more he demands, the more enthusiastic the Assembly becomes in its support of the expedition. Such a large force must surely be invincible.

The debate in the Assembly turned on whether they would be true to themselves, or not. Like the Bush administration's critique of 'old Europe' the young Alcibiades derides the 'do-nothingness' (*apraynosyne*) approach of Nikias and his friends. Alcibiades himself exemplified a kind of American 'can-do' approach; what Thucydides himself called 'the yearning for the far-off, the need for the extraordinary'. Indeed, he tells us that the Sicilian expedition became famous not for its intended purpose—the defeat of a city-state that was in all respects far inferior to Athens—but precisely because it reinforced the disparity in power between the two cities. The expedition was admired 'for its overwhelming strength as compared with the people against whom it was directed'. It was undertaken with 'great hopes for the future' especially for fame and honour (Shankman, 2000, p. 113). Thucydides paints a majestic description of the expedition setting out. The citizens of Athens, torn by fear and hope, go down to the Piraeus to see its departure, while Thucydides, hard-headed as ever, estimates its cost. What the Athenians learned about themselves from the disaster was their almost limitless capacity for self-deception: they discovered this not in reaction to war so much as in collusion with it. Their tragedy was that of a deeply cultivated society which, though superior in all respects to Sparta, was corrupted by its own vanity: its belief it could attempt any task.

The parallels with the American invasion of Iraq in 2003 are many and disturbing. But like all historical comparisons, they are not precise. The opponents of the invasion within the administration also traded in the language of risk. 'If you break it, you will own it', Powell warned the President. They also talked of the cost of rebuilding Iraq and questioned the prospects of successful post-war planning. The Assembly (the neo-cons) were not persuaded, and for them the most compelling argument was simple: because the US could not be defeated, there was no risk, so why not invade? Insurance companies call this a 'moral hazard'—insurance itself is paradoxical; it often encourage reckless behaviour. As insurance companies know, clients with life insurance policies take more risks knowing that their families will be provided should they take one risk too many. Formula One racing drivers—because they are better drivers than the rest of us—also drive cars at speeds that can be fatal. A moral hazard is invoked in war when the most powerful side is so self-confident that it takes risks it really shouldn't; or when the weaker side, faced with a strategic impasse, comes up with a plan that is tactically brilliant but strategically flawed.

This was the case with the attack on Pearl Harbor that showed poetic flair but little common sense, and its chief designer, Admiral Yamamoto, was not only a successful gambler in his private life but also something of a poet. The combination was fatal, writes Clive James, for strategy requires a 'considerable appreciation for the mundane'—or the do-able. It is worth quoting him at length:

A poetic flair has an impatient mind of its own: it likes to make an effect and it has a propensity for two qualities that can easily be inimical to a broad strategic aim.... Yamamoto's plan for deciding the war on the first day was not only the equivalent of a roulette player betting his whole bundle on a single number, it was also the equivalent of trying to cram the whole of *The Tale of Genji* into a single *haiku*. There was bound to be material that didn't fit. Even if the American aircraft carriers had been in harbour they would not have sunk far enough in the shallow water to be beyond salvage. One way or another the American fleet was bound to come back. (James, 2008, p. 817)

Paradox 2: Thucydides' story also conforms to Aristotle's insistence that the tragic hero should be a divided one; neither all good nor all bad. He should be as complex as his own fate. And the audience only pities the hero whose fate is to some degree unmerited. His downfall arises from a tragic flaw in an otherwise heroic character, or from some fatal misjudgement by someone whose judgement we have come to trust. We tend to find the Athenians admirable because they remind us of ourselves—despite the slaves, the misogyny, the piety and the superstition they are remarkably 'modern'. Unlike most ancient people they were highly innovative. They were risk takers. Other peoples, such as the Persians of course, were capable of great deeds, which Herodotus set out to record, but even he conceded that they could never attempt the unexpected.

The Sicilian expedition fascinates for that reason—it constituted a leap in the dark. No one had dispatched an expeditionary force of such size and at such great a distance before. But then the Athenians prided themselves on their daring. Thucydides himself makes the point in contrasting Athenian innovation with Spartan conservatism. The Athenians thought of themselves as a particularly experimental people: it was one of the indices of their own exceptionalism.

What also impresses us about the Athenians was their swiftness in executing their decisions. As the Corinthian envoys observed at Athens in Book 1, 'they alone are unable to call a thing hoped for, a thing got by the speed with which they act upon their resolutions' (*History*, 1:70.7.8). All of these characteristics are described by Thucydides with justifiable pride. We associate many of them with the United States today. The problem is that innovative powers frequently overreach themselves—they are often too successful to be successful. The Greeks called it *hubris*—overwhelming pride, an arrogance which was ultimately self-destructive. The word is derived from another, *hyper* (meaning 'over'). It meant stepping over the bounds that the gods have established for us: nothing should be done in excess. The inevitable consequence of *hubris* is *nemesis*—from the root *nemei*: to allot a due portion, the same root from which was derived another word, *nomos* (the law) (Booker, 2004, p. 329). The implication Thucydides expected us to draw is that pride comes before a fall.

After reaching the heights a fall is inevitable: it is a matter of *ananke* (necessity). No one can save a tragic hero. He cannot even save himself. A falling man cannot use his legs to counter the force of gravity (Warrington, 1980, p. 181). This is what is paradoxical: the higher you reach, the further you may fall. But a strategic mishap is tragic only if a country does not deserve its defeat: the fall of Hitler was not tragic for that reason. The fall of Athens was like that of Oedipus who is undone because he is too successful in finding his predecessor's killer. A less worthy man might have pressed the issue less relentlessly and thus escaped the fate of discovering that the murderer is himself. As Sophocles tells us, life is paradoxical; both Athens and Oedipus are the victim of an ill-fated pride in a very real achievement.

The Athenians took one risk too many because strategically they were too innovative; the Spartans were not. Nikias had warned them of 'that mad passion to possess that which is out of reach' (*History*, 6.13). The tragic hero oversteps the mark. *Hubris* is inevitably followed by *nemesis*. The Sicilian expedition observes all the unities of tragedy, ending in a reversal (*peripetia*). Aristotle remarks (*Poetics* 2:1452b) that in the best tragedy the reversal is always followed by a recognition (*anagnosis*) and in Thucydides' *History* the catastrophe of Sicily is followed by recognition on the part of Athenian soldiers at Syracuse (as they are led off to captivity) that they themselves had been the architect of their own misfortune. The fate of the Athenian army, isolated and hopeless on the island without their fleet, was indeed terrible, and Thucydides vividly describes their sufferings on their final march, 'especially when they remembered the splendour and pride of their setting out and saw how mean and abject was the conclusion' (*History*, 7.75).

This is another way of saying that knowledge does not always translate into wisdom. In *Oedipus* the Chorus has all the threads in its hands—the likelihood that Oedipus killed Laius, the prophecy that he will kill his father, the exposure of the child—and yet it is impossible for them, or Oedipus himself, to link them up in order to establish a pattern. They are confused and in their confusion pray to Zeus to solve the puzzle. They find themselves praying for something that will bring disaster to the King who has earned their loyalty. The ultimate irony of the play is that the most intelligent of men who solved the riddle of the Sphinx cannot read the riddle of his own destiny (Warrington, 1980, p. 203). The Athenian Assembly experienced the same fate: they knew all the facts—the distances involved, the logistic challenges, the danger of sending an expeditionary force so far from home. Despite all this the citizens allowed themselves to be swayed by Alcibiades and his supporters; they could not see that the chances of success were so slim that it was not worth incurring the risks involved.

WAR AND HUMAN AMBITION

Paradox 3: Thucydides also tells us of another paradoxical feature of war—the quest for security can result in even greater insecurity. States are often in danger of over-insuring themselves. When it came to deploying a force as far as Sicily the Athenians were operating at a logistic extreme: what strategists call the 'culminating point of operations', the point at which a force in the field can no longer be logistically re-supplied. The fact that the Athenians could send an expeditionary force so far was a strategic disaster in itself.

In the course of the two-year campaign the Athenians voted twice to send out reinforcements. The final losses may have amounted to almost 50,000 men (both soldiers and oarsmen, among whom were Nicias and both the generals who were dispatched on the second wave of reinforcements). Even if the campaign had been successful, disaster would have not been far off. For Alcibiades made no secret of the fact that he wished to conquer Carthage as well. Success can breed failure when it encourages a country or commander to attempt too much. For 2,600 years later two geo-political thinkers, Haushofer and Oskar von Niedermayer, found themselves at odds with the Third Reich. Both were professional soldiers who had rightly concluded that an invasion of Russia would be disastrous. Niedermayer had served as the German army's representative in Moscow in the 1920s. In 1942 he was recalled to duty to command an infantry division in the Caucasus. In the same year he summed up the desperate situation in which the Germans now found themselves. 'The geographer has the right to warn when an overestimation of the power of human ambition leads to under-estimation of the physical and spatial realities and to a neglect of the relationship between space, time and human strength' (Kassimeris, 2006, p. 80). But it did not take a geographer to point this out, nor for that matter a geopolitician. Thucydides had sketched out the peril in the first scientific western book on war. As a moral philosopher he had gone much further: he had warned of the dangers of human ambition.

Thucydides actually got Alcibiades to say in the debate that it is not possible to think of imperialism in housekeeping terms—how much empire does Athens want? The mantra ran, 'we may fall under the power of others unless others are in our power'. This was power for its own sake. In Thucydides power is the object of effort held and retained by those who have it, and envied and hated by those who do not. In itself, however, it is without moral content; it is pretty characterless (Knox, 1989, p. 109).

This is what the historian Polybius later intuited about the fall of Carthage in 146 BC, which he witnessed in person. The victorious Roman commander intuited it too. The destruction of Carthage did not make Rome feel more secure. It might have been better to have contained Carthage rather than destroyed it. What transpired instead was that the Romans became less fearful after the destruction of their rival, but more anxious than ever. In this regard, the ever sensible Montesquieu has some good advice in *The Spirit of the Laws* (Part 2, Chapter 10): 'When a neighbouring state is in decline one should take care not to hasten its ruin, because this is the most fortunate situation possible; there is nothing more suitable for a prince than to be close to another who receives in his stead all the blows and outrages of fortune. By conquering such a state, one rarely increases as much in real power as one loses in relative power' (Montesquieu, 2008, p. 137). Wise advice indeed, so rarely followed. It is advice that—looking back—the US might have followed in Iraq.

Let me conclude with one other parallel between the Sicilian expedition and the invasion of Iraq that illustrates Socrates' insistence that wisdom and knowledge are not the same. The Athenians blundered into a situation they simply did not understand. It is not that they were ill-informed about the relative strengths of their allies and enemies in Sicily—they chose to believe what they wanted. The Athenian ambassadors who came back from Sicily fixed the intelligence to get the Assembly to make the decision they wanted (*History* 6.46 and 6.55). Falsified intelligence has played a similar role in recent wars. Take Douglas MacArthur's dash to the Yalu River which brought the Chinese into the Korean War and prolonged it by another two years. Only the incomparable Matthew Ridgway who replaced MacArthur and got the UN Forces eventually back in the 38th parallel, where the conflict had begun, saved the Coalition forces from complete disaster. MacArthur paid dearly for his miscalculation. If the Inchon landing was his great moment in history, the decision to press ahead to the Yalu River ended his career on a disastrous note. Had a historian examined MacArthur's career up to the eve of the Korean War, wrote one sympathetic biographer, he would have concluded that he had passed the first and foremost test of any great commander: he had luck on his side. After Inchon, his luck finally ran out (Halberstam, 2008).

Employing the most tragic analogy any American officer could use, Ridgway later wrote that, like Custer at the Little Big Horn, MacArthur had neither eyes nor ears for information that might deter him from the swift attainment of his objective—the pacification of the entire Korean peninsular. His staff doctored the intelligence to permit his forces to go where they wanted to go militarily, in the process setting the most dangerous of precedents for those who followed him in office. For the process was to be repeated twice more in the years to come. In 1965 the government of Lyndon Johnson manipulated the rationale for sending combat troops to Vietnam by exaggerating the threat posed to America by Hanoi. Deliberately diminishing any serious intelligence warning of what the consequences of American intervention in Vietnam would be, it committed the US to a hopeless, un-winnable, post-colonial conflict. Then more recently, in 2003, the administration of George W. Bush—improperly reading the situation in the light of 9/11—completely miscalculated the likely response of the indigenous people. Wanting for its own reasons to take down the government of Saddam Hussein, it manipulated Congress, the media, the public and, most dangerously of all, itself, with seriously flawed and doctored intelligence with disastrous results (Halberstam, 2008).

War is often tragic for that reason, at least in the classic understanding of the term. In tragic perspective (writes Jean-Pierre Vernant), war has a double character. On the one hand it consists of taking counsel with oneself, weighing for and against certain decisions and doing the best we can to perceive the order of means and ends. On the other hand it is to bet on the unknown; we take a risk on terrain that remains impenetrable to us, for we simply do not know whether we are preparing for success or disaster (Williams, 1994, p. 19). And war is tragic in a way that no other political decision-making really is, because it involves quite literally matters of life and death.

The study of war is deeply philosophical for that reason. History tends to show that we often act foolishly and irrationally. We find victory is elusive or not worth the cost. War does not always produce significant gains. Yet war has one great virtue; it is a means to self-knowledge. It reveals us to ourselves in a harsh and often unflattering light. It enables us to explore, as practically no other human activity does, what de Tocqueville called 'the habits of the human heart'. And those habits of the heart are there in all their vivid detail in Thucydides' description of the Peloponnesian War. He is the first psychologist that we know of. And it is no accident he was Greek, because what the Greeks found most interesting was themselves. They interrogated themselves for that reason more vigorously than any other contemporary people.

For us war has become much more of a problem in and of itself than it ever was for the Greeks. For us it reveals in all its tragedy the unanticipated consequences of our own actions. We have become reflexive, not only reflective. We don't only reflect on our plight; we internalize it knowing that we ourselves may pose the greatest danger to our own interests. We have become a theme and problem for ourselves as we constantly address the unintended consequences of our own actions. We have become self-critical and confrontational as never before, knowing that doing too little or too much can both be equally dangerous. In Thucydides' world the tragic arose from ignorance (lack of knowledge or self-knowledge). In our world it is the consequence of the unhappy relationship between ignorance and unawareness: we are not always aware of the dangers or risks out there, and knowing this we are always wary of side-effects. We are self-endangered in the way the Sophoclean hero wasn't. Yes, we are different from the Greeks and we are like them at the same time. But there is one critical difference which is crucial. As Niklas Luhmann puts it pithily, 'we no longer belong to the family of tragic heroes who subsequently found that they prepared their own fate. We now know it beforehand' (Luhmann, 1998, p. 156).

6

WAR AND THE SOUL

WHY WAR IS TRINITARIAN
(PLATO (1) C. 427–347 BC)

Socrates: Our job, it seems to me, is to select, if we can, the kind of nature suited to guard the city.
Glaucon: It is.
Socrates: It is no trivial task that we've taken on. But in so far as we are able, we mustn't shrink from it.
Glaucon: No, we mustn't.
Socrates: The physical qualities of the guardians are clear, then.
Glaucon: Yes.
Socrates: And as far as their souls are concerned they must be spirited.
Glaucon: That too.
Socrates: But if they have natures like that, Glaucon, won't they be savage to each other and to the rest of the citizens?
Glaucon: By god, it will be hard for them to be anything else.
Socrates: Yet surely they must be gentle to their own people and harsh to the enemy. If they aren't they won't wait around for others to destroy the city, but they will do it themselves first.
Glaucon: That's true.
Socrates: What are we to do, then? Where are we to find a character that is both gentle and high-spirited at the same time?

(*The Republic*)

Of all the major philosophers, Plato took war more seriously than most. In one of his last works, *The Republic*, the term 'war' and its cognates, such as 'waging war', 'warrior', 'the art of war' and 'enemies' occur nearly ten dozen times, not to mention others like 'manliness', 'strife' and 'the hated'. It is not unreasonable to conclude, suggests one writer, that *The Republic*'s treatment of politics, philosophy and justice is 'painted primarily in the colours of war' (Craig, 1994, p. 15). Peace, by contrast, is mentioned less than a dozen times, and usually only in order to accentuate war even more.

The Republic was probably written around 376 BC, when Plato was in his early 50s. It is conventionally divided into ten books. The leading character is Socrates (who has now broken free of his historical personality, and is most definitely Plato's mouthpiece). The dialogue begins with him going down to the port of Piraeus, just outside the city of Athens, to pray. The action takes place entirely at night, which gives it a certain conspiratorial aura. The fact that it also takes place outside the city allows the citizens to dream of other dispensations—and *The Republic* is the first work of fantasy which enables us to imagine a future state not yet brought into being.

Plato was the product of his age. We cannot escape the times in which we live. And the most pressing challenge that the Peloponnesian War had thrown up was the need to control violence, to ensure that never again did *polemos*/war become *stasis*/warfare. *The Republic* contains, in fact, the first plea we know of for a more humane regime between the Greeks themselves. Plato, like Thucydides, had seen what happened when war becomes civil strife. He hoped to prevent this from ever happening again by inventing a rudimentary system of 'international law'—by drawing up rules to mediate the worst features of conflict. True to his own beliefs, he wanted to make war *dialogic*. Socrates' interlocutor in the dialogue suggests that war should be tamed by a 'more civilized state of mind'. Plato adds, interestingly, that conflict between city-states should not be seen as war at all, but more as a domestic quarrel. Defeat and victory, too, should be seen in dialogic terms—as a way of bringing the enemy round to one's point of view (getting him to see reason, or at least to concede the argument for the time being). As always, the philosophers wanted war to be 'reasonable' (by which they meant not more humane, but more rational).

The purpose of all Plato's dialogues is not to produce a consensus through reason, but to strengthen the bond between the participants through the free exchange of ideas. The decision to abide by the results (even to accept a decision one does not agree with) shows the respect one has for the dialogue itself, and the people one is in conversation with. But the chief purpose of any dialogue is not to see the other point of view, so much as one's own point of view through the eyes of other people. A dialogue is not only a conversation with someone else, it is a conversation with oneself. It promotes, or is intended to, greater self-understanding. With luck, this may allow one to master one's own emotions or passions. The main purpose, insists Gadamer in his masterwork, *Truth and Method*, is a hermeneutical one: it allows one to transcend one's own instinctive biases and prejudices, and sometimes even world views, through a radical break in subjective self-understanding.

But Plato had another objective—to ensure that the social discord that the war had produced within Athens and that had led to Socrates' death should never break out again. Emerson called Plato 'an American genius'—he was referring to the fact that generations over time had drawn from his work whenever they had made any distinctive contribution to their culture. All civilized nations were his posterity, and were 'tinged with his mind' (Blackburn, 2006, p. 3). It is a bold claim, but not an unreasonable one. For he established a *dialectical* method which is central to the western tradition—western philosophy tries to establish truths dialectically. We are talking, writes Simon Blackburn, about the modes in which people think about themselves and their actions. It is those ways of thinking, he adds, that help to determine who has the land, and the food, who picks up the guns, and where the money gets spent. And Plato is the first writer on the very real dialectical relationship between three realms: the instrumental, existential and metaphysical.

As the quotation at the top of this chapter suggests, a problem for the Greeks was how to ensure that no one group dominated another. In Plato's day the warrior is no longer the individual engaged in face-to-face combat with his peers, or even (which Homer tells us is the reality) a butcher hacking, maiming his way through the battlefield, often for hours on end; the Greeks called war work (*ergon*) and it was pretty unceasing. By Plato's day, the battle space had also, much to his dismay, become democratic. The rowers of the triremes were *thetes*—poor, landless people, paid a pension for their service to the state. He even suggested that since the battle of Salamis (which was their victory in part) Athenian life had become more 'trashy'. The wrong people had come to predominate in political life; the same might be true in the future of professional soldiers.

BARBAROUS PHILOSOPHERS

For Plato man is defined by his work; we are *homo faber*. In his ideal city each man has a calling or occupation (he doesn't say 'income groups', whose concept is a modern invention). Other animals perform a function; they do not work. The members of a monkey colony, for example, do not work, they perform certain roles, such as territorial display, vigilance, and look-out behaviour. They punish intra-group aggression and lead in-group movements. But there is no subdivision of labour here—even the vigilance role-players are not soldiers: they are not there principally to warn of the presence of predators, still less engage those predators in battle. They are largely interested in picking quarrels with other monkey bands: a useful function, no doubt, in avoiding overcrowding and protecting scarce resources, without which a colony could not survive for long. But this is in no way work, any more than the behaviour of street gangs in our own inner cities can be described as an economic function. The members of those gangs are not soldiers in any sense of the world, despite having honour codes of their own.

The central theme of Plato's *Republic* is social disharmony and how to alleviate it, and his discussion is perfectly in keeping with the insight of evolutionary psychologists that human nature is not in harmony. The brain areas governing emotion bring into play an inefficient mix of personal survival, reproduction and altruism. Consequently, they tend to tax the conscious mind with ambivalences whenever we encounter stressful situations: love can conjoin quickly with hate; fear can provoke aggression. These blends, writes E.O. Wilson, are designed not to promote happiness, but to favour the maximum transmission of controlling genes. And we have to choose, for emotional conflict is endemic; it cannot be eliminated (Wilson, 1998, p. 4).

Plato's city does not eliminate conflict. It takes emotional conflict to be at the centre of life and tries to forge a 'life-world' with conflict at its heart. Its goal is not happiness, but harmony, an efficient mixture of personal survival, reproduction and altruism. There is no either/or. Plato had the disadvantage of not knowing about genetics. We know that stress or change can bring out unsuspected tendencies latent in our nature, but played down by our culture. Plato's age was not unchanging, but it was not modern either: the changes that occurred were slow. The Greeks certainly had an idea of 'progress' although it was not ours. They could certainly see change at work in history, and they knew that war often brought it about. But in the absence of any knowledge of genetics, still less a knowledge of pre-history, they were forced to privilege culture. What we find disagreeable in *The Republic* (even more so in *The Laws* where Socrates' humanistic voice is finally silenced) is the 'cultural' programming. We know that intellectual schemes that we invent do not always address our true emotional needs.

But Plato had one advantage—he was not a socio-biologist. For the Greeks, harmony was not an end of life, but merely a condition. And if harmony brought happiness (which Plato does not, unlike Aristotle, claim), the happy man is virtuous because he is productive. Discontented or unhappy people, we know, are usually unproductive. Happy people tend to live longer and have more children (in part because they are more optimistic about the future).

In *The Republic* the citizenry is divided into three groups: the soldiers or the Auxiliaries are a subdivision of the rulers, the Guardians; the former are the first professional warriors we encounter in philosophy. At the bottom of the tree are to be found the people, mostly merchants and farmers, who don't form a specific class as such (for they include rich and poor alike, and some even are property owners though the great majority are not). At the centre of Plato's understanding of the nature of war is the idea of a trinity which we are more familiar with from the work of Clausewitz.

Let us take just one class—the Auxiliaries, the soldiers who, as Plato recognized in the passage I have quoted, could pose a threat to the city if they succumbed to their appetites. By his day they were no longer citizen-soldiers but professionals, but they were still 'warriors' who practised war (as opposed to warfare which is one-dimensional). In war warriors live a multi–dimensional life.

1. As an *instrumental* concept, war refers to the ways in which force is applied by the state, the way in which it is used to impose one's will upon another. War, as such, is a rational instrument employed in a controlled, rational manner, for purposes that are usually political or economic.
2. As an *existential* concept, the term refers to those who practise it: warriors. As Hegel always insisted, war would only end when warriors no longer needed it to affirm their own humanity.
3. As a *metaphysical* concept, war translates death into sacrifice—it invests death with a meaning. And it is the metaphysical dimension which is the most important of all, precisely because it persuades

societies of the need for sacrifice. It is sacrifice which makes war qualitatively different from warfare, and every other act of violence. We rarely celebrate killing, but we still celebrate dying when it has meaning, not only for the dead, but for those they leave behind. It is the sacred that makes claims on us and demands sacrifices (the etymology of the word is telling: sacrifice is derived from sacred). It is in the presence of the sacred that our lives are ultimately judged.

In the instrumental sphere the soldier has a knowledge of how to use weapons and practise in their use. He has the requisite expertise (as we would call it today). He also knows—if he is properly trained—the limits of the possible. The instrumentalization of the warrior involves calculation (both literally and figuratively). That is why Plato insists that warriors should be trained in arithmetic—they need to know how to calculate so that they can arrange troops in the field. Geometry, too, is useful, which is why Socrates warns Glaucon to tell the citizens of his own city never to neglect its study (527 C2). Of the two, arithmetic is the more important—it makes us quicker at all our studies, and requires more hard work than the rest (536 A1–C7). Socrates also tells us that gymnastics is important in military training. It is not a sound body that makes a soul good, it is a good soul that makes for a sound body (self-discipline as opposed to self-indulgence). Soldiers in Plato's ideal republic are trained to protect justice, but to do so they have to be 'sound' in both body and soul (403 C8–E3).

In the existential sphere, what makes *The Republic* so distinctive is that it talks of the warrior in a mediating role between intelligence and desire. We are driven by our desires to maximize our possessions, but we must do so within the mean. The unity of the soul requires a distinction to be drawn between spiritedness and desire (Rosen, 2005, p. 396). Socrates tells us that spiritedness is by nature more inclined to reason than to desire, which is primarily sexual or involves money making or glory hunting. If spiritedness is not distinguished from desire, it will be infected by it soon enough; if spiritedness is identified with the intellect, we may open the door to the subordination of intelligence to the will.

In the metaphysical sphere, Plato also insists that warriors should have a special relationship to the sacred. Philosophers have been interested in war from the beginning because most thought is grounded in the contingency of life. Death is the great backdrop to life; it is what throws it into vivid relief, for it is only in its absence (whether real or imagined) that life can be fully lived. Take W.B. Yeats' famous line: 'man has created death'—knowing you are going to die is one of the essential qualities of our humanity. We are the only species aware of our impending death, the only animals to be distressed by what the theologian Paul Tillich calls 'ontological anxiety'. We know our days in the world are numbered and that all we will leave behind, perhaps, is just a memory. Some of us seek to lead a better life in this world in preparation for salvation in the next. Others seek to live a better life on the understanding that it is the only life we have. Still others, including warriors, find death in certain circumstances life-affirming. There is a striking line in Shakespeare's *Henry V*: 'By my troth, I care not; a man can die but once; we owe God death.' Death settles the account for some. For all of us life itself is a debt that eventually has to be repaid.

For the Greeks, the discussion had particular force because many did not believe in an afterlife, and those who did had a depressing view of what it promised (as Odysseus discovers after interrogating an angry Achilles in Hades, who still resents his early death with unconcealed bitterness). Homer's Underworld is a shadowy world, it is not a place of torment, and it is certainly not hell, but it is a kingdom in which men who once have been people exist as insubstantial shadows of themselves.

This is why Socrates specifically insists that soldiers should be taught that Hades actually exists, and that it is a good place to go to. Although he agrees it is not 'poetical and pleasant for the many' to hear about the domain of the dead, soldiers must be taught that for the decent man death is not a terrible thing. They must not fear death (nor for that matter must they desire it), as they throw themselves into battle. Courage is aroused in those who believe themselves to be facing death in defence of virtue and justice. Plato goes to great lengths especially in condemning excessive mourning for the dead. We mourn the dead not out of some kind of morbid over-indulgence, we mourn them to celebrate their life. Not to mourn is to make life unimportant, and the political existence that it entails (Rosen, 2005, p. 97). In order to accommodate soldiers to death, Plato even encourages the children of the soldier-guardians be taken to the battlefield to observe it early in life.

The importance of Plato's discussion of the warrior (the first that we have in philosophy) is that it shows the warrior is not tamed or emasculated within the state; he appreciates, instead, that war is not the be-all and end-all of life; it is not the highest good, or the highest human calling. In his argument with Protagoras, Plato challenged whether man was the measure of all things. We can apply his argument to the warrior. If one makes the warrior the measure of all things, war will soon become the measure of life, and the warrior will come to regard everything else as a means to one end: his own existence. Instrumentality is not to be understood as subordinating the warrior to reasons of state. It is much more closely related to the object (the 'what') it is designed to produce. Its human value is restricted to the use made of the warrior by society. In war the warrior serves a larger human purpose; he puts himself at the disposal of his city, to enhance its power or secure its ends. Through his deeds he can even bring it glory. *Klea* means 'glory', *kleos* 'glorious'. The Greeks designated the muse Kleo (our Clio) as history's patron goddess—for until very recently the warriors' deeds were celebrated in every culture.

Now, of course, we find much of Plato's vision of the ideal city unappealing. Karl Popper even found it totalitarian. Did he think it was possible to found such a city? It makes no difference in the end, as Socrates himself tells us. The ideal city is intended as a subject for reflection. In the end, *The Republic* should not be seen as the blueprint for a perfect society, a utopian dream, though *The Republic* is (on one reading) the first Utopia or Dystopia we have. We should see the book as a thought-experiment.

The main criticism of the experiment was made first by Aristotle, namely that in *The Republic* the three dimensions are not as interconnected as they should be in real life. Plato's analogy does not work, as it is elaborated in his dialogue. Courage is not exclusive to the army, any more than spiritedness—you can have a spirited merchant easily enough. And desire is not exclusive to merchants any more than their desires are uncontrollable, for clearly traders can display courage too. It is also hard to say that soldiers have no desires. What Socrates means is that desires can be tamed by what Stephen Rosen calls the 'instrumentality of spiritedness'. But that is the point: warriors do have desires. They have to moderate them and match them to society's needs. And if they need courage, it does not follow that the courage of the rulers (the philosopher kings), or the common people, is not important too. When an army loses a battle, it is society that determines whether to continue to fight (Rome found itself in this position after

Cannae; Britain after Dunkirk). The soldier class does not embody courage, it reflects it. Through its action it can even inspire the rest of us to fight on. It gives even merchants spiritedness, too.

In the end, if we are to make more sense of Plato's analogy than he managed to make himself, we must reject the 'causality' he imposes and translate it back into the poetry that he banned. The relation of the parts of the soul and the classes of the city is not, in the end, causal, but metaphorical. For it is irrelevant, anyway, whether in the real world his social divisions would work. Plato himself is not always consistent. Take his checklist for the rulers. He requires them to be 'quick on their feet and strong'—the virtues we do not usually associate with philosopher kings, though they are the very virtues that Socrates' fellow citizens admired in him as a man. Why did Plato say philosopher kings must be strong? Because even the philosopher had to be a potential soldier. Socrates tells Xenophon that it is part of the citizen's duty to keep himself fit, and ready to serve the city at a moment's notice. An unhealthy citizen makes for a bad soldier (Steiner, 2001, p. 166).

In 433 BC at the siege of Potidaea, Alcibiades and Socrates were messmates. Not only did he prove himself brave in action (he saved his friend's life when they were on their way home from the siege); he recalls him as the best kind of soldier—he recalls his exceptional fortitude in enduring the bitter winter months, and his self-control when times were good, and there was plenty of food. In the end, in Plato's ideal city, the soldier is involved in a dialectical relationship, in a kind of harmony because he is a citizen. In Rosen's words, 'the individual citizen is not a unity, but a harmony, a kind of ancestor of the Hegelian unity of opposites' (Rosen, 2005, p. 396).

This unity is always changing with the changing character of war. In the ancient Greek world no distinction was drawn between the government and the military; there was no political division of powers between the executive and legislative branches of state. By Clausewitz's day the character of war had changed. 'War is more than a true chameleon which adapts its characteristics to a given case. As a total phenomenon its dominant tendencies always make war a paradoxical trinity—composed of primordial violence, hatred and enmity which are to be regarded as a blind natural force; of the play of chance and probability within which the creative force is free to roam and of its element of subordination, as an instrument of policy, which makes it subject to reason alone.' Clausewitz went on to add that the first of these aspects mainly concerns the people, the second the army and the third the state—or as he wrote, 'political aims are the business of government alone' (Clausewitz, 1976, p. 101). Long before Clausewitz put pen to paper, Plato had got there first (even though it seems unlikely Clausewitz knew this).

In Clausewitz's day, strategy was the result of a process that was much more complex than it was in the ancient world: it now involved a Trinitarian relationship between government, army and the people. Even in Aristotle's world, however, the Assembly embodied public opinion (a term not yet invented). Given that the people play a major role in a democracy, we have to ask whether democracies can think strategically? Plato was the first to ask the question; in *The Laws* the Athenian stranger has nothing but contempt for the *nautikos ochlos*, the sailor rabble that crewed the city's triremes. As he remarks rather tartly, although the city's land battles had won it moral virtue, those fought at sea had had precisely the opposite effect. And Plato had every reason to express his misgivings, for he had witnessed at firsthand what happened when the Assembly allowed itself to be swayed by emotion. At Aegospotami (406 BC) the Athenian navy won a great victory, but a storm blew up and twelve sailors were left to drown. They were *thetes*—rowers who were paid out of state funds. In its anger the Assembly voted to execute twelve admirals—it was one of the greatest disasters in military history, and it probably confirmed Plato in his belief that the *demos* had surrendered to passion in defiance of common sense. The people had failed, in a word, to think 'strategically'.

Striking though this example may be, a democrat is still likely to put his faith in Aristotle, not Plato. His main criticism of democracy was that it was based on a flawed, even dangerous relationship between knowledge and the exercise of power. In dispatching a fleet to Syracuse the Athenians had shown bad judgement: they had failed to grasp what was best for the common good. Plato contended that the majority are never in a position to make such judgements: only philosopher-kings can (in the real world, he conceded, such judgements were best left to experts). Aristotle, by contrast, saw that democratic systems have their own strengths:

The many of whom none is individually an excellent man nevertheless can when joined together be better than those [the excellent few], not as individuals but all altogether ... For there being many each person possesses a constituent part of virtue and practical reason and when they have come together, the multitude is like a single-person, yet many-footed and many-handed and possessing many sense-capacities; so it is likewise as regards to its multiplicity of character and its mind. (*The Politics*, 3.1281a40–b10)

Like Aristotle, we still tend to think that each individual is the best judge of his or her own interests, although we allow a much larger area for experts to debate each other, and for non-experts to decide in the end who to believe. Popular gut instinct is often sound. And besides, we tend to think that democracies wage war better than other political systems; they tend to win their wars. Stakeholders are more likely to fight longer for what they hold dear; those who own their own ground do not readily yield it. And citizen–soldiers are more likely to fight for each other (peer pressure requires them to fight on even when all is lost).

But our real objection to Plato touches more generally upon his views on the role of reason. Philosophers still tend to view wars as conflicts of belief that can be easily resolved through debate, through dialogue or the exercise of reason. The philosopher Bernard Williams was always telling us that conflicts of desire are more common and that they are not so easily resolved (see *Problems of the Self* (1973) and *Making Sense of Humanity* (1995)). Human beings are not always principled, or consistent—they have an emotional life. Many are inconsistent and make up their principles as they go along. As remarkable as Clausewitz' dictum was that war is an extension of politics, he did not stop there. While war is a political activity he insisted that it cannot be understood simply by focusing on the dialogue between a country's ruler and its army. War involves a dialectical relationship between the units of a paradoxical tinity: the passions of the people; military thinking (the play of chance and probability within which the creative spirit is free to roam); and political aims drawn up the state (Clausewitz, *On War*, Book 1, Chapter 1, # 28, p. 101). Each unit of the trinity adds its unique character to war and each is required to complete the puzzle.

For the people's passions may run to 'primordial violence', but they also can include emotions of a more positive kind. If the people are unduly fearful of their opponents, or not passionate enough in defence of their own rights, the outcome of the ensuing battles may differ from what we would expect, given the relative strengths of the belligerents. And the twentieth century put a particular premium on the peoples' ability to show unusual fortitude under attack from aerial bombing. They were sustained not only by reason, but also passionate defiance.

Note also that the army's creativity and talent, rather than just the notion of chance, are stressed in the passage I have quoted. In effect, what Clausewitz is saying is that chance in and of itself does not always determine a war's course. Rather it is what a commander is able to do within the framework of uncertainty that is important; passions here are important too in allowing soldiers to recover from defeat, to defy the odds in battle, to carry on when the day may appear lost.

The point Clausewitz is making, which he emphasizes again and again, is that the passions cannot be ruled out of the political realm. As Williams regretted, unfortunately many philosophers feel conflicts can be resolved by nullifying one of the elements: the human factor. Williams advised us to read Greek tragedy for that reason. It presents us with what he called 'a tragic dilemma', in which the heroes are confronted with two conflicting moral requirements, each of which are equally pressing. For Williams the great tragedians did what they set out to do: to tell us that we are creatures of our emotions as well as reason. It is the balance between passion and principle (not the exclusion of passion) that distinguishes war from warfare. And it is the political community that keeps the passions in check, and different principles in balance. And it just so happens that democracies tend to do this better than most other political systems precisely because, instead of suppressing the passions, they channel them in more creative ways.

Neither Plato nor Aristotle grasped this fully but Plato, perhaps surprisingly, was on this occasion the more perceptive of the two. He disliked the poets, as we shall see when discussing a passage from an early dialogue, the *Ion*, because they presented a world in which tribal and urban forces, family and state, are in a constant state of conflict, a world in which the passions cannot be resolved, only managed. This was not the message of harmony that he wanted to promote and he found an easy way out by banishing the poets from his idealized republic. Aristotle's solution was to promote tragedy on the curious misunderstanding that the aesthetic evocation of pity and terror made poetry out of them. As a result, we leave the theatre happier people. The experience has proved cathartic—it has purged us of dangerous emotions and desires, and so secured the social order (McIntyre, 1996, p. 95). Unfortunately, life is not like that. Nor is war. It is the philosophers' task not to simplify life but to reveal its disturbing complexity.

7

WAR AND ART
WHY WAR ENCOURAGES IMITATION (PLATO (2))

Socrates: ...in judging a general's art, do you judge as a general or as a good rhapsode?
Ion: To me there appears to be no difference between them.
Socrates: What do you mean? Do you mean to say that the art of the rhapsode and of the general is the same?
Ion: Yes, one and the same.
Socrates: Then whoever is a good rhapsode is also a good general?
Ion: Certainly, Socrates.
Socrates: And whoever is a good general is also a good rhapsode too?
Ion: No, I can't agree to that.
Socrates: But you do agree that whoever is a good rhapsode is also a good general?
Ion: Certainly.
Socrates: And you are the best of all the rhapsodes in Greece?
Ion: By far the best, Socrates.
Socrates: And you are also the best general, Ion?
Ion: You can be sure of it, Socrates, and I learned it all from Homer.
Socrates: But then, Ion, why in heaven's name do you who are the best of generals as well as the best of rhapsodes in all Greece, go around reciting rhapsodies when you could be a general? Do you think that the Hellenes are in grave need of a rhapsode with a golden crown and have no need at all of a general?

(Plato, *Ion*, 541 b-c, trans. Benjamin Jowett)

Plato's written words are still the foundation stone of the western philosophical canon. When the philosopher Alfred Whitehead famously called all philosophy merely a footnote to Plato's work, he was referring not to the systematic scheme of things which scholars have extracted from his writings, but from the wealth of general ideas scattered throughout them. He also insisted that we do not call an enquiry philosophical unless it revolves around some of the distinctions that Plato drew between 'found' and 'made', 'absolute' and 'relative', 'real' and 'apparent'—they are all part of the binary thinking that was distinctive to the Greeks. This bringing forth into the light that which is distinctive is what Novalis meant when he wrote that 'to philosophize means to make vivid'.

In an early dialogue, the *Ion* from which I have quoted, we find the classic use of Plato's greatest contribution to western philosophy—dialectical thinking. The word dialectic is derived from the same source as *dialogue*—the ground rules are spelled out in the *Protagoras* when one partner asks a question and another provides an answer. Both must be willing to be truthful. This is not a court of law with one advocate spinning a tale for the jurors, and hoping it is the one they will believe. In a philosophical discourse both parties must be prepared to acknowledge the superior reasoning of the other, to find their positions reversed, or simply to find that they are left without an argument in which (with a good conscience) they can still believe.

In the *Ion*, Socrates converses with a highly successful rhapsode (a performer of epic poetry). This is an early dialogue and shows that early in Plato's career he had already begun to question whether Homer should be the be-all and end-all of Greek thought, or that *The Iliad* should be treated as the main repository of knowledge, especially about war. Ion is the supreme authority on the poet but he is also not very bright. Socrates even manoeuvres him into claiming that thanks to his knowledge of Homer he is the nonpareil of military commanders (despite admitting that he has never witnessed a real battle in his life).

We have to see this particular dialogue in context of the great preoccupation that ancient philosophers had with war. In the ancient academy (unlike the modern) philosophers were expected to have a view about war, its function and meaning. Plato just happened to have more interest than most. But we also have to locate the dialogue in another contest altogether: the long battle between philosophers and poets which was peculiar to the ancient Greek world. (In *The Republic* Plato speaks of the 'old quarrel' (*The Republic*, Book 10).) Poets existed centuries before philosophers and were the traditional purveyors of knowledge of the world. Indeed, Plato's critique of poetry was inspired by his suspicion of its links with philosophy. In the pre-Socratic world the *logos* was poetic—Parmenides communicated his thoughts in the form of poems. Like Homer he wrote in hexameter verse, the metrical form familiar from the epic. Even Plato cast his own work in the form of dialogues which could be re-enacted on stage, but for the crucial fact that the interlocutors have no character development—but then, why should they? He wanted us to see ourselves in the characters he portrays.

At its most moving, philosophy is deeply poetic (think of Hegel's owl of Minerva, or Kant's dove that, told about air resistance, thought it could fly faster by abolishing the air). And in a supreme irony no philosopher was ever more aware than Plato of the poet within himself. No philosopher was trapped so much within his own biography. His metaphors sparkle still. In her monograph *The Fire and the Sun*, Iris Murdoch located his artistry partly in the metaphors he used: 'The cave, the charioteer, the cunning homeless Eros, the Demiurge cutting the *Anima Mundi* into strips and stretching it out crosswise. ... He wanted what he more than once mentions, immortality through art; he felt and indulged the artist's desire to produce unified, separable, formal, durable objects ...' (Bloom, 2002, p. 124). It is the encapsulation of philosophic insights in literature that moves us to imitate the actions of wise men.

For Plato the philosopher's task was to demystify, to invoke reason (not revelation), to be mundane (conceptual, not poetic). In the rational world of war (and he tells us in *The Laws* that every city-state is at war with each other (*The Laws*, 626a) the poetic has no place. If war were ever allowed to become poetic the state would lose control. War should be discussed in a cold, dispassionate light without the enthusiasms and passions which animate it. His objection to Homer was that of a 'responsible' artist towards a fellow artist who had no concern for what the power of his own language might lead to. *The Iliad*, he claimed, had locked the Greeks into a *carmen perpetuum*—a perpetual song (the term is Ovid's) from which they could not break free. They had been seduced into fighting war by the wish to imitate the exploits of Achilles and Hector. Even now we are seduced by the power of his artistry to admire a man like Achilles who is no way admirable, a man whom we would be ashamed to resemble in real life.

BARBAROUS PHILOSOPHERS

The great poet Pindar tells us that valour dwells in the darkness for the need of a story. War is a story, it is the story we sing. But there's the rub. 'I fancy Odysseus' story has become greater than his suffering because of the sweet poetry of Homer' (Sandywell, 1996, p. 82). Plato concluded that his contemporaries had ignored (or air-brushed out) the suffering because they found war poetic. The Victorian poet Matthew Arnold put it very well:

> These things, Ulysses,
> The wise Bards also
> Behold and sing:
> But oh, what labour!
> Oh, Prince, what pain!
>
> They too can see
> Tiresias—but the Gods
> Who gave them vision
> Added this law,
> That they should bear too
> His groping blindness
> His dark foreboding.
> His scorned white hairs;
> Bear Hera's anger
> Through a life lengthened
> To seven ages.
>
> ...such a price
> The Gods exact for song;
> To become what we sing.
>
> (Huxley, 1986, pp. 256–7)

Plato was concerned that in becoming what we sing, we might find ourselves locked in a vicious circle: war in reality will never measure up to what we have read, and by the time we discover this it is already too late.

Plato was the first writer to suggest that what makes war distinctive from warfare—what is a central feature of its nature—is the involvement of the Muses. It inspires imitation, which is why it persists. In today's language, we might see it (to quote Barbara Ehrenreich) as a 'self-replicating pattern of behaviour'. Its warriors and their deeds inspire young men to copy what they read (or now see at the movies)—even tragic heroes are seductive (Ehrenreich, 1997).

WAR AND ART

Iris Murdoch gets near to saying something similar when she writes that it is impossible to write a prose tragedy—i.e. no historical account can be tragic because much of real life is not. The extreme horrors of real life (its pogroms, massacres and cases of ethnic cleansing, its grand and petty brutalities) cannot be expressed in art. Art offers some consolation, whereas the most dreadful ills of history offer none. No account of warfare can be tragic, which is why no account of a brutal encounter between hunter-gatherer tribes will excite anyone outside the two tribes. But then she admits that an historical account which is great literature can *as literature* be tragic. She writes that it is the cool tone of a historian, like Thucydides, that moves us when reading of the fate of Athenian prisoners of war in Sicily as they are led into the Syracusan quarries. What moves us most is their backward glance at the recklessness which had brought them to their fate, the *anagnorisis*, the recognition of the truth. Later still, she concedes that Thucydides' account is 'great, cold, tragic writing' (Murdoch, 1977, pp. 93–6). It does not inspire us, but it moves us. For inspiration war requires more upbeat stories, but they can—and do—include the stories of defeat. The defeat of the 300 at Thermopylae is rendered real by Herodotus, and what makes it truly inspiring is that the Spartans were forbidden by law to retreat. The column subsequently erected to their memory in its terse simplicity, even in translation, is the most moving of all military memorials:

> Go tell the Spartans, reader
> That here obedient to her laws, we lie

Herodotus took the trouble to learn the names of all 300 because they 'deserved to be remembered' (Burrow, 2007, p. 16). We remember the heroic sacrificial act.

But poetry can mislead. How many poets (or rhapsodes) have seen a battle? Most don't even have the historian's gift of arranging a story into a meaningful pattern which may afford the reader an overview, or access to war's 'meaning'. And if they should happen to hit upon a valuable thought or insight, unlike the philosopher they cannot convey a universal truth or engage in a sustained argument for long, as Socrates shows by arguing Ion into a corner. Poets cannot develop arguments, they can only spin tales which are 'patterned' only for the purposes of story-telling. To the narrative attitudes of epic poetry Homer could not hope to oppose the analytic procedures of philosophy. It is philosophy (not poetry), Plato insisted, that alone can define the good life (*The Republic*, Book 10, 595a-620).

Plato called art 'a waking dream', and the nature of a dream state lies in mistaking a resemblance for the thing in question. The artist is so absorbed in his subject that he imagines himself among the scenes he describes (*Ion* 535B). He forgets the wide gap that separates him from reality. Ion admits to Socrates that he is ignorant of war as a field of study but that he can still give a good account of a battle. Why? Because he is inspired by the muse. He is quite literally a man possessed. The eighteenth century would later speak of enthusiasm; we speak of the subconscious. We used to speak (as does Simone Weil commenting on another Platonic dialogue, *The Phadeus*) of 'God seeking out man' (Steiner, 2001, p. 45). In Plato's world there are no Muses—we are on our own, so we had better see reality for what it is.

The most recent art form, the novel, highlights the predicament that many young men frequently discover too late. When Pierre Bezukhov wanders on to the battlefield of Borodino he expects to find the sort of neatly arranged battle scene that he has seen in paintings and read about in books. Instead 'nowhere was there a field of battle such as his imagination had pictured: there were only fields, clearings, troops, woods, the smoke of camp fires, villages, mounds and streams; and try as he would he could descry no military 'position' in this landscape teeming with life. He could not even distinguish our troops from the enemy's'. In this case Tolstoy drew from his own experience as a professional soldier. In a nod to Tolstoy, Andrei Makine opened his novel *A Hero's Daughter* with the description of a Second World War battlefield that echoes *War and Peace*: 'before the war, from books, he used to picture battlefields quite differently; soldiers carefully lined up on the fresh grass, as if before dying they had time to adopt a particularly significant posture, one suggested by death ... which is why when he was first skirting that meadow covered with the dead he had noticed nothing'. There is no dignity in death: in war everything is reduced to a brownish porridge (Sebastian, 2008, p. 13). Pondering this dilemma in *The Thin Red Line*, the author James Jones depicts a soldier called Bell who finds himself in the middle of a vicious fire-fight in the Pacific theatre. 'In a film or a novel they would dramatize and build to the climax of the attack ... It would have a semblance of meaning and a semblance of emotion ...[but] here, there was no semblance of meaning, and the emotions were so many and so mixed up they were indecipherable. They could not be untangled. Nothing had been decided; nobody had learned anything ... Art, Bell decided, creative art, is shit ...' (Jones, 1998).

Ultimately, the issue for Plato is one of responsibility. His criticism of the poets is essentially ethical. It is the task of the philosopher to instruct. His real objection to art, he tells us in *The Republic* (606a), is that the artist makes the soul 'relax its guard'. Artists delight in sensation; they delight in illustrating the demonic, the fantastic or the extreme. Truth, by comparison, expresses itself in quiet contemplation. And it is the philosopher's supreme task to allow us to keep control of war—control is its ultimate legitimizing principle, the final break with the lawlessness we associate with warfare. Artists in Plato's eyes are essentially *irresponsible* because they play with reality; they tend to refashion it to suit the aesthetic demands of their own art. We must all see reality for what it is, not what we would like it to be. In *Phaedo* Socrates fears that the sun will blind him, but in *The Republic* (516b) the just man looks at the sun and 'is able to see what it is, not by reflection in water or by phantasms of it in alien abode, but *in and by itself, in its own place*' (Murdoch, 1992, p. 38).

Telling though Plato's critique is, I suspect few of us today would entertain it. He recognized that we all need to live by myths, but he believed we translate them into very banal aspirations. On the contrary, however, we are often inspired by art because it reaffirms our humanity; and it does this not by getting us to escape our own contingency but to confront it. It is our willingness to be heroic or to sacrifice ourselves for others that makes life itself heroic. It reassures us that our individual mortality can be overcome—that the memory of the doer or the deed will live on. Faith in the redemptive power of war is what gives it its universal appeal—should it lose that appeal or should art be incapable of capturing it then war would indeed be in trouble.

Indeed, Plato is often accused (not entirely unfairly) of not recognizing the specific character of artistic creation. Good art can make the real more real. Iris Murdoch claimed that Tolstoy and Homer both show us aspects of the real world (our own) which we do not always see. Harold Bloom prefers a variant. They show us aspects of reality that otherwise we would not see unless they showed them to us (Bloom, 2002, p. 647). George Steiner makes the best case I know for art. True art is an enunciation that 'breaks into the small house of our cautionary being' so that it is no longer habitable in quite the same manner as it was before. It is a transcendent encounter that tells us in effect 'to change our lives' (Steiner, 1990, pp. 142–3).

The case for art is not that it offers us an escape from reality; on the contrary it animates it (Brodsky, 1987, p. 123). It makes the real more real. It helps us transcend experience precisely because our understanding is limited in the finite world. We adhere to fixed reference points in the field of experience as a condition for the possibility of knowledge, but that in turn requires us often to transcend sensory perception. Art is there to help us go beyond the immediate. It is all about seeing; artists get us to see things anew. For children, seeing comes before words. They see the world before they can explain it in words, or try to use language to tease out some deeper meaning to life itself. Language is an attempt to capture either literally or metaphorically what we are actually seeing. As Dr Johnson said, 'Imitation produces pain or pleasure, not because they are mistaken for realism, but because they bring realities to mind.' None of which necessarily invalidates Plato's case. Artists do encourage mimicry; they get us to imitate our heroes. This is the greatness of Homer, the man who single-handedly invented the western warrior type. In imitating our heroes we change reality. He goes on to add, and it is a vital insight, that our heroes are not larger than life. They are life's largeness, which is why we admire them and seek them out (Bloom, 2002, p. 4). And this can be dangerous. It is—in short—in the nature of war to be mimetic.

And these days war only becomes real for many when its images are diffused through film. As Volumnia (the mother of the greatest of Shakespeare's soldiers, Coriolanus) remarks, 'Action is eloquence and the eyes of the ignorant more learned than the ears' (*Coriolanus*, 3.2.76–77). The young Ron Kovic was inspired to join up by the movie version of Audie Murphy's memoirs, *To Hell and Back*: he never forgot the scene of Murphy (the most decorated soldier in American history) playing himself, blasting away into the German lines. But Kovic had a bad war: he came back a paraplegic and his own *Born on the 4th of July* became an anti–war movie. Except for the fact that it is difficult for any movie to be anti–war. So concludes another disillusioned soldier, Tom Swofford:

> Vietnam war films are all pro-war, no matter what the supposed message, what Kubrick or Coppola or Stone intended. Mr and Mrs Johnson in Omaha or San Francisco or Manhattan will watch the films and weep and decide once and

for all that war is inhumane and terrible, and they will tell their friends at church and their family this. But Corporal Johnson at Camp Pendleton, and Sergeant Johnson at Travis Air Force Base, and Seaman Johnson at Coronado Naval Station, and Special 4 Johnson at Fort Bragg, and Lance Corporal Swofford at Twenty Nine Palms Marine Corps Base watch the same films and are excited by them because the magic brutality of the films celebrates the terrible and despicable beauty of the fighting skills. (Swofford, 2003, p. 7)

In *Jarhead* (2005), the cinematic version of Swofford's memoir, we see life imitating art. Swofford and his friends are seen watching Coppola's epic, *Apocalypse Now*, and cheering wildly when the helicopters roam through the Wagnerian sky en route to their mission. It is the power of music which intensifies and heightens the audience's emotional response.

What Plato would have disliked about the cinematic depiction of war we can only guess—but I will make an attempt. He would probably have found fault with the everyday sadism and cruelty displayed: it is estimated that by the time he is eighteen an average American will have seen 18,000 murders on television, not to mention those seen on the computer screen. Everyday violence was central to Greek depictions of war too: Homer tells us of 148 different ways to kill a person, but the Homeric battlefield is embedded in a consistent fable with a moral, even religious, message. Deaths on screen are often unanchored to anything more than 'shock and awe'; they are the product of spectacle: special effects, and they are usually accompanied by music which is not cognitive, but rhythmic, and often relentless in its rhythm.

War, unlike warfare, exists at the level of presentation and representation and the two feed off each other. In the end, however, 'war' is not unadulterated violence precisely because it is mimetic. One way to appreciate this better is to translate the idea into the currency of our own age. For every age tends to frame and reframe the old philosophical questions in its own distinctive language. Evolutionary psychologists tend to do so in Darwinian terms. As biological creatures we are necessarily social animals. Culture is programmed into us as a species, and war is an especially interesting cultural product. We must ask why so many young men are still susceptible to what the writer Luis Borges called 'the moral and ascetic charms of war' (he was writing about the cinema) which Ion and other rhapsodes conveyed in their own day through poetry (Manguel, 2005, p. 84). It is easy to explain away their willingness to kill. Anthropologists can find good instrumental reasons for taking another person's life, such as the competition for women or scarce resources. But dying is difficult to explain away in Darwinian terms, for each of us is programmed to avoid pain and especially an early death (and war is usually a young man's calling).

Those who object to Darwinian explanations are often deeply opposed to any proposals to re-cast questions in the social sciences and humanities in terms of cultural evolution. But war does seem to have evolved in a way that Darwinian theory would suggest. It has such a wide appeal not only across the centuries but across cultures that it prompts us to ask whether something corresponding to natural selection is taking place. Are some ideas such as war more competitive than others because of their intrinsic appeal, or do they persist because they compete with other ideas (peace), survive the competition and spread? In her book *Blood Rites*, Barbara Ehrenreich reaches the conclusion that war is contagious. It spreads from one culture to the next. In some senses, she adds, it can be seen as a loose assemblage of algorithms or programmes (in the computer sense of the term) for collective action. The idea that it is glorious to die for one's country persisted for centuries. In that respect, culture cannot always be counted upon 'to be on our side'. 'In so far as it allows humans to escape the imperatives of biology, it may do so only to entrap us in what are often crueller imperatives of its own' (Ehrenreich, 1997, p. 235).

Is war, she asks, a 'meme', a word which is an abbreviation of another word, *mimene*, which in turn is derived from the Greek *mimesis* (imitation). The word appears in the most recent edition of the *Oxford English Dictionary* where it is defined as 'an element of culture that may be considered to be passed on by non-genetic means'. A number of writers now employ the term 'mimetics'—the theory that much of human social evolution is based on the differential spread of units of culture called memes (a notion originally proposed by Richard Dawkins in his 1976 book, *The Selfish Gene)*. Memes are said to resemble genes in that they produce cultural change through a process similar to natural selection: those memes that are passed on by imitation and learning tend to dominate social life. As Dawkins writes:

A meme should be regarded as a unit of information residing in a brain. It has a definite structure realised in whatever medium the brain uses for storing information ...This is to distinguish it from phenotypic effects which are its consequences in the outside world. (Dawkins, 1976, p. 192)

In other words, a meme is merely a set of instructions, the blueprint, not the product.

If war is indeed a meme, it is a persistent one. Memes can be carried by literature and art, they are a product of representation, as well as presentation (intellectual reflection). But ideas are also ways of giving us an illusion of control: the dominating influence that spawned the arts was the need to impose order on the confusion caused by the growth in human intelligence, writes E.O. Wilson (Watson, 2002, p. 771). If this is true, artistic ideas help us to re-order the world by promoting imitative conduct. In the case of war, nature really does imitate art: it channels mimetic impulses along certain lines. We imitate our role models, our heroes; role-playing is the ordering principle.

Of course, there are many objections to seeing war as a meme transmitted across the centuries through (for example) epic poetry. Perhaps, the most serious challenge is that it is difficult to demonstrate experimentally that they actually exist. Biologically, a gene is a distinct part of the chromosome. Chemically it consists of DNA. Physically it consists of a double-helix. As Dawkins himself acknowledges, memes have not yet found their Watson or Crick. Memes—we have to presume—are to be found in brains where they are largely invisible to observation (McGrath, 2005, p. 123). Memes are hypothetical constructs inferred from observation of behaviour rather than observed in themselves. Does this make them useless at the explanatory level? Nothing would please meme supporters more than to present the world with a list of detailed, experimentally testable examples. Unfortunately, there is no way to establish whether memes exist experientially. But remember it is difficult as well to prove much of quantum physics through experimentation. We know that we can divide matter into atoms, that those atoms can be divided, in turn, into the subatomic particles: electrons, protons and neutrons, and possibly that these particles can themselves be divided into quarks. I say 'possibly' because quarks have never actually been observed (Greene, 2000, p. 231).

In the end, it is a matter of faith that memes will one day be demonstrated to exist, although the world is beginning to make money out of taking them seriously. In 2004 a group in California carried out an experiment in meme production by launching on the market (or the 'meme pool') the term 'bright' as a popular word for an atheist, just as the word 'gay' has been almost wholly appropriated by the homosexual community. So far they have not had much success. The evolutionary psychologist Paul Marsden has launched a company called Brand Genetics to help firms identify and clone strong memes in the marketplace (Strathern, 2007, p. 301). And then there is Bill Wasik's *And Then There's This: How stories live or die in viral culture* (2009), a study of how ideas 'catch on' in the marketplace. Wasik invented the first 'flash mob' in June 2003 when he used e-mail and text messaging to invite hundreds of young New Yorkers to converge on a store in the city. His book is the latest search for the holy grail of the Net—why certain things and ideas propagate themselves and are passed on a like a virus to be seen by an audience that numbers in the million. It is the search for what IT wizards call the 'internet meme'.

In the case of war one suggestion is the role of 'intelligent design'—it is deliberately implanted in our imagination by states or political leaders. War has always been designed by politicians and poets involved in what the contemporary philosopher Slavoj Zizek calls 'the military-poetic complex'. But philosophers have sometimes colluded too. Alexander the Great took with him on campaign a copy of *The Iliad* annotated by his teacher, Aristotle. Perhaps a more plausible explanation is that memes are passed on from one generation to the next rather like viruses: they *infect* a host. 'I'm firmly convinced that not only as great deal but every kind of intellectual activity is a *disease*'—comments a character in Dostoevsky's *Notes from Underground*. The spreading of religion, wrote William James, which he believed was also transmitted culturally, was due to what it called a 'mystical germ'—it was, he claimed, a very common germ for it had created 'the rank and file of believers' (Dennett, 2006, p. 84). Religion appeals to many because it creates a sense of belonging. James's 'mystical germ' was not a gene, it was a germ, and germs are caught by infection. So, in that sense, we may say that war replicates itself contagiously. Language, claimed William Burroughs, is a virus communicated by mouth—poets do indeed sing a song and we become the songs which they sing.

But there is one other explanation which I find much more convincing. It is offered by Ehrenreich: war persists because of its capacity to *compete* successfully with other memes. Assuming memes exist, it is possible to maintain that the survival value of any cultural instructor is the same as its function: the survival and replication of itself. A meme, writes Daniel Dennett, is 'an information packet with attitude—a recipe or instruction manual for doing something cultural' (Dennett, 2006, p. 350). Memes persist because they can be transmitted or copied, and it is their persistence which is most remarkable of all. They persist because they are so adaptable, which is what Clausewitz meant when he wrote that every era fights war differently; in every age war has its own distinctive 'cultural grammar'.

And the memes that survive interact co-competitively and combine with others. They have trans-cultural appeal, or flourish in the presence of other memes (such as religion) and thus give rise to 'meme-complexes'. In the earliest days, simple memes probably survived by virtue of their universal appeal to human psychology. When war became more organized and structured, as society became more complex, we reached the memeplex stage. In that sense memes are like genes: to admit to their existence is not to argue that they determine behaviour, or that they instruct us how to behave. Memes switch each other on and off; they respond to the environment or the context. Sometimes they will fall on barren soil; societies may prefer to cooperate, not compete. Sometimes they embed themselves deeply. They are both the cause and consequence of our actions. The meme of war is operative only in a memeplex (or marketplace of other memes): the connections are vitally important.

Of course, the main reason I suspect that people object to meme theory is that it is deemed to attack the principle of free will. Whatever argument we prefer, writes Midgley, meme theory is still rather bleak because it suggests that our thoughts do not always aim at our own advantage, but rather their own. We are left with the prospect that some memes like war discourage the exercise of judgement that might decide that peace is actually better for us, just as faith disadvantages—or so many atheists claim—the exercise of the sort of critical judgement that might decide that religion too is dangerous for our health in so far that it may lead to inquisitions, witchcraft trials and religious wars. Thus Dawkins claims that when you plant a meme in a mind you literally parasitize a brain, turning it into a vehicle for the meme's propagation in just the way that a virus may parasitize a genetic mechanism of a host cell (Dawkins, 1976, p. 207). He takes religion as a key example. Many religions teach the objectively implausible but subjectively appealing doctrine that the soul survives our death (Dawkins, 2006, p. 190). The idea of immortality has spread because it caters to wishful thinking, and wishful thinking counts because human psychology has a near-universal tendency to let belief be coloured by desire. It is the idea that the soul persists after death that animated the Crusaders to go on campaign, and that animates today's suicide bombers to take their own life, as well as the lives of others.

Dennett prefers a different metaphor: symbiosis. A meme can be symbiotic in that it encourages sacrifice and altruism without which we would not, as humans, have achieved so much. He is aware that in claiming that memes are only interested in their own fitness (i.e. their own reproduction) this is an argument against human agency, but he reminds us that memes are complex too. Some are parasites whose presence lowers the fitness of their hosts; others are commensals whose presence is neutral; finally, there are mutualists whose presence enhances the fitness of both the host and the guest (Dennett, 1996, p. 340). We should expect memes to come in all three shapes. Some enhance our fitness (child-rearing and food preparation); some are neutral but are important for us in other regards (music/literacy); and some may be positively harmful, such as war. But when we look at the history of war in detail we find that it fulfils all three functions at the same time. It has made many societies more competitive; it has inspired great art, and enhanced the richness of life; it has inspired others to great deeds which do not always require a battlefield, of course, for their transmission.

Midgley voices another objection. If we need only explain any war by reference to a meme that successfully invades a population that has no immunity to it (the metaphor is telling) then do we not excuse ourselves from having to understand human psychology: such as peoples' intentions, nightmares and dreams? Do we not need, however, to look into their hearts (Midgley, 2004, p. 70)? But is this objection really as compelling as she claims? All memes evolve in human consciousness. 'Being involved in thinking', writes Dennett, is a meme's way of being tested by natural selection. It tries to have broad appeal (Dennett, 2006, p. 350). War has had an enormous appeal over the centuries, but its appeal is clearly diminishing even in terms of those aspects of war that for the philosopher and psychologist William James gave it its moral force, or romance.

Meme theory is still in its infancy. I suspect it is unlikely to be widely accepted as demonstrably true. But then does that really matter? Just thinking about war as a meme is in the end useful. At one point Dawkins himself speaks of them simply as an analogy. While making stronger claims to their scientific status, Dennett also adds that 'whether or not the meme perspective can be turned into science in its philosophical guise it has already done much more good than harm' (Midgley, 2004, p. 68). And the good it has done, I would contend, is that it bears out Plato's essential claim that what distinguishes war from warfare is that the former is mimetic.

What makes our world human, of course, is imitation, and that applies in all states of being, including the state of nature. The reciprocal imitation of desire, not originality, is the definitive mark of our species. Recent scientific exploration of imitation (such as Vittorio Gallese and Giacomo Rizzolati's research on 'mirror neurons'—neurons that fire both when one performs a particular action and when one observes another performing it) suggests that imitative behaviour is about to become a new paradigm in the behavioural sciences (Girard, 2007, p. 4). Dozens of published studies in recent years have attributed to them what mirror theorists call 'embodied simulation'—it is through mimicry that we experience others. Empathy, for example, feeling the experience of another, is not just something that we are capable of; it is woven into the very cloth from which we are cut (Bentley, 2008, p. 66). Mimicry is so central in the way we live, writes Herbert Simon, that humans are probably genetically predisposed to be imitation machines (Surowieki, 2005, p. 59). And never before has imitation been so encouraged, and so quickly, through new technologies such as the internet, television and cell-phone cameras—ours is a deeply imitative age.

In the state of nature, of course, there are none of these mechanisms of transmission—there are 'no arts, no letters, no society' (Hobbes tells us). There is culture of a kind, such as rituals and social taboos. There are sympathies, loyalties, needs and customs which reinforce ethical bonds within the tribe, but they are narrowly framed, and they have no appeal outside the primary group. And because there is no art, none of these sympathies can be translated into a Hegelian spirit (or Geist): into concepts such as freedom, or rights (liberty), or values (justice) or even sacrifice. Warfare has no mystique even for its participants.

Once something has a mystique we copy it: what makes war mimetic is that taboos are translated into codes of chivalry, or into an ethos (the warrior's honour). These are not necessarily our codes, of course, and what one age finds chivalrous another may find barbaric—the role models of one era are not those of another. But some role models are so inspiring that they have appeal across the centuries ('Achilles and

Hector slain/ fight, fight and fight again/ in measureless memory,' wrote the poet Edwin Muir).

It is through imitation in war that we are reminded of our shared humanity. Only in war do we recognize ourselves in our enemies. Artists remind us that our humanity is shared—not only do we all feel pain, we also feel shame; war is a product of nature and nurture, and the enemy is not some alien 'other' that it is impossible to comprehend let alone communicate. For what a truly *de-politicized* discourse might look like, let me cite an episode from *Star Trek: The Next Generation*, in which the captain of the *Enterprise*, Jean-Luc Picard, debates his fate with the Borg Collective. The Borg is a collective entity in which all individuality has been repressed and everybody works for the good of the whole. It represents everything humanity is not. It is the ultimate alien, writes Adam Roberts, the true 'other' because it is not even worth considering what makes for its 'otherness'.

The Federation which Picard represents is centred on one planet—the Earth (Sector 001 in the series). It is also metaphorically centred on core human values and beliefs which are still at the heart of our concept of self. The Borg, by contrast, have no centre, no purpose or sense of meaning. 'They have neither honour nor courage,' complains the Klingon warrior, Worf. They are a meme-less just as they are a gene-less community, as Picard finds out for himself after he is captured.

Picard: I will resist you to my last ounce of strength.
Borg: Strength is irrelevant. Resistance is futile—your culture will adapt to serve as ours.
Picard: Impossible! My culture is based on freedom and self-determination.
Borg: Freedom is irrelevant. Self-determination is irrelevant. You must comply.
Picard: We would rather die.
Borg: Death is irrelevant.

The text is pretty banal, especially when it appears on the printed page, but the importance of the exchange lies in the total 'otherness' of the enemy. For the Borg do not claim that they are stronger than the Federation. They simply say, 'strength is irrelevant'. They do not have different values; they have no values that we would recognize as human. They do not say, 'your strength is insufficient', which would actually mean by implication, 'we value our superior strength'. Instead, they insist that it does not figure or compute. And they do not value life because they cannot imagine the concept of sacrifice, which is why for them death really is irrelevant. Picard, concludes Roberts, cannot enter imaginatively into their world any more than they can enter into his. There can be no exchange and no negotiation (Roberts, 2000, pp. 166–7).

It is impossible to imagine a similar dialogue taking place between a hostage and a hostage taker in Beirut in 1983, still less between a suicide bomber and his acquired target in Israel today, should he survive to be interrogated. Our world sees a clash of wills involving different understandings of sacrifice, different meanings of death, as well as different concepts of honour. We live in a dangerous and deeply divided world because we avenge ourselves when we feel dishonoured, but it is still one that is recognizably human.

Meme theory is useful in illustrating one other reality. There are no Kantian solutions (democratic peace theory) or magic bullets that will bring war to an end. For war must not be seen in isolation. Hence the importance of the memeplex as a concept, whether or not it is 'real'. Midgley makes this point when discussing genes. We cannot eliminate war through genetic means by targeting, for example, the gene for aggression. That such a gene exists, she has no doubt. There is good evidence, after all, that there is a centre of the brain specifically concerned with it. But a gene should never be seen in isolation. Our capacity for anger is deeply interwoven with our capacity for fear, love, respect and contempt. The clue to ending aggression is not genetic engineering. Instead, it demands that we extend the sympathies we feel to a circle wider than our immediate family, tribe, community or even nation. It asks of us that we be less fearful of the 'other'; it asks that we be more charitable to strangers, more respectful of other peoples' customs, and less contemptuous of the mores of 'tribes' other than our own (Midgley, 1985, p. 61). In the meantime we will continue to fight wars. Only when or if war ceases to inspire young men (and even these days women)—only when it ever loses its mimetic appeal—will it finally have exhausted its possibilities.

8

WAR AND POLITICS

WHY WAR IS A CONTINUATION OF POLITICS BY OTHER MEANS, AND NOT ITS NEGATION (ARISTOTLE 384–322 BC)

Statecraft is what determines which forms of practical abilities undoubtedly must be represented in a certain community, further what kinds of skill and to what extent the ordinary citizen must perform. We see that even the most popular skills are subordinate to statecraft. For example, the art of war ... because statecraft then uses all practical skills as its means and also legislatively determines what we are to do and what we have to leave, then the goal of statecraft encompasses within itself the goal of all other skills, and its goal is then for all people the highest good.

(Patočka, 2002, p. 201, *Ethics* 1094, A.28)

Unlike Plato's dialogues, Aristotle's books are not literary works—they are lecture notes or summaries of the lectures he gave at the Lyceum in Athens at the end of his life. Even his students were called peripatetics because they did most of their studying not in a library or lecture theatre, but on foot. Aristotle's work, like Plato's dialogues, makes for easy reading. It is only in the last two hundred years that philosophy has become remote for many of us because of its arcane language. The trouble began when the philosophers became professionals, addressing other professors using the argot of a freemasonry of scholars. Language matters: poetry and its metaphors used to be part of philosophy's appeal. In recent years philosophy has lost its way together with its poetry. Even when we do come across a genuine work of literature (Nietzsche's *Zarathustra*), we tend to find it embarrassing. Richard

Rorty (who wrote elegant and transparent prose himself) thought it comic, and advised us to read novelists if we wanted to tap into the regenerative power of the imagination.

Of course, Rorty is right: novels do extend our sympathies by amplifying our experience and extending our range of acquaintance beyond the rather small circle of friends and neighbours we tend to meet in real life. It is no coincidence that the rise of the novel in the eighteenth century was accompanied by discussion of sympathy by philosophers. Take Adam Smith's *Theory of Moral Sentiments* (1759), which argues that 'the source of our fellow-feeling for the misery of others' is mobilized by 'changing places in fancy with the sufferer'—by imagining ourselves in their place (Wood, 2008, p. 130). Rorty's argument was that philosophy has indulged in too many language games and forgotten its chief function: to educate us in the virtues as novelists still do.

Indeed, philosophy used to be a highly practical activity, especially for the Greeks. Aristotle insisted he wanted to make his readers better people. No philosopher would advance such a claim today, which is another example of the gap which has opened up between philosophy and the rest of us. But the ancients did, and they were perfectly serious. What they wanted to impart was good practice, which is why Plato wished to banish the poets: what did the poets know about war? When Plato and Aristotle discussed the subject, they expected to be read by their fellow citizens, who could also expect to be sent into battle. And for Aristotle what made a good general was the link between the good and the goal. Every practical ability, he tells us, aims at some kind of good (Patočka, 2002, p. 200). For that reason, it is right to determine the good as the goal. As he also writes, there are two kinds of goal: mere activity and the deed (defined as an outcome). 'The goal of the general's art is victory, just as the goal of the economist's art is prosperity.' And then he takes the argument further by informing us that although there are many goods (i.e. goals), there is one supreme one: the good of the whole community, which brings us back to the quotation with which I began.

It is taken from a book traditionally known as the *Nichomachean Ethics*, which was either dedicated to, or edited by, Aristotle's son, but its subject matter is declared to be 'politics'. And the work which is called *The Politics* is presented as the sequel to *The Ethics*. The latter is devoted to finding the good, the former to the particular form of constitution necessary to make the good realizable. In one of the most famous passages in *The Politics*, we read the following:

> Hence it is evident that the state is a creation of nature and that man is by nature a political animal. And he who by nature and not by mere accident is without a state is either a bad man or above humanity: he is like the 'tribe-less, lawless, hearth-less ones' whom Homer denounces—the natural outcast is forthwith a lover of war (*philopolemos*); he may be compared to an isolated piece at draughts. (*The Politics*, 1253a, 2–8)

A little further down, Aristotle adds:

> For man when perfected is the best of animals, but when separated from law and justice, he is the worst of all; since armed injustice is the more dangerous, and he is equipped at birth with arms, meant to be used by intelligence and excellence which he may use for the worst ends. (*The Politics*, 1253a, 32–5)

Now, of course, in reality man is not equipped with arms at birth, unlike all the planet's other major predators. Mary Midgley speculates that the only thing that might have made us less murderous towards each other is that unlike the animals that once preyed on us we didn't come into the world equipped for murder: we have no talons, no horns, and only indifferently sized teeth. Murder has always been an exhausting business for human beings. But we do, of course, have larger brains: we are a highly inventive species. We have made up for what we lack in physical prowess by inventing weapons. Add to this, she adds, another innate human institution: vengeance, and we have a potent mix. Humanity is the most murderous species on the planet when it comes to violence within the same species group: especially when we avenge ourselves for wrongs (real or imagined) (Midgley, 2006, p. 27).

The point is that it is culture (in the case of intra-species conflict) that helped us to turn murderous warfare into controlled war. Konrad Lorenz is not as popular a writer today as he was in the 1950s, but his speculations about our cultural evolution still resonate. Every species, he contends, (but especially predators) are equipped with inhibiting mechanisms which make it difficult to kill members of the same group: think of the submissive postures in pack animals, such as wolves, which involve exposing that part of the body which demands the greatest protection. Even when contending for mating rights, alpha males rarely kill each other—the loser usually backs off and adopts a posture of submission. Usually he is not even forced to leave the pack.

There is a certain ritual in such contests which is a product not of culture (social conditioning) but nature; it is a biological mechanism that enables the game to end while the losers are still ahead. When we domesticate animals we do not breed out these savage instincts, we merely control them. We separate them from their families, breed them selectively over generations, and provide them with food so that they do not have to forage for it themselves.

Our own evolutionary history, Lorenz contends, follows much the same pattern. But we also have culture. Its purpose is not to domesticate us, it is to limit the damage done to us through domestication by channelling instincts into a collective good. The defence of family becomes the defence of the state—sacrifice for the larger community; killing is sanctioned usually by the state. Culture provides us with a moral code and social norms that are intended not to emasculate us but to replace our instincts with collective desires. Culture, writes Leszek Kolakowski, should not be regarded as Freud did in one of his last books, *Civilisation and its Discontents*, as a tool for repressing instincts; instead, we should think of it is as a tool which replaces instinctual abilities and channels aggression into more useful social ends (Kolakowski, 1989, p. 115). Our moral sensibilities which we hold so dear may be the way by which we limit the degenerative effects of domestication. This is why our moral heroes still include warriors, and why the sacrifices we value most highly are often those incurred in battle.

This is why Aristotle tells us that the ends we set ourselves can only be successfully attained if we are trained to understand what the collective holds to be good for its own survival. Unlike biological instincts (self-preservation) they are not an unambiguous good. Survival presumably is—it is programmed into us. It is there for a reason, the survival of the species. Later we learn to identify the things that are harmful to us (such as food that is poisonous), but the teaching in such cases is usually pretty basic because most of these we know instinctively anyway. The willingness to engage in collective violence may be instinctive too but we must be taught what courage means for the rest of us, and what sacrifices make sense for the community as a whole. The courageous person, Aristotle writes, must feel and act 'according to the merits of the case and in whatever ways reason directs'. But it is society that determines the 'merit' of a particular case (or cause) and reason can only be developed through education.

WAR AND POLITICS

The only merit of war, adds Aristotle, is to yield a *political* result. It must advance the goals of the state in whose name the warrior is fighting. This can only be achieved through education too—through statecraft. Good practice must be taught; and the object of all teaching is to help us to detect and diagnose failure in the attempt to reach our goals (McIntyre, 1998, p. 73). It is politics—a dialogue conducted within the city and only within the city—which makes this possible. When Aristotle writes of the *polis* he was writing not just of a city, or even a city-state, but a place in which history happens, out of which history is made, and for which history exists to be narrated by historians and interpreted by philosophers like himself. Only in the city can we ask the most fundamental of questions: what are the goals we should aim at; what is the best way to achieve them; and what is the best way of managing the consequences of failure, for politics like war is never predictable? The last question is one of the most important: it should be the purpose of statecraft to ensure that even defeat can be managed.

Let me illustrate this last point by taking one of Shakespeare's lesser known plays, *Troilus and Cressida*. If called upon to define Shakespeare's chief faculty, Carlyle insisted that he would claim it was superiority of intellect (Bloom, 1998, p. 1). Hazlitt wrote that anyone who bothered to study *Coriolanus* could save themselves the trouble of reading Burke's *Reflections*, or Paine's *Rights of Man* (Hazlitt, 1991, p. 345). No philosopher equals him in wisdom or his profound understanding of human nature; no other writer has ever achieved his psychological insight. So although he may not have been a philosopher (in the whole Shakespearean concordance the word 'philosophy' is found only ten times), he was a consummate thinker who also had a pretty good grasp of the nature of war. In *Troilus and Cressida* Shakespeare is more technically philosophical than in any other work. Aristotle even makes a brief appearance (anachronistically, of course, in a play set during the Trojan War—it is a rather poor joke, a reference to the philosopher's belief that young men were unfit to hear moral philosophy) (Nuttall, 2007, p. 208).

I want to take the argument between Troilus and his older brother, the renowned warrior Hector, over whether to send Helen back to her husband, and thus save further lives in a conflict which has long since lost its political rationale, if it ever had any:

Hector: Brother, she is not worth what she doth cost
    The keeping.

111

Troilus: What's aught but as 'tis valued?
Hector: But value dwells not in particular will
   It holds his estimate and dignity
   As well wherein 'tis precious of itself
   As in the prize. 'Tis mad idolatry
   To make the service greater than the god
   And the will dotes that is attributive
   To what infectiously itself affects
   Without some image of th'affected merit.
                (*Troilus and Cressida*, 2.2. 54–60)

Hector is an Aristotelian before his time: all value, at least, in politics is to be determined by the value attached to the prize. Troilus memorably retorts that we cannot judge the correctness of an act by only thinking of its consequences. Hector rebuts this with what Nuttall calls 'magnificent ethical objectivism'. If every value were free-standing there would be no point debating it. We argue about the rights and wrongs of any war because of the consequences—intended or unintended, foreseen or unforeseen, because of the 'worth' of the particular enterprise. 'To make the service greater than the god' is pure idolatry—we expect it in a state of nature; when we escape it we enter a world of politics where value must be a goal and the goal must be the common good (Nuttall, 2007, p. 215). Troilus will have none of this—honour is more important (in this case the high opinion others have of Troy and its leaders). Hector finally buckles and Shakespeare gives him only one reason for not following his own logic to the end: handing back Helen to the Greeks would compromise their 'joint and several dignities'. Hector has to lose the argument, of course, because we all know how the war ends: in his own death and the city's destruction. But does Shakespeare leave us with the words he gives because he believes them: i.e. opinion is different from truth? Consequences don't matter that much—what is important is one's reputation, or less reductively, perhaps, honour and truth must be conjoined for the former to have value? Did he think that a dishonourable outcome is to be avoided whatever the cost?

Hector's original argument, I suspect, Shakespeare wants us to know is the correct one—for it is political in inspiration. The language he employs is very different, of course, from Aristotle's. William Elton treats the discussion between Priam's sons as an expression of a change in the idea of value—a change of mindset from the medieval scholastics (who were indebted to Aristotle) to the world of Hobbes—the transition from a fixed, divinely sanctioned concept of political value, to one that we associate with the market-place in which (to quote Hobbes) 'the value or worth of a man is, as with all of other things, his price' (Arden Shakespeare). Hobbes himself meant by this that a man's value is determined by 'as much as would be given for the use of his power'. When we fight for honour, we are actually fighting to gain power: to be respected is to have it. Hobbes again: '*honourable* is whatever possession, action or quality is an argument and sign of power ... Dominion and victory is honourable because acquired by power.'

We must read Aristotle, of course, in his own historical context. The same applies to reading Shakespeare too. Neither of them was writing about power, they were writing about the good. Aristotle does not talk of profits, but he does talk of prudence—the need to assess every action in the light of its consequences. Again, the terms can be translated into a Hobbesian terminology if we wish. Prudence can be seen as thrift—the husbanding of resources, the calculation of balance and loss (the 'virtue', writes McIntyre, 'that is embodied in life insurance') (McIntyre, 1998, p. 71). But Aristotle is not talking of prudence in terms of profit (doubling one's income, or speculating against a short-term loss in the expectation of a long-term gain). He is talking in the philosophical terms of his own age: he is extolling virtue when allied to practical intelligence. Virtue is knowing how to apply general principles in a practical situation. Prudence is not only in itself a virtue, it is the basis of all virtue. The city is strong when it listens to virtuous politicians (like Pericles) who warn its citizens not to over-extend themselves. It is in grave danger when it allows itself to be swayed by the passion of man like Alcibiades, when it allows reason to be trounced by desire (especially when it involves gratification, or the short-term gain over the long).

Aristotle accepted that war could have a profit motive—he defined it at one point as 'a form of acquisitive activity' (*The Politics*). But what is being acquired should benefit the city as whole (the abduction of Helen benefited only Priam's son, Paris). Thucydides also tells us that even the Sicilian expedition involved an economic sub-text. Alcibiades voted for war because he was in debt. He had been living beyond his means and the expedition offered a way of restoring his fortunes. The poor who rowed the triremes also were paid for their service, which is why Plato so disliked them—they profited from war, too (Thucydides, *History*, 6.24). But we also know that whatever the folly of Athenian ambition, the citizens never lost sight of statecraft in this respect if no other. One of the reasons why Athens proved so effective for so long was that as a democracy it never defaulted on its debts even when facing defeat: not only did it insist on repaying them, it was also willing to tax its own citizens more extensively than was any other city-state (Ober, 2008).

Aristotle would have gone much further than we do: it is the willingness to tax oneself to maintain a reputation for financial probity that makes one 'happy'. The ultimate end of every action, he insists, is happiness; and he defines it (and the definition is central): a life that fulfils the capacity to act in accordance with our rational human natures. In the *Eudemian Ethics*, happiness is defined in more specific terms, such as intelligent contemplation; and also as the exercise of moral virtue. The key point is that Aristotle believes that what constitutes our humanity is not merely the use of reason, and it is not merely its use in selecting one course of action over another (whether for example to remain at peace with a neighbouring city-state or go to war). It adheres precisely in the use of reason in *action;* in war it adheres in the exercise of prudence, the demonstration of courage, the application of mercy, all qualities that set us apart from other animals, and remove us from the animal-like condition of being which is to be found in the state of nature.

Hector was therefore right to ask the otherwise demeaning question: shouldn't we cut our losses and return Helen to the Greeks, and so end the war while we still can. Prudence involves soundness of political judgement. It involves more than merely choosing the right means to the attainment of set ends: it involves choosing the right end in the first place. And the right end is that which is attainable, that which it is right to seek to attain. In the case of the Trojan War the Trojans had overstepped the mark: they are faced in the ninth year of the war, when *The Iliad* (and Shakespeare's play) is set, with the prospect of a disaster they had brought upon themselves.

Now, the quotation with which I started this chapter is the genesis of what we call strategy. Strategy is the military realization of statecraft. The first strategic plan we know of is the one Pericles designed to win the war. His plan was at once strikingly simple and highly original: he knew that Athens had insufficient manpower to fight the Spartans on land. His plan was not even to contest the inevitable Spartan invasion of Attica, but to take refuge behind the city's walls. The Spartans would fail to starve out the Athenians because their fleet would supply them with grain; and the imperial tribute they raised from their allies would pay for the war indefinitely. The Spartans could not match the Athenian navy at sea. In a word, the Athenians could not lose. As the power that had provoked the war, they would win by default.

Thucydides himself was of the opinion that the strategy would have worked if Pericles had not died when he did, so early in the conflict. But in the event the plague that killed him also reduced Athenian manpower critically. Although Athens rallied, eventually the Spartans realized the war could be won if they changed their strategy and extended their theatre of operations. Persian subsidies allowed them to build a navy and challenge Athenian command of the sea. In the end, all that Pericles accomplished was to force the Spartans to think strategically, too.

It is interesting, however, to read Aristotle's explanation for Sparta's own decline which followed soon after its victory. The following passage appears in *The Politics:*

> It is notorious that the Spartans themselves, while they alone were assiduous in their laborious drill were superior to others, but now they are beaten both in war and gymnastic exercises. For their ancient superiority did not depend on the mode of training their youth, but only on the circumstances that they trained them when their only rivals did not. Hence we may infer that what is noble, not what is brutal, should have the first place; no wolf or other wild animal will face a really noble danger. Such dangers are for the brave man. (*The Politics*, 1338a, 24–31)

What Aristotle is saying here is that the true training of a citizen is in reason, and that reason will direct us to aim for a final end. If reason is employed to train the irrational element in man (as it was in Sparta, where there was an exaggerated fondness for brutality), it will fail us. We should all be able to reason out that the only purpose of war is peace—the state trains its citizens for war to obtain peace, which it recognizes (or should) is the highest good. Sparta's mistake had been to reverse the order: to train its sons for war as an end in itself, and to treat peace quite cynically as only a preparation for combat. Sparta had trained its young men in desire, will, spirit and appetite. It had directed these emotions and desires to victory, but had been unable to use the peace it had won, and therefore found it could not live at peace with others. Of the great virtues, it had cultivated only two—self-control (or discipline) and courage. And these had been cultivated only so that they could be used in battle. Because they had not been trained in justice or wisdom, the Spartans had not acted as nobly in peace as they had in war. Aristotle asks the ultimate question: what does it profit a society to win a war if it goes on to lose the peace that its victory had secured?

9

WAR AS PACIFICATION

WHY WAR CAN BE SEEN AS POLICING
(TACITUS AD 54–120)

'Men make a wilderness and call it peace.'

(*Agricola*, 30)

If only we had that epigram and nothing else of Tacitus' work, it would be worth it even if we did not know the context. In its sentiment, if not expression, it is thoroughly Tacitean. According to the Stoic philosopher Epictetus, it is not deeds that shock humanity but the words describing them. To call peace a 'desert' is even more disturbing than to deny that pacification can produce it—in this case it is disturbing because it is to acknowledge the reality of Roman rule (Koselleck, 2004, p. 75). 'They produce a desert and call it peace' is one of the best things ever said about war, and it took Tacitus to say it so directly and unforgettably. The words are put in the mouth of a British chieftain, and for him there is no philosophy to extract from it, but there is for us. Pacification is a form of peace, but it can end up being self-sustaining, and it is alas not untypical of imperialism. Just as it is the responsibility of the influential citizen, even in a tyranny, to exercise independent moral judgement, so Tacitus is arguing it is the responsibility of all informed observers to pay war the same respect we pay politics: what exactly are we fighting for, or think we are fighting for. In another work he gets the defeated British leader, Caractacus, to say, 'if you want to rule the world, does it follow that everyone else welcomes enslavement?' (*Annals*, xii.36). War offers a window into the character of the society waging it. Even the Romans, from time to time, had reason to feel unsettled.

Above all, Tacitus reminds us that we must be brave enough to acknowledge that peace can be ruinously destructive—*Peace Kills* is the provocative title of a book by the American writer Patrick O'Rourke (O'Rourke, 2005). We must always have the courage to see ourselves through the eyes of others, even—or especially—our enemies. And we may not always like what is reflected back. As so often in Tacitus' work, the reality of empire is placed within a framework of observation and analysis which does not sterilize or excuse. His view of human life is wholly unsentimental, which is why it must have pained his contemporary readers to have read about themselves in such an unflattering light.

There is method here, of course. As Erich Auerbach claims, the vividness of Tacitus' speeches is 'sheer display'. We should not expect any sympathy for the barbarian case. But the rhetorical *genre* of writing speeches allowed the historian to enter imaginatively into the world of those from whom, in all other respects, he was probably far removed in sympathy and sensibility, whether he is writing of mutineers in the Roman army elaborating their grievances before their general, or barbarians complaining about the cost of Roman rule (Auerbach, 1953). In reality the British chieftain could have been a Roman senator complaining about Nero's Rome, with its state trials and purges, and the indiscriminate burning of the early Christians. We should not expect any real sympathy here for the 'lesser breeds beneath the law'. Tacitus is really addressing his own countrymen's vices. As always his warning is addressed to his readers—all of them Romans, not barbarians. He is also employing a typical rhetorical device: inversion. In revealing their own *feritas* (ferocity) and a complementary lack of *humanitas* (humanity) he is claiming that the Romans have become warlike by nature. He is making a point. His history, after all, shows Romans preying on each other; barbarism, we learn, begins at home.

The concerns of ancient historians are not ours, of course. We prefer to focus on the things they don't mention such as the poor and slavery, and the things we know really mattered like the economy about which they are largely silent. It may also be asked what has the Roman Empire to do with us—everything has gone, everyone is dead and has been for centuries. But historians know, of course, that this apparent emptiness is an illusion and that the past is still present, if not always

WAR AS PACIFICATION

visible. And in the case of Tacitus' reflection we have reason to reflect that if war is a means to peace it is also a form of peace—peace as pacification. It is a product of the state of war, not warfare. And it is still apposite—we continue to pacify the frontiers of the world, the wild zones, the *zones grises*, the no-go areas or Kalashnikov zones of the developing world (and urban ghettos of our own).

The main reason why pacification is a theme of his books, Tacitus himself tells us, is that his choice of period gave him no great conquests or triumphs to record—the period was one of consolidation, peace-keeping, and policing. At the beginning of *The Histories* (1.2), he writes: 'the work I begin is splendid in disasters, ferocious in battles, anarchic with plots and savage with peace itself'. 'Savage wars of peace' was what Kipling, the great songsmith of the British empire, called their own wars of pacification. As Tacitus recognized, his contemporaries might talk of the Roman Peace but the empire was at peace neither with the barbarians nor with itself. Periodically it was convulsed by civil war; it was also permanently at war with the outside world. Violence was always just beneath the surface. The Romans, it should be said, could probably have subdued the German tribes had they really wanted to, but potential taxes from a conquered German province would have paid neither for the costs of the conquest nor for its subsequent garrisoning. Pacification was the cheaper option, not to bring the tribes within the Roman Peace but to keep them in a permanent state of warfare. So when we look at Tacitus' statement we should see it as an aspect of the nature of war; peace as pacification.

Tacitus is the second historian to appear in this book, and for the same reason as Thucydides—Gibbon called him 'the philosopher's historian'. The quotation I have extracted from his work is a paradox, and philosophers love paradoxes. A paradox is something which appears true, but is in fact contradictory, or something which appears contradictory but is actually true. Bertrand Russell once remarked that the mark of good philosophy is to begin with a statement that is regarded as too obvious to be of interest and from it to deduce a conclusion that no one will believe; and there were many of Tacitus' readers through the centuries who have not wanted to believe what he told them. By his day the great hope of pacifying the whole world had vanished; the civilizing mission no longer had universal appeal. Peace stopped at the frontier. Rome still had a duty to police that frontier to preserve the peace within but that peace was now exclusive, literally and metaphorically. 'Withdraw into yourself', advised Marcus Aurelius. He spent much of his time as emperor keeping invaders at bay, and seems to have thought of philosophy as a similar exercise in self-defence (Gottlieb, 2000, p. 314). War, in that sense, is at one with the cosmos—it is the ordering principle. The desert we call peace may be regrettable (Tacitus can appreciate this—just), but it is one with the 'collateral damage' that war always brings in its wake, and there was no reason why the damage or its extent should have troubled a Roman emperor's peace of mind.

Marcus Aurelius spent over half his life on the frontier. 'Don't hope for Plato's Utopia, but be content to make a very small step forward and reflect that the result even of this is no trifle' (*Meditations*, ix, 29). There is a passage in the *Meditations* in which he tells us without a trace of irony that like the spider which exults when it has caught a fly, and the huntsman who celebrates his success in killing a wild boar, so a general may exult if he has conquered the Sarmatians (as Marcus himself had just done—he took the title 'Samarticus' in AD 175 to celebrate his triumph). But he derived no personal pleasure from the victory, or so he tells us. 'Are not all robbers alike if you examine their sentiments?' The sentiment could have been put in the mouth of one of Tacitus' barbarian chieftains, if it were not for the stoicism that underlies it. Marcus had no sense of accomplishing anything other than shoring up an empire that was now permanently on the defensive. Empires, writes Robert Kaplan (thinking of his country's own), are works in progress with necessity rather than glory the instigator of each outward push (Kaplan, 2005, p. 6). This was not true of the empire builders like Pompey and Caesar, but it was certainly true of the Roman empire by the time of Marcus Aurelius after the 'push' had stopped. Rome's consolidated peace was real but fragile; keeping it together was a constant work in progress; the later empire was in the business of deterrence and credibility, not glory.

Maintaining the peace was a duty that was not meant to bring much pleasure to the rulers, any more than the ruled. Stoicism has as its essence a dogged determination in accordance with the dictates of reason. Since the Stoic acts in accordance with reason, he is possessed of the only true good, which is why he cannot be depressed by the vicissitudes of fortune. Empire, like everything else, is not meant to bring much happiness, but it does secure us from the primal night. If we wish to secure an even greater peace—peace of mind—we must disregard all the attractions of external goods, including glory in the thrill of battle, and thereby not expose ourselves to the pain of their loss (McIntyre, 1998, p. 103).

The Stoic philosopher Seneca saw the empire as a *moral* concept for that reason—the frontier was a moral barrier between people who were born to bring peace to the world and the barbarians who were warlike by nature. The *Pax Romana*, in other words, was a moral idea. It offered the vision of a world free from war, but a world that had to be constantly pacified. As Greg Woolf writes, we should see the peace not as the absence of violence but providing a carefully balanced economy of violence, i.e. violence channelled to a just or moral end (Woolf, 1993, p. 191). In the high Middle Ages the poet Dante took justice to be the key to the distinction between warfare and war: any war undertaken for the common good must be just. The very idea of justice requires a concept of law. Just wars are fought to restore the law of nations, to correct a rupture in the cosmological order, to restore the status quo. Such thinking is entirely alien to warfare, where lawlessness obtains as a condition of existence. In the state of nature injustice is the rule, either because order has broken down or because it has not yet been forged. In Dante's eyes the conquest of the world by Rome was unquestionably just—it had brought law to the barbarous fringes of the known world by incorporating them in the *Pax Romana*. If one takes such a view, adds Alberto Manguel, then how can one complain about 'collateral damage': creating a desert and calling it peace. Let justice be done though the heavens fall, is the motto.

Can the same be said of the United States today? When it first embarked on the War on Terror it too saw military power as a morally transformative agent. In 2003 it thought it had a mission to pacify the Greater Middle East so that it would no longer provide a breeding ground for terrorists. 'We have a choice', Rumsfeld reminded the American people a few days after 9/11. 'Either they change the way we live, which is unacceptable, or we change the way they live, and we choose the latter' (*International Herald Tribune*, 22 October 2008). Here was a grand mission for a new century. Out went the duty of containment and deterrence that had been imposed on Americans during the Cold War. In came a new style: shock and awe and preventative pacification. 'We must extend our peace by advancing our technology', declared President Bush, which meant spending money on mobility and swiftness of response, and advances in the three-dimensional imagining of battles. 'The best way to keep the peace is to redefine war on our terms.'

After the disappointments in Iraq the Americans no longer saw the use of force in terms of a civilizing mission; they saw it in terms of risk management. Clausewitz called war a moral contest (i.e. a clash of wills) conducted by physical means (or force) (Clausewitz, 1976, p. 127). But pacification can be potentially endless: a country may have constantly to reimpose its will on another. Yet to remain a moral contest, force must be measured. The Romans were masters at imposing their will, especially within the Empire. Tacitus saw it (or encouraged his readers to see it) from the other point of view—just once. He encouraged them to ask 'what is the message being sent?' For an empire then at the height of its power, miscalculations did not really matter. Imperial powers recover even from serious setbacks and defeats. But over time an unmeasured use of force will fail, as power weakens, as it did eventually in the case of Rome. In fact, at some point one begins to see life from the other side of the hill, and it is at that point that we may even lose our self-belief. Tacitus, at least, had the consolations of Stoicism. Life was grim. We are not so stoical and we do not have the same self-belief (though the Americans can still claim more than most).

The true impact of Tacitus' warning could be seen in Iraq when on two separate occasions (April/November 2004) the US Marines tried to pacify the city of Fallujah. The first battle was joined in April after the mutilation of four American contractors evoked a great deal of anger in the US military. The army commanders resolved on the total destruction of the enemy in an act of revenge, or intended intimidation. The result was the destruction of an entire city. About two-fifths of the buildings did not survive the fighting. At times, the house-to-house fighting conjured up the battle of Stalingrad—one Marine company took sixteen hours to capture a single mosque. The Americans soon found that hearts and minds cannot be won, even in the Middle East, by using Abrams tanks, armoured personnel carriers, fighter bombers and C-130 gunships within the confines of a modern city. A city cannot be reclaimed for the forces of good by flattening it. By the time the second battle took place in November, most of the civilians had already fled—Fallujah was already a desert before fighting began.

We have to give the Bush administration the benefit of the doubt. No one set out to create a desert in 2004. But what does an imperial power do when its success in ridding the world of an old criminal (Saddam) attracts new ones (insurgents and Al-Qaeda) drawn to the challenge of engaging the imperial power wherever it finds it? Is the cost of pacification too high? Will the amoral villain (Al-Qaeda) win the moral ground and perhaps the whole fight? It did not in Iraq, where Al-Qaeda was in the end soundly defeated, but it might in Afghanistan and Pakistan where it has relocated, because of course the war on terror has no end. America is involved in an eternal mission (one which President Bush told the American people would last their lifetime). Its enemies are likely to be eternal too (and almost protean-like in their ability to reinvent themselves).

In the end Tacitus' message, as communicated through his imaginary British chieftain, is one that the armies have had to re-learn again and again. After the battles of Fallujah the US was no exception. The US army now sees its mission as 'armed social work', to quote its revised field manual FM 3–24 *Counterinsurgency*. Its objective has changed from regime removal to 'nation building'. 'The "terrain" we are clearing is human terrain, not physical terrain,' said David Kilcullen, one of General Petraeus' key advisers, at the time when the new counterinsurgency doctrine was developed. The strategic aim, as always, however, is to persuade the enemy to admit to defeat. In some wars (especially 'savage wars of peace') it is also to win the hearts and minds of the local population. A tactical success, won at great cost to the civilian population, can deny a victorious army any significant or long-term political gain. And nothing is more frustrating, as the United States found in Vietnam, than a series of hard-won battles such as those fought in the streets of Hue and Saigon that fail to deliver a decisive strategic result. Fallujah was not a defeat, but it was hardly a triumph. As one general acknowledged, 'we cannot afford many more like it' (Ricks, 2006, p. 405). Violence is discursive; it tells a tale and the tale we tell must be plausible, especially when the deserts we create in the future will be in the cities.

In that regard, the savage fire fight in Mogadishu in 1993 portrayed in Ridley Scott's film, *Black Hawk Down*, was for the US Army a trial run for the future. The challenges this will present are many, but Tacitus' warning requires us to face up to the most pressing. When pacification loses its political purpose or rationale, an army is likely to find that its objectives are tactically driven. And the problem there is not only that it will undermine the political process; it may become the political process. For their part, insurgents are usually eager to reduce war to a Hobbesian state of nature in which the 'political' disappears altogether, and war becomes warfare, not an instrument to peace, but a condition of being. From that anarchy, the political landscape is often reshaped. Violence produces change; it forces people to flee from their homes and thus reshapes the ethnic or sectarian landscape; it creates new political allegiances and realignments. It should be the object of the pacifying country to do the same but within the rules of war (Feldman, 1991).

Perhaps it is just as well the US has forsworn a civilizing mission. The army chaplains ministering to the Marines as they went into Fallujah in April told them that they were 'tools of God's mercy'. A remark like that doesn't end the discussion, but it certainly starts one. It adds force to another conjecture of mine: that there is in the American psyche something quite absent from the Roman and British, an incipient desire to destroy what cannot be redeemed. When facing defeat there may be an unconscious desire on the part of the redeeming nation to return to a state of warfare. It is when a people are considered unworthy of our efforts that the real problem often arises.

Let me develop this theme by passing out of the realm of fact into that of fantasy. A work that captures the difficulty of nation building with a satirical force characteristic of its author is Mark Twain's novel *A Connecticut Yankee in King Arthur's Court*. Its hero, Hank Morgan, finds himself by a trick of time transported to the early medieval world of Camelot. By profession, Morgan is the superintendent of a company that makes Colt revolvers, and he is every bit the efficient rationalizer for whom management is a prevailing passion. He is also a modernizer who sees Arthur's kingdom through the lens of a nineteenth-century liberal reformer. He has entered history to redeem King Arthur's subjects, to give them a 'New Deal', a term which actually appears in the novel, but which we can be fairly certain Franklin Roosevelt did not lift for his own purposes forty years later.

Confident in his own 'civilizing mission' the Yankee sets out to drag King Arthur's kingdom into the modern age. He introduces schools and factories and even a printing press, together with modern ideas. As a classic utilitarian he is only interested in what he calls 'the business part of social arrangements'. In this he was very much a product of a culture which took utilitarianism further than any other. Two centuries later, American thinking still remains highly consequentialist in spirit. The utilitarian mind is given over entirely to instrumental reason, and war has no higher good than its utility. In keeping with the logic, one of Morgan's first reforms is to establish a military academy based on West Point. It too is essentially an engineering school whose instructors have no time for the romance of war, or the Knights' traditional calling. Ever the machine-minded technocrat, for Morgan programming is everything. 'Training is all there is to a person. We have no thoughts of our own, no opinions of our own; they are transmitted to us, trained into us.' The over-zealous Yankee is as tone-deaf to the music of war as he is to the rhythms of medieval life.

What Twain's hero discovers too late is that reform does not always deliver what it promises. The defeat of a traditional way of life is not always followed by cooperation; it often provokes sullen non-cooperation and occasionally active resistance too. When there is a clear loss of the legitimacy of existing authority, people try to find security in a sense of identity offered by old kinship groups. Such a group can be a clan or a tribe, or even a nation—whatever defines the ethnic *survival group*. In the case of Arthur's Britain, the group is social; the knights are a warrior caste.

One of Hegel's fundamental theses is that it is the essence of 'being' to manifest itself in a crisis. In Twain's novel, the Knights of the Round Table have no wish to be civilized or pacified or, in their particular case, tamed. And as warriors they are willing to risk all for honour, the essence of their 'being'. The outcome is a battle which ends in a bloodbath. 'Within ten short minutes after we had opened fire, armed resistance was totally annihilated—25,000 men lay dead around us.' At the end of the brief engagement, all that is left of the cream of the Round Table is microscopic fragments of flesh raining down from the skies onto the head of the victors below, an horrific outcome that reminds Morgan of a steamboat explosion on the Mississippi. All that is left to identify the dead is 'an alloy of brass and buttons'. At least, the old muskets and rifles of Twain's youth had demanded some skill in their use; only a few shots could be fired before the enemy was encountered face to face. But the machine gun required just a steady hand on the trigger. Marksmanship requires excellence, a machine gun only minimal competence. Twain regarded all modern wars as a 'wanton waste of projectiles', but it was the further improvements in the accuracy of guns that concerned him most about the future of war.

Of course, the novel must not be taken too seriously. It is meant to entertain, which is why it has never been out of print since it was first published. It has gone on to spawn three Hollywood films, as well as a Broadway musical. But it is striking that not one of these productions includes the horrendous battle at the end of the novel when the flower of Camelot is mown down by the Yankee's machine guns. If Twain himself was unwilling to spare his readers' sensibilities, Hollywood is far more squeamish.

In discovering new worlds and returning, we often get a clearer glimpse of our own. Twain's fictional Camelot shows how pacification can wreak havoc upon a traditional culture still steeped in the old verities of warfare. It is significant perhaps that Twain came from the American South, which had witnessed the very first attempt at modern regime change. The Reconstruction period that followed the collapse of the Confederacy in 1865 had presented Washington with an especially intractable challenge. The South had lost two-thirds of its wealth and a quarter of its white male population of military age. The plantation colony did not survive the abolition of slavery. Reconstruction, perhaps, offers no exact parallels to American state building programmes (or pacification) in the late twentieth century, but it does offer the first example of democratic regime change through the exercise of military power. Germany and Japan were likewise pacified in 1945. Both societies 'embraced their defeat'—the phrase is John Dower's. In none of them did pacification have to continue into the post-war phase. In neither country did the occupying forces have to confront a popular revolt as the Yankee does in Arthur's kingdom, or the US did in Iraq after Saddam Hussein had been toppled from power.

The American empire is ageing fast, but there is life in it yet; the legions may be deployed for years to come on frontiers even further afield than North West Asia. And I have no doubt that when the unforgivable errors of the War on Terror have been forgotten, America's critics will still be expecting it to rescue them from the latest folly which, for the most part, they will probably have brought on themselves. The main criticism to be made of American imperialism (if that is what we want to call it) is impatience to finish the job and move on. Americans deal with exit strategies; the Romans didn't, although they were forced to exit all the same. Michael Ignatieff might have been writing of Hank Morgan when in his book *Empire Lite* he remarked that the trouble with the Americans is that 'no other imperialists have been so impatient for results'—hence the provocative title he gave to his book (Ignatieff, 2004, p. 8). It is a provocation, of course, that Tacitus too might have relished.

10

WAR AND PEACE

WHY PEACE IS A CONTESTED CONCEPT
(ST AUGUSTINE AD 354–430)

Wars themselves then are conducted with the intention of peace, even when they are conducted by those who are concerned to exercise their martial prowess in command and battle. Hence it is clear that peace is the desired end of war. For every man seeks peace even in making war; but no one seeks war by making peace. Indeed, even those who wish to disrupt an existing state of peace do so not because they hate peace, but because they desire the present peace to be exchanged for one of their own choosing. Their desire, therefore, is not that there should be no peace, but that it should be the kind of peace they wish for.

(*The City of God*, Book XIX, Chapter 12)

Augustine is an excellent example of how philosophers' lives run parallel with their thoughts, and how their thoughts are shaped by events in the outside world. James O'Donnell's *Augustine* (2005) is a fascinating new study which places his thought firmly in its historical context. Augustine was traumatized, as were so many of his contemporaries, by the breakdown of the western Roman world. The tone was set by St Jerome, then living near Bethlehem. 'In one city, the whole world has perished' (Moorehead, p. 39). Jerome made the point by punning on the Latin words for city (*urbs*) and world (*orbis*). It was a clever turn of phrase, but Jerome probably borrowed it from Ovid who had written four hundred years earlier.

It is even to be doubted that, but for the acute anxieties the collapse of the western empire had raised, fifth-century Christians would have given so much prominence to life after death, crystallized in Augustine's unforgiving God of the last chapters of his book. Two centuries earlier, Christians had worshipped a much more forgiving deity. Every generation forges God in its own image, it gets the God it desires (or fears). Augustine's view of Christianity is Pauline—dark and forbidding. In his world, few are saved. It was Augustine who gave Christianity the concept of original sin at its most stark: none of us merit God's grace, but a few gain it (and even then not through their own efforts, but in a kind of eternal lottery).

The pagans quite naturally blamed the collapse of the social and political order on the Christians for persuading Rome to desert its traditional gods. Augustine's response was to write *The City of God*. One of the first works to be serialized, it appeared in sections over the next fifteen years (its author was over seventy by the time it was finally completed). Augustine took the more optimistic view that the empire has been shaken rather than transformed. Except that it hadn't. The 'transformation' of the later Roman world was a stock phrase when I was a student studying history in the 1970s. More recently, historians have rediscovered how catastrophic was the collapse for the great majority of Roman citizens who had to struggle on as best they could. It is still fashionable to call it a transformation, but the word, while true technically—life was transformed, and it was transformed slowly, does little justice to the impact on social life. Contemporaries knew well enough they were living through dark times. In north-western Europe urban life virtually disappeared after AD 400—a town like Lyons shrank from 160 hectares to a mere 20 (Freeman, 2008, p. 174). Trade patterns were disrupted; the market in mass-produced goods largely disappeared. Living standards may even have fallen below those of the Iron Age. As Pope Gregory the Great wrote in despair 250 years later, 'What goes on in other parts of the world I do not know, but here in the land in which we live, the world no longer renounces its common end but shows it forth' (Freeman, 2008, p. 176).

Whatever the scale of the destruction, life went on and, as a Christian, Augustine went to great pains to remind his readers that even the Roman Peace had been imperfect. We construct empires in the hope of greater security; the only real security however is that offered by our compact with God. At times he must have remembered the lines of Paul to the Thessalonians: 'Since we belong to the day let us be sober and put on the breastplate of faith and for a helmet the hope of salvation.' The good citizen in this life sallies forth in armour, knowing that peace constantly has to be fought for. Only in the next life is it safe to take off one's armour. Only in the City of God can we expect to find eternal permanence and perfection. As Koselleck adds, Augustine found in a just peace in this world no guarantee of its maintenance and even in the striving for such peace no guarantee of its fulfilment (Koselleck, 2004, p. 102). Even what we think to be a Just War may appear deeply unjust in the eyes of others.

These days we are so keen to categorize everything—and identify specialists who know the categories inside out—that we are in danger of losing sight of Augustine's insight. There is a framework for understanding peace, and it is not necessarily to be found in the peace institutes, or in the conflict resolution courses taught in universities, or for that matter in government think tanks or Departments of Defence. There is a professional deformation at work here (or at least the threat of it). The professional affliction is expertise: we specialize these days: some of us do 'war', others do 'peace'. Each community is immured in its own epistemic ghetto. As a result, each understands neither war nor peace as well as they should.

Augustine is an important writer for many reasons, but one is that he breaks with the tradition that we are so violent by nature that we can never aspire to peace. The reality, he writes, is very different. We are constantly at war with each other because we are the only species that dreams of peace; we are the only species that can imagine a world that is finally at peace with itself. What is in our nature is our constant disquiet and striving for what is out of reach. In fighting to secure peace for ourselves we often make the world more unlivable in for the defeated. What is Heaven on Earth for some may be seen as Purgatory by others.

Peace is not easily definable: nothing that has a history can be defined, Nietzsche tells us. What do we mean by the word 'peace', asked Susan Sontag in her Jerusalem Prize acceptance speech (2001). Do we mean the absence of strife, or forgetting or forgiveness? Or do we mean the great weariness or exhaustion that often follows war, which can be followed, but not necessarily, by an emptying out of rancour? What most people mean by peace is victory: the victory of their own side. Calls for peace for the defeated often appear fraudulent (Sontag, 2007, pp. 145–6).

Augustine, in the passage I have quoted, presents us with yet another paradox to add to the many others in this book. Paradoxes are important in philosophy. The juxtaposition of two contrasting ideas gets us to think, it challenges orthodox wisdom. And what Augustine forces us to confront is that war is what philosophers call a contested concept. To employ another term, it is aporetic—it is our peace, not someone else's. Peace is never final. It is reinvented or renegotiated every time a conflict erupts between the victors and those they have defeated. Peace is only final when war together with warfare has been eliminated in the city of God.

This perspective reveals the extent to which Augustine never completely broke with Plato. In *The Republic* Plato is the first philosopher to offer a model city: the city of Pigs (*The Republic* 369b-376). Here peace is automatically guaranteed because the state exists purely for the provision of need. Such a state is without history and therefore without human truth. The city of Pigs stands outside history because there is no growth (or decay). It endures in the same state from generation to generation. In the real world, states grow and decay: citizens also have imagination and dream beyond their immediate human needs. But they grow often in a distorted form. Peace, Augustine realized, is not to be found in some immutable state of being in which the relationship of citizens to each other inheres in their reciprocal appetites or needs. Peace inheres in concepts of justice and the good, and stems from a demand that injustice be avenged, or wrongs righted. The state is always renewing itself for that reason; peace inheres in bringing back citizens to living in a more peaceful communion with each other. It emerges from human discontent. For we all attempt to become more contented by realizing our dreams. It is precisely because we dream that peace is an aporia.

It is important to grasp, writes Peter Brown, that Augustine was a man steeped in neo-Platonic ways of thinking. The whole world appeared to him as a world of 'becoming', as a hierarchy of imperfectly realized phenomena which depended for their quality on 'participating' in an intelligible world of Ideal Forms. The universe was in a state of constant, dynamic tension in which the imperfect forms of matter strove to realize their fixed, ideal structure (Bloom, 2002, p. 88). As a Christian, Augustine believed that the only genuine peace is to be found in the City of God—the next life, not this. The Roman Empire had aspired to the perfection of an ideal order on earth, but it had failed, as every human endeavour must. Empires are always at war for that reason; they are always struggling to impose an order. And they usually fail in the long term. In fighting for justice, we rarely attain what we wish. As William Morris wrote, we fight and lose the battle, and the things we fight for come in spite of our defeat. But when they come they turn out not to be what we understood, and other men have to fight for what we meant under another name (Hill, 1969, p. 485).

As Reinhart Koselleck reminds us, Augustine's insight was actually gained from postulating another world (the City of God). It is only by standing outside history (by looking at the world from outside) that one can make sense of both history and the world. For Augustine, we can never know real peace in the life from which we transit from birth to death. The only real peace is God's. In *The Confessions*, xvii he writes, 'You touch me and I am set on fire to attain the peace which is yours.' It is a peace which transcends human understanding. What Augustine derives from his Christian vision is a rather autumnal reflection on life: *The City of God* is a mournful work sustaining a relative good in the face of a greater evil (Koselleck, 2004, p. 101). The greater evil is original sin (which we carry within us from the state of nature into the state of war) and anything that prevents our return to it should be considered a blessing of sorts.

Bringing the argument into the present day, we could say that Augustine was the first writer to understand that peace is a *contested concept,* a term popularized by the philosopher W.B. Gallie in the 1950s. In Gallie's formulation, there are a number of conditions to which every contested concept must conform (Gallie, 2004, p. 161). Let me mention three. The first is that it must be appraisive in the sense that it signifies or accredits some kind of valued achievement. And nothing could be more appraisive than peace—it is what everyone aims at, or claims to. As Aristotle told us, peace is the only purpose of war. War is merely an instrumental means to an existential end. There are a few exceptions: Hitler is one of them. He refused to conclude peace treaties with the countries he defeated; he signed armistices instead. Hostilities were suspended—for a time, but in the Nazis' world view societies were in a permanent and necessary state of war with each other.

This theme was not exclusive to Fascism: it was part of the spirit of the times. In his early novella *The Time Machine*, H.G. Wells paints the sad picture of humanity grown 'indescribably frail' and decadent through many years of peace. The Eloi—like cattle—'knew no enemies and provided no needs'. Their end was the same—their fate was to become a source of protein for the vicious and aggressive Morlocks, living in their subterranean kingdom, venturing out only at night for food. At the end of the book the time traveller comes to the conclusion that moral strength is the outcome of a need, or a danger, and that security sets a premium on feebleness.

Peace is aporetic for other reasons too. Some societies, in John Dower's felicitous phrase, actually 'embrace their defeat' (he is talking of Japan after 1945) (Dower, 1999). There are times when defeat can come as a great release from suffering. For many it may be better than a continued state of conflict. But there is the rub. Is it a peace of exhaustion? Is a society shell-shocked into it? Is it desired or desirable, or even very real? Peace is an appraisive concept for that reason. And the consequences in Japan were not quite what the United States had intended. As Dower reminds us, the occupation is seen by the Japanese themselves as the country's 'American interlude' (Dower, 1999, p. 24). Inevitably winning has defined the moment ever since. It is the victors who still command attention; it is the occupiers and their agenda which still hold pride of place. Looking back today, however, we can see that Japan remained under the control of fundamentally military regimes from the early 1930s to 1952—General Tojo was followed by General MacArthur. The Americans continued to run the country through a bureaucracy that had been there before the war, and it was infinitely stronger when they left. Democracy as such was confined to what Dower calls 'a box', an unelected elite. Which is not to deny that the Americans introduced significant changes (Dower, 1999, p. 561). Militarism was defeated and Japan became more egalitarian, but real accountability and political pluralism were stifled by the occupiers themselves, who decided to play safe as the Cold War unfolded. Ironically, when Japan eventually bounced back, it did so in a way the US found disturbing. The quest for economic growth at all costs was reinforced by a siege mentality and characterized by an almost pathological series of protectionist measures. These too were a response to defeat.

Gallie's second condition for a contested concept is that the achievement must be of internally complex character—is it a concept desired by all, or only by some. *Cui bono*—who gains? A society or an elite, a part or a whole? Not everyone welcomes peace, and others who do are not prepared to accept it on the victor's terms. Some may lose out. It is because there are both winners and losers that the term 'peace' is contested. We may assume (to revert to Dower's book) that the Japanese people gained from peace. Another twelve months of conflict would have seen mass starvation and social collapse. But the real winners were the big corporations (the ones that have since become household names) who consolidated their operations after 1943 when the country went on a total war footing, thus enabling it to hold out as long as it did. They not only survived, but prospered under the American occupation.

Gallie's third claim is that a concept is contestable when the value attached to something changes over time. For want of a better word, value is often 'open-ended' in character. What may be seen as desirable at the time it is negotiated may be bitterly contested afterwards. A peace can appear punitive. The German army marched back in good order to Berlin in 1919; it was not disarmed as it was in 1945. Shortly afterwards the settlement forged at Versailles came to be seen as a punitive or 'Carthaginian' peace. Not every society embraces a peace settlement. Claims of a stab in the back are not uncommon. Civilians blame the generals, and the generals the politicians, and historians spend their time critiquing both.

All three conditions illustrate why peace is one of the most contested concepts of all. Our own age differs from Augustine's in one crucial respect—we can imagine a 'perpetual peace' in this life, not the next. You have to be modern to imagine the human race living sufficiently long that it is actually worth constructing a permanent peace (and you have to share a modern sense of catastrophe to think of permanent peace as an urgent project). On 11 April 1945 President Roosevelt formulated his testament to the American people and held out for them a unique vision, 'peace, more than an end of this war, an end to the beginning of all wars' (Kosellek, 2004, p. 203). The central charge against the 28 defendants of the Tokyo trial (1946) was not that of committing crimes against humanity (the charge levelled against the Nazis in Nuremberg), but crimes against 'peace'. The defendants were accused of planning, preparing and waging a declared and undeclared war of aggression; they were punished accordingly.

Liberals and Marxists held out the hope of a permanent peace as a teleological promise. An ideological age defined everything in terms of its own first principles. The ideal of a world at peace was the Holy Grail, the attainment of which in the second half of the twentieth century brought the two most important political religions of the day (liberalism and Marxism) into conflict with each other. The liberal idea of a world at peace was formulated by Reinhold Niebuhr in 1930.

'The civilized world is fairly well developed and permits its life to be ordered and its social and political relationships to be adjusted by the use of economic force without recourse to the more dramatic display of military power ... Our imperialism reveals ancient motives, but the technique is new ... we are able to dispense with the soldier almost completely; we use him only for a few under-developed nations' (Iriye, 1995, p. 35).

Even so, the US felt it could not be at peace until the world had been made safe for democracy against all other challenges (especially Marxism, which preached that democracy itself was merely a bourgeois conspiracy against humanity).

For their part, Marxists saw the promise of peace for what Niebuhr called it, 'imperialist'. For Lenin imperialism was the 'highest state of capitalism', and he contended that imperialism was also the main cause of war. The democratic peace promised by Woodrow Wilson offered only a perpetual state of warfare between classes, between nations (developed and underdeveloped) and, of course, states which deemed themselves to be 'civilized' and those deemed not. In blurring the distinction between war and peace, Wilson joined Lenin as a characteristically twentieth-century figure. In calling US entry into war in 1917 a 'crusade for peace', it was not clear where war ended and peace began (Iriye, 1995, p. 37). Peace was contained in the act of war, and future war was always possible until a permanent peace had been secured.

But the peculiar contribution of the late modern age to the concept of peace was made by Fascism. For it was Fascism which devalued peace altogether and maintained that war was an absolute value, and peace at best an instrumental end—a 'strategic pause', an entr'acte—at best an interval between rounds, while the belligerents recovered their strength for the next encounter. War was no longer conceived as an instrumental measure for the protection of the state, it was considered to be the supreme end of statecraft. True to form, even the Nazis expected the Third Reich would fall one day (even if it survived its allotted thousand years). (Albert Speer even designed the great monuments of the Reich with the idea that they would be no less impressive or grandiose as ruins in the far distant future—he even developed what he called a 'theory of ruin value'.) (Nelis, 2008, p. 483).

In their separate ways (and the distinctions were morally important) all three of the last century's political theologies preached a kind of Orwellian logic—War is Peace. After 1989 only one country was left to dream of this order: the United States. The Wilsonian tradition was still pervasive. It took the US to war against Iraq in 2003; it is the basis of regime change and nation building. The Americans still dream for other people. Some societies are even happy to be part of their dream. Others would rather be left to dream for themselves.

For all of us today peace is no longer other-worldly. We may still dream of the City of God but it is the City of Man in which we live. Unlike Augustine, we have come to distinguish between two kinds of peace: one conformist, the other meliorist (Gallie, 2004, p. 197). One peace is attainable in the here and now, based on order, conventions and rules. Frequently that order is forged by war; on some occasions peace is indeed pacification. On other occasions peace can be negotiated between two equal powers on terms acceptable to both.

The other ideal is meliorist. Truman promised the American people in 1945 not only peace in our time but peace for all time. The meliorist elements inhered in the vision of a New World Order. Every American President since Wilson has taken his country to war on that promise. George W. Bush was the first to break with that tradition. All that he promised his countrymen was that they could manage the Global Disorder through military action—war has become risk management under a different name. For the neo-conservatives the war in Iraq was meliorist—the threat of terrorism, stark and ineluctable in its form after 9/11 could only be eliminated, they believed, by 'draining the swamp', cleansing the Middle East of the dictators and dictatorial regimes which made life so desperate for so many young Arabs. In their own way, the neo-cons were no less fundamentalist in their thinking than their radicals in the Islamic world. The US soon found it did not have the power to take the Iraqi people into the brave new world of its own imagination.

Instead, at the beginning of the twenty-first century we find that the world is divided into the two cities of E.L. Doctorow's novel *City of God*. First, there is the city of consolidated institutions, the jewelled wonder we see from airplanes at night, floating like an ocean liner on a sea of darkness. You wonder how much God has had to do with this creation: how much of the splendour and insolence of the modern city comes from the inspiration of God. This is 'the city of the un-remarked God, the sometime-thing God, the God of history'. And then there is the city of the teaming masses whose sustaining social rituals are always in danger of breaking down, the city that has begun to lose its shape, the city which sees the emergence of prophets speaking of evil, irreverence and blasphemy, calling the pious to rise up. This is the city in which 'the un-remarked God, the sometime-thing God is alive once again, revealed in all His fury' (Doctorow, 2000, p. 271).

11

WAR AND SOCIAL NORMS
WHY WE STILL DISTRUST MERCENARIES
(MACHIAVELLI 1469–1527)

If anyone supports his state by the arms of mercenaries, he will never stand firm or sure, as they are disunited, ambitious, without discipline, faithless, bold amongst friends, cowardly against enemies; they have no fear of God and keep no faith with men ... The cause of this is that they have no love or other motive to keep them in the field beyond a trifling wage, which is not enough to make them ready to die for you. They are quite willing to be your soldiers so long as you do not make war, but when war comes it is either fly or decamp altogether.

(*The Prince*, pp. 54–5)

No other writer before or since has had the impact on language that is associated with Machiavelli. Think of such words as 'Machiavel', 'Machiavellize', 'Machiavellian', 'Machiavelline', 'Machiavellism', 'Machiavellist' (Angelo, 1969, p. 245); these are some of the contorted forms in which the author's name has passed into the common currency of the English language. Inevitably, they are cast in a negative light; they are usually terms of abuse, not praise. But the one attitude of Machiavelli's that has met with ringing endorsement since his death is his uncompromisingly negative attitude towards mercenaries.

Machiavelli himself is a paradoxical if important thinker. On the one hand, he was simply too busy in politics to have the leisure Aristotle advised was necessary for prolonged and profound philosophical reflection. He was also in less demand during his lifetime as a writer than as a public servant. He was commissioned only once to write a book. His patrons, the Medici, asked him to write a history of Florence. The commission, we may surmise, owed more to his ability as a historian, not a political thinker, but it may have had a more practical purpose, of keeping him out of mischief in the public realm. If so, the family was merely following one of Machiavelli's own philosophical precepts: an able statesman out of work, like a huge whale, will endeavour to overthrow the ship unless he has an empty cask to play with.

Machiavelli had neither a satisfactory political career nor a satisfactory intellectual one. For a man who is credited with a peculiar insight into the baser motives of politicians, it is strange that he should have invested his hopes of preferment in some of the worst politicians and his hopes for Italy's future in the unmentionable, including the Borgias. He was not, as it happens, even a particularly gifted politician—he was not trusted. In truth this was our good fortune: he was forced to write because his services were not in high demand at home.

Technically, Machiavelli is not even a philosopher in the formal sense of the word, but he was unable to dispense with theory altogether. He imbibed concepts that were in current fashion and which historians see as vital in the formulation of the modern mind. One was the rebirth (or Renaissance) which contemporaries were fully aware of at the time. It is important to remember that it is not a term that historians have applied to the period, looking back. If ever there was a period that was self-consciously conceived, it was the Renaissance—Machiavelli himself would not have been in the least surprised by the word (although it is not one he actually used). From the time of Petrarch with his call for *rinascimento* to Giorgio Vasari two centuries later, the Italians were acutely conscious that their civilization had been reborn in the dialogue between themselves and the ancient world.

The world into which Machiavelli was born was reinventing everything. Alberti had rewritten the rules of painting with the invention of perspective in 1435. Gutenberg revolutionized the communication of ideas by inventing the printing press twenty years later. Luther's Reformation would have been impossible without it. Columbus' 'discovery' of America changed Europe's view of the world: it extended its horizons. Copernicus' rediscovery of a solar-centric universe revolutionized the way the Europeans thought about the cosmos. What is important about all these intellectual breakthroughs is that they occurred at the same time. The Renaissance in that sense can be said to have given birth to what we would now call 'lateral thinking'. We should remember that even Leonardo da Vinci and Michelangelo regarded themselves primarily as military engineers. Even the arts fed into the making of fortresses and war machines, such as Leonardo's designs for a rudimentary tank and submarine. So we should not be surprised that the age also witnessed an intellectual revolution in war. Of all of these discoveries which served to increase the scope of human ambition, the invention of perspective in art was probably the most important. In allowing the viewer of a painting to see an object extended in three dimensions it re-educated the viewer's eye to see a new world. This transformation of pictorial technique cannot be understood merely as a technical process. On the contrary, it corresponded to a revolution in perception in all fields of activity, including war.

The invention of perspective was truly revolutionary, for it introduced the world to the metaphysical as well as artistic idea of the vanishing point beyond which the world ceases to exist, because it is beyond the range of our senses. The facts of metaphysics shifted to a cosmos in which the human perspective was everything. In theology as well, the Reformation asserted an unmediated access to God, and the responsibility to judge our actions by the light of our own conscience. In politics there was an infinity point, too: there were no limits to human ambition. It introduced another revolutionary idea from which there was no going back: it is human beings who give the world the form it possesses. And in war the early modern era recognized that a finite source of energy, muscular power, had given way to an infinite source that was chemical—gunpowder. War had become an instrument of rapid social transformation.

Machiavelli was acutely aware of how war was being reshaped increasingly by modern inventiveness. He appreciated the importance of technological change (the old canard that he was dismissive of firearms is simply untrue—you won't find this in *The Art of War*, which is why the book has never been out of print since its publication; indeed, it remained the mainstay of learning in military academies well into the eighteenth century). He appreciated Rome's strengths but he also recognized its weaknesses. He was aware that the Roman army had been vulnerable to non-western militaries, such as the Numidian horsemen of Africa and the mass cavalry of the Parthians, precisely because it had failed to devise a technological solution to the problems both posed. He recognized that in the matter of modern artillery Florence was more innovative than Rome—it was this emphasis on technology that expressed the modern world-view.

In short, Machiavelli recognized that his age was witnessing what we would today call a significant 'paradigm shift'—and such shifts, Thomas Kuhn reminds us, (though he himself never used the term) occur not in the minds of individual innovators, but in particular conjunctures of social and intellectual circumstances which challenge existing structures of knowledge and open up space for new ideas. As Kuhn tells us, what makes particular writers so fecund in their ideas—and so original to those of us looking back at their times—is their recognition that they are living in times that were out of joint. This tends to unsettle existing structures of knowledge about the past and its relation to the present.

And Machiavelli's world was modern in being acutely sensitive to the fact that change was occurring more quickly than in the past. What makes us modern is our ability to revive, renew and revalue the legacy of the past, which is why there is nothing after modernity—the modern age is the last (to be 'post-modern' is still to be modern but in the 'latest' way). The Renaissance may have rediscovered many of the ancient classics, but it did not attempt to copy the ancients—the Renaissance itself was a contrapuntal argument between the ancient and modern world, a taking further of western thought. The classics inspired competition, not mimicry. This contrapuntal moment of abandonment and revival has been the style of the modern world ever since.

Again the point is not that war was substantially transformed, but that contemporaries thought of it in a revolutionary way: it could initiate major changes. Gunpowder did not radically change the face of battle until the early seventeenth century, but it allowed the Europeans who mastered it to think about war differently. Gunpowder armies were too expensive to be controlled by private individuals: they had to be financed by the state. In the course of the next century governments no longer relied on subcontractors, whether private warlords or private bankers—they raised professional armies and paid for them out of taxation. Machiavelli died a good half century before this began to change the political landscape, but he and his contemporaries were aware that power was becoming increasingly *instrumentalized*; it was being directed to new political purposes as the state saw fit. Morality too was becoming an instrument of that purpose; moral principles were becoming technical rules. It was obvious to Machiavelli that as the power of the state grew so it would impinge on the moral choices of the citizen. It was beginning to erode the private space/sphere in ways that neither Plato nor Aristotle could have imagined.

Both philosophers, although they had lived in an age when the *polis* was in decline, nonetheless had taken its form and institutions for granted: Machiavelli living through the Renaissance—a time of remarkable change—recognized that all political institutions were potentially ephemeral, including a city-state like his own (MacIntyre, 1998, p. 125). And it is this which makes his appeal to the permanence of human nature so striking. Like Aristotle, he accepted that Man is not by nature a political animal; he becomes one when he leaves the state of nature. Man is born 'without a city, through nature rather than choice ... without clan, without law, without hearth' like the person reproved by Homer, for 'the one who is such by nature has by this fact a desire for war, as if he were an isolated piece in a game of draughts' (Machiavelli, 2003, p. xxxii). Like Aristotle, he accepted that warfare is the natural condition of the human race; war is the invention of culture (or human nature tamed). War has value, warfare has none. But Machiavelli knew something that Aristotle did not, that the character of war is always changing; that its cultural grammar reflects changing times, and that the norms of war are perpetually in flux too.

In this paradigm shift, Machiavelli believed there could be no place for mercenaries. We find this argument developed at length in *The Art of War*, the only prose book to be published in his lifetime. Appearing in 21 editions in the sixteenth century alone, it was a revolutionary work because it was the first of its kind to link war to the art of government. It was popular with the new ruling class of Europe who were interested in raising regular armies, paid for by taxation to augment their own rule at home (absolute monarchy), and to advance the interest in what was an emerging European state system.

Machiavelli's view of mercenaries was not unique to the man or his time—it had become even something of a commonplace before he was born. The success of foreign *condottieri* in Italy served merely to heighten the indignation of many thinkers about the decline of military *virtù*; even the rise of native Italian mercenary captains brought scant comfort, for it became apparent that the old citizen armies represented a vanished age. Mercenaries were not considered to be good soldiers; they were businessmen only interested in profit; they did not take risks because they wanted to survive to old age to enjoy their wealth, rather than die when still young on a battlefield for civic glory. Whenever they were employed (or so many of Machiavelli's contemporaries believed) campaigns were always feebly waged; victory if ever obtained was always unexploited; defeats were never disastrous, and battles were invariably bloodless. Mercenaries not only ignored the all-important training of recruits; they were disorganized in battle and cowardly when on the run (Angelo, 1969, p. 121). 'For the wars of Italy were brought to such a degree of futility as to be entered into without fear, waged without danger and ended without loss' (Burrow, 2007, p. 290).

Most of these complaints were made in the name of 'realism'—words like *reason* and *necessity* dominated the day-to-day administration of the Italian city-states. Writers such as Guicciardini made political realism almost axiomatic in their writing, and in a realist world power could never be subcontracted to private contractors without the state incurring a cost. War was now too important for governments to subcontract it out to others, though many of Machiavelli's contemporaries found it difficult to imagine an age that could do without mercenaries altogether. Even in Thomas More's *Utopia* (1516) mercenaries are on hire, and the explanation is clear enough: if there must be wars then only they should be asked to fight them. 'You see, the Utopians are just as anxious to find wicked men to exploit as good men to employ' (Strathern, 2007, p. 21).

The historical record—it should be noted—does not actually bear out any of these criticisms. Mercenary captains did incorporate the latest military thinking into their campaigns, as they did the latest technology, especially firearms. The art of war was pioneered in Italy, not Spain or France, and it owed a lot to the fact that most mercenary captains knew their trade. But all this misses the point. For it matters not whether Machiavelli was 'economical with the truth'; the picture he paints is one that instinctively we believe to be true—such is the power of his writing. War unlike warfare is anchored to what we imagine or would like it to be—it is in that sense profoundly *normative*.

Warfare has no norms because, unlike war, it has no value. We recognize this today in the killing fields of the developing world. One British newspaper editorial claimed that the *genocidaires* in Rwanda were 'driven by that atavistic fury that goes back to the times when human beings moved in packs and ate raw meat' (Allen and Eade, 2000, p. 499). Robert Kaplan has described the killing grounds in Africa as 'nature unchecked'; William Pfaff, the celebrated columnist of *The International Herald Tribune*, as evidence of 'apocalyptic nihilism' (Kaplan, 1994, p. 10; Pfaff, 1995, p. 3). It is because war, by contrast, is still considered to have value (as I discussed in Part One) that war is an inherently normative activity. Norms are the institutional expression of our values. All cultures translate underlying values into norms of social behaviour. In many cases they immediately proceed to confuse the two, so that criticism of a given social norm is regarded as an attack on the values it is supposed to represent. Criticism of the use of mercenaries, for example, is not to be taken as a criticism of war. It was precisely because Machiavelli valued war that he believed mercenaries had no place on the battlefield.

In *The Prince* he declares that the ruler should have no other object, and no other thought, than waging war or preparing for it in peacetime. The most important task of politics is to shape citizens into soldiers and to employ them well. As Quentin Skinner adds, Machiavelli brought the Aristotelian figure of the armed and independent citizen willing to fight for his liberties once again into the centre of the political stage (*The Art of War*, p. xx). For Machiavelli, war was an inherently *normative* exercise because it is only through war that the citizen can become a good soldier, and only a soldier can be a good citizen.

So we can see that his objection to mercenaries stemmed from his understanding that they live outside the political realm: they are a band of people whose appetites are untrammelled by a sense of public spirit. It is the fact that they are creatures of appetite that makes them so dangerous even to the states which employ them. In his book *Terror and Consent*, Philip Bobbitt cites several examples of mercenaries 'bezerking': a mercenary force, ostensibly loyal to its paymaster Charles V, sacked Rome in 1527 because they had not been paid. Echoing Jerome's famous lament on hearing of the fall of the city, Erasmus wrote that not only a city but a world had perished (Bobbitt, 2008, p. 28). The mercenaries of choice in the seventeenth century were often to be found at sea. Many of the buccaneers who raided settlements and shipping in the Caribbean, Bobbitt reminds us, often served the states in which they had been born, but their leaders tended to think of themselves as free kings, masters of whatever they possessed (the words are Hobbes', writing of men in a state of nature in the absence of a real king, or sovereign) (Bobbitt, 2008, p. 32).

Machiavelli's belief that mercenaries were particularly wicked derived from his view of human nature (admirably elaborated in the *Discourses*, 1:37). His central insight was that human beings are continually striving for what is forever out of reach. Human desire is infinite because it lacks a finite object. Every time an object is acquired it is accompanied by a dissatisfaction so great that it demands that a new objective be set. This dissatisfaction, both with self and the object acquired, is at the root of all human striving. It is also at the heart of warfare. War is notably different because soldiers (citizens) are not creatures of appetite. Throughout the *Discourses* he refers again and again to the dependence of political stability on the creation of what we today would call 'public spirit'. By this, Machiavelli means nothing more than a recognition on the part of the citizen that his own selfish interests and those of the Commonwealth do, in fact, overlap sufficiently to justify the restraint of the former. This is what Machiavelli meant by liberty. It is not so much a form of government (such as a democracy) but a way of life which makes citizens virtuous. Freedom, reason, law and glory are embedded in force, desire, change and necessity. While these polarities may at times overcome one another, they also reinforce each other. Life presents us with the opportunities (what Machiavelli called 'occasions') to realize order and value, and we must learn to grasp them before they lapse back into the chaos from which they emerged (Mazzeo, 1967, p. 115).

For all his criticism of Plato's utopianism, the two writers were not that different in this understanding. For Plato, war transformed the city from a political unit into a political body: its unity was reinforced by the participation of its citizens and became meaningful only through the citizens' input. Thus in *The Republic*, he spins a famous myth in which citizenship arises from the birth of a warrior class that is the first to think and act 'politically'. For Plato, the man who cultivates knowledge in himself and reconciles his knowledge with his violent desires is particularly virtuous. For the warrior, work is the only form of work which is not aimed at the production of something one needs and which does not consist in merely performing a skill (Gadamer, 1980, pp. 55–6). On the contrary, his skill is knowledge: knowing who is the enemy of the commonwealth and who is its friend; knowing against whom he should he apply his craft and on whose behalf he should act out his role as a 'guardian'. It is precisely because he has it in his power to oppress his fellow citizens that he needs to exercise remarkable self-restraint. For the warrior is asked to defend his fellow citizens even when he may not always respect them, and he is asked on their behalf to fight enemies whom he may personally admire for their martial virtues.

For Machiavelli, the good citizen directs his life to the good of the republic, which by the fifteenth century had replaced the Church as the best institution to protect men from the most extreme consequences of the unrestricted indulgence of their appetites. The citizen-soldier is even prepared to dedicate his death to it as well. Plato had tamed Achilles by warning us not to imitate him, which is why he is still the hero most warriors want to resemble but dread they might become. For both Plato and Machiavelli, sacrifice is that curious dialectic at work in war: a citizen can find meaning in death, and another, seeing this, can find his faith in life restored. The difference is that Machiavelli did not believe in a distinctive warrior caste. But both men were of one mind: it is safe only to arm fellow citizens. <u>Mercenaries are not disinterested enough to be trusted; nor are they willing to sacrifice themselves or enter into a covenant with the nation, precisely because it is their appetites, not reason of state, that propel them into war.</u>

Machiavelli's position, of course, was in itself highly normative. It is grounded in a very specific European tradition that dates back to Aristotle, the tradition of 'civic militarism'. Clearly the citizen must love his country enough to fight for it. A country cannot exist without liberty; nor can liberty without virtue, nor can virtue without citizens (so concluded Rousseau in his *Discourse on Political Economy*) . The mercenaries who fought in the Roman civil wars, he complained, were proud of their debasement (they were only too willing to hire themselves out). They were contemptuous of the laws by which they were protected, and they were even more disdainful of their fellow citizens whom it was their duty to protect. They believed it more honourable to be Caesar's hirelings, rather than Rome's defenders (Percy, 2007, p. 129).

By the beginning of the nineteenth century this 'norm' had become entrenched in western thinking. Sarah Percy quotes de Tocqueville, to the effect that a nation that cannot raise a citizen army ceases to be great in the eyes of its enemies. It lacks 'the will to grandeur' (Percy, 2007, p. 162). Similar normative views can be found in fiction. In Norman Mailer's classic World War II novel, *The Naked and the Dead*, General Cummings makes much the same point, if cast in a language distinctive to a particular age. 'There are countries which have latent powers, latent resources, they are full of potential energy so to speak, and there are great concepts which can unlock that, express it. As "kinetic energy" a country is co-ordinated effort…' What Cummings advances is a peculiar mid twentieth-century notion of the 'will to power'. Not for nothing does he invoke the latent power of his own country, which was quite simply the century's most powerful country.

'We shall be giving the word for everything: industry, trade, law, journalism, art, politics and religion from Cape Horn clear over to Smith Sound ... The world can't help it, and neither can we.' So declaims the Yankee businessman in Conrad's novel *Nostromo* (1904), which anticipates by fifty years the coming of what Henry Luce would later name 'the American Century'. In Mailer's day great concepts were needed to unlock that power—Mailer's own age was intensely ideological. And of all the century's ideologies it just so happened that liberalism was the most persuasive. Every other appropriated its institutional forms (parliaments) and even paid lip service to its ideas: elections, references to the rights of man, etc. Above all, Cummings grasps the point that a country is kinetic energy. The material resources of a nation must be harnessed to contemporary ideas through the medium of war. 'Historically the purpose of war is to translate America's potential into kinetic energy' (Mailer, 1992, p. 326).

Cummings is an authentic voice of his age; he is a proto-Nietzschean figure. Mailer certainly portrays him as one in touch with the 'fascistic' tendencies to be found even in the liberal west when it came to waging war as personified in the 'terror bombing' of Japanese cities. He recognizes that the world has become a laboratory for releasing reserves of energy, and that a powerful state, provided it has the courage of its convictions, can sweep aside all the old conventions that had inhibited the release of human energy in the past, including most religious taboos and social conventions. War is the instrument by which energy moves from its promise to its ultimate realization. To this end, individuals and individual states can become tools of destiny. 'We are out of the backwaters of history', remarks Cummings, to which his interlocutor remarks ironically, 'We have become destiny, eh?' What makes Cummings such a Machiavellian figure is that he advances the philosopher's claim that the nation-state is a self-overcoming of a people's appetites, one which enables them to turn their desire for power against itself. In war they learn to obey their own self-imposed commands. In obeying them they become 'a people' for the first time.

In other words, whether we listen to Machiavelli (the voice of the Renaissance), or Rousseau (the voice of the Enlightenment), or the fictional General Cummings (the voice of the American Century), we have taken to heart the idea that civic virtue is essential to war and that mercenaries violate the norms of war which allow us to distinguish it from warfare. They embody the explosion of unfocused energies and appetites for purely personal ends. It just so happens, adds Percy, that the anti–mercenary norms of the nineteenth century *institutionalized* Machiavelli's insight. To ignore the importance of norms in the nineteenth-century shift away from mercenary use is to ignore the fact that war itself had become in institutional terms deeply normative. The norms had now been codified and translated into legal conventions and have remained in place ever since (Percy, 2007, p. 162). Norms have always been part of the cultural grammar of war, however, and the ongoing debate about mercenaries should be seen in this light.

As Alasdair MacIntyre recognizes, war has always been normative; it has always been conducted and debated within the context of norms which a community shares (MacIntyre, 1998, p. 250). Every age will continue to have its own norms of war, as long as war itself is valued as central to the conduct of political life. And, of course, norms are always changing as the character of war changes too. Sometimes citizens are called upon to fight; at other times the state raises professional armies; and sometimes it contracts out to others. Where Machiavelli was in error was thinking that a city like Florence, even if it had managed to raise a popular militia, could have defended itself against the national armies of France and Spain. But his work lives on. So important was the idea that mercenaries were antipathetic to the norms of a modern community that they have been discredited in our thinking ever since. Only the state, we still believe, should claim the monopoly of violence and only the state can sanction violence against other states.

Today, of course, war is no longer central to the life of the political community; accordingly our social norms have changed once again. War is progressively being divorced from political life. The citizen-soldier is now a figure of history. Civic militarism is alive in some areas of American life but in an adulterated fashion. And ironically mercenaries are back precisely because of the unwillingness of the citizen to serve his country. I don't think Machiavelli would have been surprised, however, to see that they have once again returned in the guise of Private Security Companies, though few if any actually engage in combat—yet. The public discourse about them is frequently framed in disparaging terms, as evidenced by Jeremy Scahill's best-selling *Blackwater: The Rise of the World's Most Powerful Mercenary Army* or Stephen Armstrong's *War Plc: The Rise of the New Corporate Mercenary*. For their part, those who argue in favour of the new corporate warriors might argue (not that they actually do) that we should understand the civil society model as one that has grown and asserted itself organically and embraced abstract social norms from which it has become impossible for individuals or nations to deviate even when the model has been shown to fail. Yet it is inconceivable, for now, that the Sudanese government could hire a company from Russia to 'pacify' Darfur, or Amnesty International hire Blackwater to defend the people of the region from genocide under the 'responsibility to protect' mandate of the United Nations.

But Machiavelli can also be engaged on a second order question: the warrior ethos. The warrior's ethos, or warrior's honour, is supposed to reflect the society which he serves. Like all institutions the military is highly normative: its sense of self-sacrifice is cultivated. In most armies soldiers are not allowed to negotiate better working conditions for themselves, or to withhold their labour until such time as they are paid more—they are not allowed to go on strike. Instead they are deemed to have entered into a covenant with society which provides them with food, housing, education, subsidized consumer facilities and medical care. They derive a sense of collective identity from a unit, or flag (Moskos, 2000). In contrast, private security companies embrace the norms of the marketplace, with its attachment to the law of supply and demand. They do not conform to the normative world, which constitutes today's 'post-modern' military. Performance is measured against the standards of the marketplace, such as efficiency and cost. Their relationship with society is highly contractual.

The challenge in future will be to marry the business-oriented view of private security companies with the military ethos of armies to which they have been subcontracted. The point about this is not that the individual soldier thinks of service as a contract, but rather that company employees tend to regard themselves as contractors, not covenanters. The point is that different values are institutionalized differently by different professions. The challenge is to marry different norms in a synergistic relationship. Can the business ethos of a private security company be squared with that of today's post-modern military? There is no reason why not as long as war is still valued as an instrument of politics, and the warrior is still held in esteem. But war probably would be devalued if the state ever decided to outsource *combat*. For there is a larger truth in Machiavelli's idea that politics is the process by which value is translated into different norms at different times. One value of war is competitiveness; this has taken many forms: glory of Machiavelli's day has been translated more recently into credibility. Another value is wealth; war has made many societies wealthy but these days it is more likely to take the form of market share rather than mercantilist zero-sum dynamic: the territorial state has been replaced by the trading state (Bobbitt, 2008). And then, of course, there is civic virtue: war still makes citizens aware of their civic responsibilities. It just so happens that in the western world today few are required to don uniform in their lives; instead they pose a potential target to terrorists (some of whom number their fellow citizens). Civic duty now translates into resilience—a willingness to show fortitude under fire, and find in the same community of fate common cause with each other.

None of this is likely to reconcile us to private companies that are called upon to do fighting, or are dispatched to foreign climes to kill in our name. Nor should it as long as subcontracting is deemed to detract from the enduring value of war, or more precisely the values a society attaches to it at any particular time. We are still likely to conclude that there is too much of 'warfare' about them; that they carry the genetic stain of our distant ancestors.

12

WAR AND HUMAN NATURE

WHY WAR (UNLIKE WARFARE) PROMOTES COMPETITIVENESS, NOT COMPETITION (THOMAS HOBBES 1588–1679)

So there in the nature of man we have three principal causes of quarrel. First, competition; secondly, diffidence; thirdly, glory. The first maketh men invade for gain; the second for safety; and the third for reputation. The first use violence to make themselves masters of other men's persons, wives, children, and cattle; the second to defend them; the third for trifles, as a word, a smile, a different opinion, and any other sign of undervalue, either direct in their persons or by reflection in their kindred, their friends, their nation, their profession, or their name.

(Hobbes, *Leviathan*)

Hobbes was the first great philosopher to write in English, and he just happened to be one of the greatest stylists. In the words of Peter Ackroyd, he 'led the English imagination into unknown paths' (Ackroyd, 2002, p. 389). He got them as a nation to think about war seriously for the first time. There is a general darkness in Hobbes' writing which is also at one with English melancholia, betrayed so often by his arresting use of language. Even when he refers to laughter as 'sudden glory', we must not be fooled—the thought sounds delightful until we realize that he means our glory at the expense of the person laughed at. But then he was also able to laugh at himself: of all the possible epitaphs to be engraved on his tombstone the one he liked most was with its pun on alchemy: 'This is the true Philosopher's Stone' (Critchley, 2008, p. 141).

Hobbes' relentless misanthropy can be off-putting, though we know that in person he was remarkably good company. People think because his work is dark his life was too. In fact, his contemporaries sought him out. He was one of the most engaging of all the philosophers featured in this book. It was also a measure of his faith in human nature that he wished to restore humanity's confidence in itself. He wished to subvert the idea that government was ordained by God, not Man. Hobbes had a fine historical sense. And it is to history, not mathematics, that we should look in determining what made the seventeenth century revolutionary. In the long run, the new critical method of the age had a greater impact than the mathematics of Newton. Mathematics, after all, had been part of the inheritance from the Greeks, whereas historical criticism was a new force, quite unknown to them. In the face of historical criticism, the authority of biblical sanction was challenged for the first time. The Bible too became 'historical', not timeless. He abandoned the old scholastic medieval hunt for the biblical text as the 'authority' on what to think. If the state exists for man, then it is the product of human reason, and therefore political science is a rational science, and its principles can easily be reasoned out.

And it was history that led Hobbes to conclude that philosophy is historical too. Leisure is the mother of philosophy, and the commonwealth the mother of leisure. Philosophy and the city are joined at the hip: city life makes philosophy possible, and the complexity to which city life gives rise makes it urgent that philosophers draw up rules for commodious living. It was his historical consciousness which allowed him to describe the state as man's invention, and not God's plan for Man. If the state was made for our convenience then it had better be strong, because the consequences of state failure are usually very disagreeable indeed. And when looking at war and peace we should not look to God's designs but Man's ambitions. Hence it was nonsense to talk of what we should or should not do in terms of Natural Law. Instead we should look to the demands of politics. And in politics, power (not right) is the key factor.

Hobbes can be over-reductive. He tends to reduce everything to power (in this he resembles Foucault), but power has instrumental ends of its own. As he writes in the *Leviathan* (Book 1, Chapter 11), 'So that in the first place I put for a general inclination of all mankind a perpetual and restless desire of power after power that ceaseth only in death. And the cause of this is not always that a man hopes for a more intensive delight than he has already attained to, or that he cannot be content with a moderate power; but because he cannot assume the power and means to live well which he hath present, without the acquisition of more.' Hobbes recognized that power is really only a means of insurance. We all want to insure ourselves; the stronger we are the more likely we are to over-insure.

Power is all that there is in the end—I cannot put it better than Geoffrey Blainey, who has written perhaps the most stimulating study of the causes of war:

> One generalisation about war aims can be offered with confidence. The aims are simply varieties of power. The vanity of nationalism, the will to spread our ideology, the protection of kinsman in an adjacent land, the desire for more territory or commerce, the avenging of a defeat or insult, the craving for greater national strength or independence, the wish to impress or cement alliances—all these represent power in different wrappings. (Blanning, 1996, pp. 26–77)

The assertion of power lies at the very heart of the use of collective violence by both state and non-state actors alike.

What Hobbes reasoned out from this deduction is that whereas competition is the cause of warfare, competitiveness is what gives war its nature. Competition is hard-wired into us. Men compete in the state of nature all the time over limited space (the territorial imperative), over access to water holes (resources), or even access to women (social reproductive needs). Darwinian natural selection is powered by competition, and there are two evolutionary reasons why it is in our nature to compete with one another much of the time. The first is Machiavellian intelligence. We are social animals because, as we evolved, reciprocating favours from others in our community assisted our survival and the passing down of our genes. We learned to identify those who would return our favours. We formed alliances to secure ourselves against attack. Our ability to empathize with those outside the immediate family group (the gene pool) such as non-family members of a tribe is not entirely unique to us, but the related concepts are: fidelity, loyalty and ultimately self-sacrifice.

These qualities that enable us to live together, however, are also a source of competition. Security in primitive societies is purchased through 'dense sociality' such as family, kinship group, the tribe, all of which separate 'insiders' from 'outsiders'. The very same propensity to be communal and socially cohesive made us aggressive to others. It also made us excessively fearful. It is our ability to identify with others that leads us to discriminate against the rest; to see them as outsiders, or strangers. It is the need to drive them out that leads to conflict. In the state of nature there are no social networks that encompass others whom we will never meet (such as the 'imagined community' of the nation). In the state of nature social relations are deep, but networks very shallow.

Competitiveness is very different. It is, as Hobbes says, a form of *quarrel*. Other species don't quarrel, they compete as do we in our pristine animal state, the state of nature. Competitiveness can lead us to quarrel even over a 'trifle' (Hobbes' word, not mine). But the quarrel is delimited by rules—it produces winners and losers, and the losers are expected to abide by the result. Both parties are expected to enter into and observe peace treaties, or to agree to a temporary cessation of hostilities. This in no way reduces the motivation for competitiveness, but it keeps it within bounds. War is often about status—Great Powers seek to secure more of it, lesser powers enter into alliance with others to secure it; political alignments are constantly in flux. Only when competitiveness escapes its bounds does it break down into competition, as for Hobbes was clearly the case in the Thirty Years War (if you are fighting for God, how can you compromise on faith?). It was also the case in the English Civil War from which he fled, adding, with his usual candour, because he cared for neither side enough to risk his own life.

The social contract which binds man to the state is therefore not an escape from war, but an escape from warfare: it represents the transformation of competition into competitiveness, which paradoxically allows us to entertain the hope of peace. For competitiveness need not be zero-sum. It can even take a non-violent form, which alas is not possible in the state of nature. In short, when we escape the state of nature we do not abolish conflict, instead we channel it into different ends—we translate competition into competitiveness. This can be seen most vividly by comparing Hobbes' three causes of conflict with respect to both warfare and war.

Take *competition*. Our DNA gives us special attributes: we recognize facial expressions, we study body language. We feel embarrassment (particularly when laughed at), and we seek to avenge ourselves against those who have made us the butt of their jokes. And then there is language, which Noam Chomsky told us over fifty years ago is genetically programmed into us. Our brains have highly developed cognate structures unique to ourselves, and language enables us to think in abstractions, to formulate rules and conventions and social taboos (against incest), which in turn permit us to *imagine* something called injustice, and the need to correct it.

And language is divisive. As Aristotle tells us, 'though we may use the same words, we cannot say we are speaking of the same things'. Two declarations can both be true at the same time in terms of justice or peace or social organization. We just happen to have different ideas for what is just for us, and we are willing to fight to win justice or punish an injustice done. Aristotle called these divergences in speech the 'discourse of humanity'. They are also the discourse of warfare, and warfare is not only endemic but bloody. Many hunter-gatherers often find themselves in a state of near permanent warfare. The reasons for this are many—they arise quite literally from the imperatives of survival. There is no politics here—which is usually the world of interest or values, not the survival of the fittest. And many hunter-gatherers are quite unforgiving. As one shaman told a western anthropologist, 'the most important thing for us is that we never end a war … it became known that you could win a war with the Yąnomamö today, but your children's children would pay for it forever … Stopping fighting is not the Yąnomamö way' (Gottschall, 2008, p. 151). Conflicts never end. A survey in the 1970s found the murder rate among the Kung bushmen was higher than in the United States. Within a worldwide sample of 31 hunter-gatherer societies (with zero reliance on agriculture and herding), 64 per cent practised warfare at least once every two years. Only 10 per cent did not experience it at all (Kelly, 2000, p. 2).

The rules that allow for discrimination in war inhere purely in the political realm—it is the *state system* which allows us to recognize our common humanity at the same time that we draw our primary identity from the tribal group into which we are born. Athenians and Spartans may have behaved badly towards each other—but *polemos* was distinguished from *stasis* precisely because when they were still fighting within the rules they recognized themselves as fellow Greeks. The English and French, even when fighting each other in the Hundred Years War, continued to recognize each other as members of Christendom. Three hundred years later they saw themselves as members of a club, Kant's 'republic of Europe'. The larger civil society to which the nation states of Europe belonged allowed them, as Adam Ferguson claimed, to 'meditate their ruin' within the context of laws and conventions. Tribes have no such conventions (though they may have taboos and act according to ritual); they recognize no obligations to each other. Tribal identity is entirely self-referential. Nation states produce nationalism; tribal societies do not export 'tribalism'.

In the absence of any understanding of common humanity, competition tends to be zero-sum. Take pre-colonial New Zealand, where the word 'Maori' meant simply 'normal' or 'ordinary'. The Maoris were usually in a permanent state of war with one another, their preferred weapons being clubs and spears. They usually took no prisoners except those they later consumed. At times, whole tribes were expunged and their oral record died out with them. In pre-colonial New Zealand, life truly was nasty, brutish and short—its ruling principle was *mana* meaning (most often) 'revenge'. Life was even more savage with the introduction of guns bought from British traders in the early nineteenth century. In the twenty years in which they used muskets against each other, a quarter of the entire native population died from one cause or other related to the conflict. In this case they did achieve what scientists would call a 'singularity'—they did recognize before it was too late that the idea of warfare as an act of revenge could no longer be sustained with the introduction of modern weapons. This epiphany was followed by the collapse of their traditional belief-system, and their mass conversion to Christianity (which the British had also imported with their guns). The Maoris chose to internalize the Christian message of the brotherhood of man (including their fellow Polynesians) by coming to terms with the fact that warfare plus guns would lead eventually to their own extermination.

Hobbes as one of history's earliest ethnographers was right to see in the Indian societies in the Americas evidence of a pre-government phase of human existence. He was also right to intuit that there is an interrelationship between warfare and society in human nature. And he was above all right to suggest that the connection could be empirically established. He was wrong, however, to think that most hunter-gatherer societies actually live quite literally in a permanent state of warfare in which 'every man is enemy to every man'. Of course, the hunter-gatherer world does know peace, even if it is episodic. Clearly the state is not essential to peace, nor is government central to its establishment. But the critical factor for us in translating war into peace that can last for years is the fact that we *politicize* war. Clausewitz tells us that politics is the 'womb of war', and so it is—for it is politics that externalizes reason, and finds in particular forms of political association (such as the *polis* or nation-state) ways of employing collective violence more effectively.

Because there is no political realm in the state of nature, there is no concept, for example, of 'social substitutability'—the anthropological term for the development of concepts of injury and group liability. Even in the raids and counter-raids that distinguish warfare, of course substitution of kin is often made (women and children are not always targeted or killed—though few are considered non-combatants and therefore beyond targeting). Many hunter-gatherer societies go in for strategies of extermination. The Mundurucu headhunters of Brazil turn their enemies into the game they hunt everyday—they speak of them not as fellow human beings (however different) but in the same language they reserve for the animals they hunt. And what is even more frightening is that the enemy is an enemy simply because he exists (Wilson, 2004, p. 113).

Greater social substitutability—putting people in uniform (creating Rousseau's 'accidental soldiers')—allows a much greater displacement of vengeance than does a feud, because it involves non-family members (many times removed from the family that has committed the original outrage). The emergence of social substitutability constitutes a watershed in human history, for it creates the preconditions not only for more general deployment of lethal violence for the attainment of a group objective, but also more selective targeting (Kelly, 2000, p. 71).

Politics also requires something else: organization. Once the group solidifies into a city (or into an embryonic state), raids continue but they become more strategic. They require rational planning and logistic back-up, and greater organization (as raiding parties are sent even further afield). They require a division of labour at home so that armies can be recruited and put into the field. In turn, this leads to the growing instrumental character of war. Logistics may also explain the emergence of economics: the economy of war was the first economy to appear and, in turn, gave rise to the market economy we know today. Pierre Clastres in his book *Society Against the State* (1974) argues that it was the war economy pioneered by the first city-states of the ancient world which turned warfare (or what he calls 'tumults') into war between states: collective organized violence directed centrally and sustained over time. The city state's fixed walls and ramparts also anchored people to permanence—they required organization and organization produced city life (the 'organization of fixed space') from which emerged the marketplace. It is in this double sense that Clastres feels confident in arguing that logistic necessity fed back into state formation, while the state as a political and social unit made logistic planning possible for the first time (Virilio, 1997, p. 20).

And the third factor in politicizing war is the rise of armies which, however fearsome for their skills, are usually the state's chief currency of power, not to be lightly put at risk, nor squandered in a day's fighting. Once armies are put into the field, the death toll tends to go down because armies need to be conserved (especially if they are the chief currency of power). The Egyptian state in 1294 BC at the battle of Kadesh (now in northern Syria) was only able to field an army of 24,000 men out of a population of 2 million. In other words, less than 2% of able-bodied men were mobilized for battle. Modern states were able to put much larger armies into the field, but again if you look at the percentage of the population killed, it is very small. At Waterloo, the most lethal battle of the Napoleonic Wars, less than one tenth of 1 per cent of the adult male European population died in the encounter. Or take the cost to Russia of the First World War which provoked the October Revolution. One decade after the fighting had ceased, the Russian population had got back to what it would have been if the war had never occurred (Harris, 1989, p. 68). The 20 million plus Russians who were killed in 1941–5 came near to levels we would expect in warfare (10 per cent–20 per cent death rate), but this was a one-off, and is an exception that proves the rule.

Indeed, the main reason why the war between Nazi Germany and the USSR was so bloody is highly telling. The Nazi version of the world posited a social Darwinist environment in which cooperation and altruism were unreal, and survival the only imperative. The Nazis did not fight war, they practised warfare. Against the west they observed the Geneva Conventions (in the main). Against Slavs they practised a war of extermination. To quote Hitler:

If we did not respect the law of nature, imposing our will by the right of the stronger, a day would come when the wild animals would again devour us ... by means of the struggle the elite are continually renewed. The law of selection justifies this incessant struggle by allowing the survival of the fittest. (Midgley, 1985, p. 139)

WAR AND HUMAN NATURE

A nuclear war too would have degenerated into warfare within hours of the conflict taking off. Fortunately, it was played out in war games and computer simulations: as a RAND analyst corrected an American general with the cheeky self-assurance of the new breed of armchair strategists, 'General, I have fought more nuclear wars than you' (Kaplan, 1983, p. 173). There was no question, however, that if the bluff had been called, if the bombers and missiles had been dispatched to their targets, this book would not have been written.

The second reason why Hobbes found warfare to be endemic in the state of nature is *diffidence* (in its original sense, of distrust). This feature has given rise to the phrase 'a Hobbesian trap'—a situation where fearing an attack upon us, we attack first. We pre-empt our enemies, or try to. This is so ingrained that it takes no notice of whether a man is stronger or weaker than another, for the weak can creep up on a strong man in his sleep; even during the day an intelligent man can outwit an opponent who is physically stronger, but not very bright. One of the problems is that human beings unlike other animals have developed weapons, and weapons that can be used at a distance. These can be deadly in hunting non-human prey, but projectile weapons also allow a small, less aggressive non-alpha male to kill from behind without fear of retaliation from the alpha male victim. In human society the strong are much more at risk than in any other species.

Outside the political realm there is not much that can be done to reduce diffidence—tribal communities are small, they lack the 'depth' of an organized collective unit such as a city-state. City-states can reduce distrust through greater transparency, which is often the product of intelligence gathering and diplomatic contacts. Alliances with other states can augment the power of both—they can act (to use a military term) as a 'force multiplier'. Hunter-gatherer tribes rarely enter into long-term associations with each other.

The third cause of warfare is *glory* by which Hobbes meant honour. 'Every man looked that his companion should value him at the same rate he sets upon himself.' Honour, Pinker tells us, is genetically programmed into us to amplify the emotions we have, such as pride, anger and love of kith and kin. These emotions are there for a reason: to help us survive in difficult local conditions. We are prone to retaliate violently against anyone who would test our resolve by signs of disrespect. This is a necessary survival strategy in the absence of a state, or the absence of law, and it is as true for the frontiers of our inner cities in

East Los Angeles as it is for tribesmen like the Yąnomamö (Pinker, 2001, p. 327). For Francis Fukuyama writing of the street gangs in the United States, in the harsh unforgiving Hobbesian world of the inner cities, 'there are still people who run around risking their lives in bloody battles over a name or a flag or a piece of clothing; but they tend to belong to gangs with names like the Bloods or the Crips and make their living dealing drugs'. Gang membership buys protection and enables one to bond with others (Fukuyama, 1992, p. 166). Both at home and abroad there is something ominously contemporaneous about Hobbes' discussion of warfare.

When we turn to the state and the invention of war we find ourselves on very different ground. The advent of a state enabled us to modify the form warfare had taken as well as change its meaning (Gauchet, 1998, p. 41). Conflict becomes *competitiveness*—the realization of human potential, a supreme act of will. It is the great event, writes Marcel Gauchet, that severs history into two: it brings human society into history, not in the sense that it delivers us from a state of inertia into one of motion, but it modifies in every way the de facto relation to change, and hence the actual rate of change. Change also makes life considerably more complex. Imposing an order means changing it. Power is not perceived any longer, it is willed (Gauchet, 1998, p. 34). Democritus got there first: 'from concord comes great deeds—and for states the capacity to wage war and in no other way' (Democritus B 250, Warren, 2007, p. 449). Great deeds are possible only in the state, and they are usually accomplished through war—war is not so much a deed but an expression of ambition, a demand of our humanity. Who could better Hegel's classic description: the great man of the age is the one who can put into words the will of his age, tell its age what its will is, and accomplish it ... he actualizes his age (Carr, 1971, p. 54). The English critic F.R. Leavis meant something similar when he wrote of great writers that they are 'significant in terms of the human awareness they promote' (Ibid.). In other words, the will has to be released and channelled, usually through the medium of war.

When we turn to war, we find causes of competition turned into causes of 'quarrel'.

First, *competition*. States, concludes the sociologist Michael Mann, have spent half their time waging war. We are instinctively territorial creatures whether we are laying claim to land, marking out a person as property, or in the last century defining the limits of someone's thoughts. The most important point about competitiveness is that it should be continuous, in the sense not that it is endless but that each competitor knows that they may once again meet in conflict. This is why, writes Geoffrey Parker, we have designed 'etiquettes of atrocity': such as laws of war, rules and conventions, and even social taboos (customary law). Even though they are breached often enough, especially in the heat of battle, states are shamed into justifying their acts to others and themselves. Competition between states, he writes, requires neither rationality (for if it works it will continue), nor trust (thanks to the penalties of defection), nor even mutual communication (because deeds speak louder than words) (Parker, 2002, pp. 167–8). What is essential is the memory of earlier encounters, the recognition that one day soon we may meet up once again with our enemies on the field of battle.

Competitiveness is endemic in other forms of social discourse. Philosophy itself is inherently competitive. Harold Bloom speaks of the 'anxiety of influence'—the extraordinary competition between writers to emerge from the shadow of some great master (hence Plato's attack on Homer and Thucydides' wish to outdo Herodotus) (Bloom, 2000). Democracy first arose in Athens from competition (arguments in the law courts) and it thrives today in the competition of political parties who vie for our votes. And competitive instincts are at their most transparent in the marketplace where companies vie against each other for market share.

But competitiveness is most vivid in the sphere of sport, which is 'war' in a different guise. The Greeks were the first people to celebrate excellence in sport as well as war. The Greeks were able to channel their competitive instincts into competitive sports (the Olympics)—the poet Pindar extolled the virtues of athletes as well as warriors. Excellence could be manifest in competition between cities in architecture and the arts, but not, of course, in the state of nature where Hobbes tells us (metaphorically) there are no 'commodious buildings.... No Arts, no Letters, no Society' (Hobbes, *Leviathan*, 1.13). Hobbes' stark dismissal of the 'natural state of mankind' as nasty, brutish and short is arguably the most quoted and best known of all ideas bequeathed to us by seventeenth-century philosophers. What still strikes the reader most in his picture of the state of nature is how plain and barren it is: there is nothing to appease the soul. The point, as Nietzsche remarks, is that war is a contest which the invention of the city makes possible, and it is only in the contest that excellence can be demonstrated and admired, even by one's enemies.

What makes war different from warfare is the game element. And games are about risk taking: but they are not in the main about chance. Chance games are ones of pure contingency: one spins the roulette wheel and finds oneself either in luck or out of it. There is no system that we know of that can beat the bank. Even 'edge work'—the increasing popularity of dangerous sports such as bungee jumping—are about risk taking on the basis of training and skill: they are not meant to be suicidal. There is of course an element of bravado, an important element of tempting fate which provides the adrenalin rush. And there is always the risk of failure. The modern phrase 'tempting fate' comes from Greek tragedy in which *ate* (the force of fate) punishes human beings for their pride, for daring once too often. But *Homo Ludens* takes risks. The world is one in which there is a place for daring.

Informed risk taking, nevertheless, is governed by fear of losses, not hope of gains. Every war involves what Richard Sennett calls 'a mathematics of fear' (Sennett, 1998, p. 82). Every war involves the prospect of defeat: not in the sense that any successful risk taking may lead one to take another risk, but rather regression to an indeterminate mean. The next risk could be profitable or disastrous. At which point the game has become one of chance. The supreme gamblers, Napoleon and Hitler, took one risk too many. It is for this reason, adds Sennett, that risk taking is something other than a sunny reckoning of the possibilities contained in the present. The mathematics of risk offers no assurances, and the psychology of risk taking focuses quite reasonably on what might be lost. The greatest loss would be self-respect. So do nothing that is likely to devalue your reputation by turning competitiveness into competition (a fight for survival). Germany and Japan forfeited their reputation in World War II because their leaders were gamblers who risked all and lost everything.

Let me move on to *diffidence*. Hobbes' very first book was a translation of the *History of the Peloponnesian War* in which he tells us that he learned all that he needed to know about human passions. And what Thucydides tells us is that the primary cause was the fear that the Spartans felt for the growth of Athenian power. Countries fear their neighbours when they think that they desire what they have. As one of the leading Athenians said during the war, the Athenians were 'seized by a mad passion to possess that which is out of reach'. This too is a form of diffidence, or fear: Athens over-reached itself not only because it was ambitious; it was fearful because it recognized that others feared its own ambition. The most powerful (ironically) are often the most fearful of all. That is why diffidence (or distrust) is so dangerous. Great powers are always seeking to subdue potential rivals 'by force of wiles to master the persons or men he can, so long till he sees no other power great enough to endanger him'. Frequently they over-insure themselves; they go to war not only against threats that are real, but those that are imagined.

In other words, in every war there are two entropic principles at work: the more security you have, the more insecure you feel. And it is in the nature of great powers to be over-competitive because they have so much more to lose than others, at least in their own mind. This was quite clearly evidenced in the way in which the War on Terror expanded very quickly from a war against one terrorist movement with global reach into a war against terrorism in general.

The way to deal with excessive competitiveness is to restore the role of politics. The problem with contemporary Athenian democracies from Plato's perspective (and, one suspects Thucydides') is that it depended for its success on the cultivation of the soul. And that meant the soul of the *demos*. But it was also clearly apparent that a city-state that chose Alcibiades to lead the expedition halfway through, and later condemned Socrates to death, was lacking in such cultivation. Only a *polis* governed by the truly philosophical temper, argued Plato, could hope to realize its ambitions. For Plato, the failure at Syracuse was evidence that democracy did not work. Plato was not a democrat: we are. The way to avoid sanctioning politically unwise expeditions in the future is to have more open debate; greater parliamentary scrutiny, and greater transparency in politics. In a word, the way to prevent competitiveness from becoming competition is to be more democratic.

Finally, *glory*. The word 'state' derives from the Latin *status* (in its sense of standing or position). Status is important, as Hobbes realized, in helping the members of a community to construct their identities. He writes about respect or value, and he writes as one would expect in the language of early market capitalism—a man's power is treated as a commodity; regular dealing in the social market establishes his price. 'The value or worth of a man is of all things his price, that is to say so much as he would be given for the use of his power; ... for to let a man (as most men do) rate themselves at the highest value they can; yet their true value is no more than it is esteemed by others' (Hobbes, in Macpherson, 1962, p. 37). The language is still familiar and presupposes, of course, a marketplace in which competitiveness thrives. The language of society and politics these days even more than in Hobbes' time is fused with market terms. We talk of 'moral capital' and 'social capital'. One British general during Kosovo even insisted that the British army could only be asked to undertake what the 'market will allow' (Moskos, 2000, p. 95).

The point is that value (or honour) involves power: to be dishonoured is to be disempowered: to be humiliated is to disrespect oneself in the eyes of others. Hobbes was putting forward an essential claim about human beings that he just happened to express in the language of a seventeenth-century Englishman. The Bastard, one of Shakespeare's first notable characters, reacting to the morally dubious bargain that has been struck by King John, the man he serves, and the King of France, complains that his master has moved 'from a resolv'd and honourable war to a most base and vile-concluded peace' (*King John*, II.1.561–98). That is often the dilemma. At times peace may dishonour those who conclude it—one thinks of appeasement in the 1930s.

The principle has been a key factor in international politics for most of the modern age. In 1914, Russia's honour required it to back Serbia; Austria's required it to issue its ultimatum to the Serbian government. The rest, as they say, is history. In 1939, Britain's honour required it to guarantee the borders of Poland, even though it was in no position to defend them. Even in the Cold War, the credibility of the United States required that a 'decent interval' should follow the defeat in Vietnam. In pursuit of that end Nixon and Kissinger prolonged the war until they achieved 'peace with honour' in 1973 (in the event the 'interval' between the time the peace treaty was signed in Paris and the collapse of South Vietnam proved much shorter than anyone had imagined).

Today war still persists, but it has been recast as risk management and the concept of glory has been *instrumentalized*. Glory can mean different things: 'honour', 'worth', 'price' or 'estimate'. Like individuals, nations are still concerned with worth because value is intimately linked to authority, especially the authority of the state. If we take glory to mean 'fame' or 'renown' then it may indeed appear applicable only to the pre-modern era. If we understand it to mean 'deference', 'just due' or 'prestige' then it is still an important motive for going to war, even though it has been recast as 'credibility'. States no longer fight to win status, but they do so to retain it. For with it goes something else which is central to power: honour. In our world honour means 'credibility' (the word which was introduced into common parlance during the Cold War). If war has become risk management, what we are especially anxious to manage is anything that puts our credibility at risk.

What is important about credibility is that, like honour, it requires the recognition of others. Hobbes told us this three centuries ago—we want to be respected because respect is the currency of power. In the words of Pierre Bourdieu, 'an individual who sees himself through the eyes of others has need of others for his existence, because the image he has of himself is indistinguishable from that presented to him by other people' (Sennett, 2003, p. 55).

Honour was especially important for the Japanese leadership in 1941. Without honour the country would have had no social existence. For the generals this was much more important than 'mere' existence that would have been put in doubt by another year of fighting. Its most extreme expression was that of the kamikaze pilots who were asked by their country to offer their lives in suicidal attacks against American warships. The atom bomb changed the terms of engagement overnight because it subverted the rules of the game: it made nonsense of the warrior code and the Samurai ethos. The A-bomb was the triumph of a different kind of rationality, the ultimate triumph of means over ends. To use another Weberian term, at that moment the Japanese became 'disenchanted' in the Samurai ethos. In the world of mid-century Japan, there was a strong contrast between the sacred and profane. The sacred involved a sacrament between the soldier and Emperor, citizen and nation. Political society itself was on a higher plane—a mystical union. The atom bomb did not destroy the will to fight, it destroyed an ethos on which the will to continue the fight ultimately depended. It made nonsense of the citizen-soldier's sacrament with the nation. The struggle now required only one outcome: the triumph of the profane.

Hiroshima forced the generals to accept that the country could simply be wiped off the map—there would be no decisive battle in which the nation's honour could be defended and the sacrament between people and nation reaffirmed. The A-bomb at least offered them an exit strategy. They could not be accused of lacking will, or showing insufficient spiritual stamina. Instead, they could fall back on the supernatural force of the atom.

BARBAROUS PHILOSOPHERS

Credibility is today's word of choice, and has been since 1945. Elsewhere more old-fashioned honour often requires that men inflict pain on others. Honour, in that sense, is a social bond, and winning it back a social obligation. And in much of the world the defence of honour is also not confined to the present. It is shared with the ancestors with whom it is important to keep faith. Cultures of honour spring up because they amplify human emotions like pride, anger and revenge, and because they reinforce solidarity, the clanship links or gang membership from which their members derive safety. They are often a sensible response to external challenges. Honour in international society represents a kind of social reality. It exists because everybody agrees it exists, and it must be constantly defended on a hair-trigger response because it is dangerous not to. To be risk-averse is to invite dishonour which, as Hobbes warns us, can be dangerous. In other words, honour and war feed off what Hobbes saw as a universal need for self-esteem. War will only end—i.e. we will only have an immunity to it—when we do indeed look into our hearts and discover that we no longer need to take revenge, or seek the esteem of others, at least on terms of our own choosing.

13

WAR AND BATTLE
WHY BATTLES ARE RARELY 'DECISIVE' (MONTESQUIEU 1689–1755)

And if the chance of battle, that's to say, a particular course, ruins a state, then there is a general course which dictates that this state should perish in a solitary battle. In a word, the principle turning point carries within it all particular accidents.

(*Considerations*, 475; Koselleck, p. 121)

If Hobbes is the father of social *science*, Montesquieu is the father of *social* science. For what interested him most was a particular society's nature and capacities—when going to war against a society culturally very different from your own you have to know what animates it or you may soon find yourself in trouble. In a striking passage the philosopher Montesquieu argued that there are no decisive battles as such. Armies may be defeated in an afternoon, but defeat is often symptomatic of something more profound: countries are rarely defeated on the battlefield; so-called decisive battles usually compound or confirm the underlying cultural weaknesses of the defeated side.

Battles define war; there are few battles in warfare, and what battlefield encounters take place tend to take the form of skirmishes or ambushes rather than a sustained clash of wills. 'Ambushes, treacherous feasts and stealthy raids at dawn—these are the characteristic modes of Yąnomamö warfare', writers the anthropologist Marvin Harris. In an extreme act of bravery the occasional young blood may enter a village and kill an enemy at sleep, thereby winning for himself the reputation of being a 'fearless' warrior. But the general intention on the part of the tribe is to kill the maximum number of neighbours while incurring no losses oneself (Harris, 1989, p. 97). In another book he recounts one such encounter in the late 1920s involving two aboriginal bands in northern Australia. At dawn hostilities began with some old men shouting out their grievances at one another. When spears began to be thrown two or three men were singled out for special attention. Since the old men did most of the throwing the spears mostly missed their target. Not infrequently the person hit was one of the screaming old women who weaved her way through the fighting men yelling obscenities at everyone, and whose reflexes for dodging the spears was not as good as those of the men. Harris does not want us to think that such encounters are slapstick comedy; the warring parties are usually in deadly earnest. According to one authority 28 per cent of deaths in these two particular tribes were caused by battlefield wounds. Bear in mind that when a band contains only ten male adults, one death per battle every ten years racks up this kind of high body count (Harris, 1978, p. 35).

But if battles 'make' war so distinctive, there are no general laws that can be adumbrated from studying them, only general propositions that, all things being equal, when applied should hold true on the day. In the second volume of *The Open Society and its Enemies* we find the author taking to task those who claim otherwise. On p. 448 we find this footnote: 'If we explain, for example, the first division of Poland in 1772 by pointing out that it could not possibly resist the combined power of Russia, Prussia and Austria, then we are tacitly using some trivial universal law such as if of two armies which are about equally well armed and led one has a tremendous superiority in men, then the other never wins'. Such a law, Popper adds, might be described as a law of the sociology of military power, but it is too trivial to raise a serious problem for students of sociology, or to arouse their interest for long. Yes, we can accept as a truism that if an army outnumbers another 3 to 1 it will probably prevail on the day. If a general finds himself enjoying such favourable odds he can probably feel confident that the odds are on his side. But you cannot remove the parenthetical qualification and transform the statement into an absolute law that applies at all times and in all places (Popper, 1972, p. 772). It is precisely because we know from history that an army with inferior numbers can win that we have to ask why some societies do not allow the loss of a battle to determine the outcome of a war, and why others do.

WAR AND BATTLE

Let me take another general 'law' in war: democracies tend to lose the first battles but win the last. In his lectures on industrial society Raymond Aron turned to Alexis de Tocqueville to discuss the democratic way of war. He reminded his readers that de Tocqueville too had admitted his debt to Montesquieu. He merely happened to be the first to apply them to the only truly democratic society of the time, the United States. Aron chose to look at one set of problems for a democracy, lack of preparedness for war (a failure to maintain a large armed establishment in time of peace). If this was a weakness it rarely proved fatal. Provided a democratic state can survive initial defeats it tends to be tenacious in pursuing war to final victory. If Clausewitz is right to argue (and I think he is) that war only ends when an enemy is prevailed upon to admit defeat, Aron is right in his diagnosis: it is much more difficult for democracies to admit defeat than it is for other regimes. It is difficult to compromise if one occupies the moral high ground as democratic regimes invariably believe they do (Aron, 1970, p. 37). De Tocqueville had warned that mass public opinion presented a new danger. Just because they have been elected, democratic governments are not necessarily right or wrong; but once they think they are right it is difficult to argue them out of it. The attempt to make the world safe for democracy launched the west on a new crusade; only recently have others come to ask whether democracy can be made safe for the world.

The force of Aron's argument is the same as Karl Popper's—there are no general laws in war, only regularities which are not scientific laws. War, Aron conceded, was not a science and no laws can be deduced except for some trivial generalizations. Democracies tend to be disadvantaged at the beginning of war, and to be more advantaged at the end. The trick, if one wishes to take them on, is to win quickly, and to do nothing that is likely to induce in them a fit of moral outrage—in 1941 the Japanese High Command understood the first but not the second. It could only hope to prevail by taking the US Pacific fleet by surprise and attacking Pearl Harbor without warning, which was calculated to turn the war from the first day into a moral crusade against lawlessness.

There are no laws of war that allow us to predict outcomes with complete certainty. Even historians now readily admit that there are many possible, subsequent turns of fortune in war, none of which is inexplicable. Hence the present popularity of counter-factual history.

The idea that the future really is open is not inconsistent with the belief that every event is determined, in so far, and only in so far, as every event usually has a cause. 'We would have to ... abandon history', writes Michael Scrivens, 'if we sought to eliminate all surprise' (Ferguson, 1996, p. 71). This is the importance of another of Popper's works, *A World of Propensities* (1990). We should remember Popper's claim, 'we learn by trial and error, that is "retroactively"'. In his essay, he presents 'the propensity interpretation of probability as a generalised dynamic':

The tendency of statistical averages to remain stable if the conditions remain stable is one of the most remarkable characteristics of our universe. It can be explained, I hold, only by propensity theory: by the theory that there exist weighted possibilities that are more than mere possibilities, but tendencies or propensities to become real: tendencies or propensities to realise themselves that are inherent in all possibilities in varying degrees and which are something like forces that keep the statistics stable.

So it is possible to discover those 'weighted possibilities'—those propensities or trends that may or may not work themselves through to a successful conclusion. This is why we try to find those regularities or rules that govern all human behaviour. We do so, knowing that the world is no longer what we once thought it, 'a causal machine'. It is a world of unfolding propensities, or outcomes. But we can still predict results. We may never know for sure where those possibilities or propensities are leading. But we can still work, Popper insists, with an 'objective theory of probability' (Popper, 1990, p. 148). Some outcomes are more likely than others, but they are not assured.

In the end, the rules that I have outlined above do structure war in a way that restricts the number of things that can happen, determines some of the things that will happen, and makes it possible to assign greater or lesser probabilities to the rest. It is in that limited but still vital respect that it is worth discovering them. This is partly why few victories on a battlefield actually 'determine' the outcome of war; instead they usually confirm a propensity that is already visible (at least to the historian, with the advantage of 20:20 hindsight). It is the historians, however, who must shoulder a lot of the blame. It is they who are always trying to identify decisive battles, an exercise which is often overly reductive.

The decisive battle, of course, continues to weave its spell. It is the stuff of popular military history—battles give war its world-historical importance. It is the stuff of cinematic and literary accounts which give war its enduring popular appeal. Montesquieu's great insight was that the nature of war is different: wars are ultimately decided by social and economic and cultural factors. His significance as a philosopher is his understanding that in a community everything is connected up so that change in one aspect of life usually affects another. It is he who introduced us to the concept of cultural complexity.

As Michael Howard observes, military victories on the battlefield rarely determine the outcome of wars: at most they merely provide political opportunities for the victors—if those opportunities are not seized, victory will be wasted. This was the experience of the German army in two world wars (Mandel, 2006, p. 14). The 'decisive battle' is not central to the nature of war: strategy is; the ability to turn a local success into a decisive political outcome—this is one of the essential unities to all strategic experience in all periods of war (writes Colin Gray) 'because nothing vital to the nature ... of war changes' (Gray, 1999, p. 1). Neither author is arguing that victory is not indispensable or even that there are not societies that are willing to abide by the result of a battlefield encounter. If a society is similar to one's own, battle probably will be causal: battlefield encounters will decide the outcome of wars. But if they are dissimilar they may be unavailing.

It is not surprising that Montesquieu was interested in the bigger picture. The *philosophes* were different from all other philosophers because the division of labour among intellectuals was not yet as advanced as it was to become. They were, in fact, the first community of public intellectuals (or talking heads) before either term was invented. The versatility of their interests is testimony to their aspiration to universality. Montesquieu was not only a philosopher but a historian, a political scientist, a social critic and sociologist, just as Adam Smith was not only an economist but a student of rhetoric and a moral philosopher as well, something we forget today. We tend to see him exclusively as an economist, the first major figure in the field. In fact, Smith always thought of himself as a moral philosopher (Gay, 1973, pp. 321–2).

For Montesquieu everything in life was connected up in ways that the social theorist, like the historian and the philosopher, must seek to uncover—this includes a country's climate, the size of its population, its moral codes and even manners. It is to his credit that he refused to claim that any one element dominates. Indeed, he believed every society had an intelligible structure, though he gave primacy to politics (not economics) as the chief point of reference in a nation's life. He did so because he believed man was a political animal by nature. This is where he outdid Clausewitz. Clausewitz too saw war as a continuation of politics, but he tended to ascribe success and failure in war to decisive battlefield encounters, and to attribute victory or defeat to the genius of a particular general.

Montesquieu derived his view of war from his wider reading of the world. He believed that certain fundamental patterns of behaviour give order to the world's chaotically diverse customs. If this were true, various actual behaviour patterns, customs and rules which we find at different times in different parts of the globe might be explicable in terms of different kinds of environment (such as climate). Conventions, moral codes and forms of government are not, he insisted, 'solely conducted by the caprice of fancy'. 'I have laid down the first principles, and have found that the particular cases follow naturally from them: for the histories of all nations are only consequences of them; and that every political law is connected with another law, or depends on some other of a similar nature to a general extent' (*Sprit of the Laws*).

In other words, Montesquieu set himself the challenging task of identifying those underlying uniformities, as well as the specific factors that produced the complex and diverse world he was studying. For him the laws of nature and society were actually the relations between one thing and another (*Spirit of the Laws* Ii.i). It is a difficult concept to grasp because of his tendency to think that a 'law' and a 'relation' are synonymous. He considered that there was an order or regularity in the world that was rational, and which could be grasped by a rational mind: 'order' inheres in the relationships we study. We too try to discover what Herbert Simon calls 'meaningful simplicity in the midst of disorderly complexity', but we don't share the Enlightenment belief that it is necessarily rational (Buchanan, 2002, p. 214).

Let us take a classic remark by one of Britain's most famous generals. In a lecture on strategy which he delivered in 1966, Bernard Montgomery insisted there were only two strategic principles that were 'eternal': never march on Moscow, never fight a war in Vietnam. The fact that he reduced the laws of strategy to two was reflective of English pragmatism—a traditional dislike of theory. In *The German Ideology* Marx and Engels distinguished between the French 'philosophical system' and the English 'registration of facts'. Montgomery was being very English in narrowing the lessons of strategic thinking down to two, and eschewing altogether any attempt to be more systematic.

Taking up his first claim, few countries have been invaded more than Russia, and the invaders have taken many forms, including the Teutonic Knights whose defeat is celebrated in Eisenstein's film *Alexander Nevsky*. More recently, Napoleon, Imperial Germany and the Third Reich have all sent their forces deep into Russian territory—only one, Imperial Germany, with success. Russia's size (and weather) do not preclude a successful attack: Germany succeeded in 1917, as did the Western Allies in limited operations in the Crimea in the mid nineteenth century. But anyone planning to invade Russia should take into account several factors that are distinctive to the society as a geographical and cultural entity. As Montesquieu would say, one must make the connections. One connection is the weather (Napoleon's army melted away on the advance to Moscow because of an unusually hot summer that spread cholera; it disintegrated on the march back because of an unusually cold winter). Another factor is the character of the regime in power. A strong Tsarist autocracy or Communist government could survive an initial string of failures; it could mobilize unusually large reserves of human capital, usually not available to its enemies. When a regime was weak (as it was in 1916–17), collapse might follow defeat in the field. In almost every case, however, no battlefield success, whether at Borodino (1813) or Kiev (1941), however admirable as classic set-piece tactical encounters, proved to be decisive. If you intend to invade Russia, your one hope is that it will defeat itself.

Montesquieu was looking at one side of the equation: why do some countries lose wars even when the battlefield encounters are not decisive? What of the other side: why do some countries win all the battles but lose the war? I am going to invoke Montgomery's second example: Vietnam. For he delivered his lecture at a time when the Americans were becoming mired in a potentially unwinnable war in Indochina.

Colonel Harry Summers recalls a conversation in Hanoi in April 1975 with a senior North Vietnamese general: 'You know, you never defeated us on the battlefield.' His interlocutor replied: 'That may be so but it is also irrelevant' (Summers, 1995, p. 1). Hanoi concluded very early into the struggle that its adversary did not possess the psychological or political means to fight a long-drawn-out war; it therefore resolved to fight asymmetrically. It had no interest in ending the conflict swiftly. On the contrary, as long as long as it did not lose, it could be said to

175

have won; the US, for its part, as the stronger side was condemned to winning, which it could not do because no victory on the battlefield could force a decision. Summers invokes another feature of war which distinguishes it from warfare—it is not always symmetrical.

Asymmetry is usually not a feature of warfare which may be complicated but not complex. When two complex societies are alike, of course, they will also think about war in the same way. As Martin van Creveld explains: 'Given time the fighting itself will cause the two sides to become more like each other even to the point where opposites converge, merge and change places ... The principal reason behind the phenomenon is that war represents perhaps the most imitative activity known to man' (van Creveld, 1994, 174). Tribal warfare is more imitative still because hunter-gatherer societies are very similar indeed in structure. As Montesquieu recognized, cultural diversity makes all the difference; some societies learn more quickly than others. Cultural diversity is what makes war so unpredictable: hidden strengths and attitudes of mind can count more than numbers, or resources. The stronger side does not always prevail.

In the case of the Vietnam War, the North Vietnamese too tried at times to fight a classic conventional war against the United States. The siege of Khe Sanh (1967) was a traditional military operation in which the Americans found themselves surrounded by a superior force numerically which could bring artillery fire to bear on every part of the base. They were only able to break the siege because they had more resources than the North Vietnamese, including B52 bombers and ground-attack aircraft.

One of the explanations for North Vietnam's eventual success is that it reverted to tradition; it exploited its cultural capital. The 'national' element in its history, for example, long predates the Vietnamese nation-state. As a national community it was the oldest in Asia as well as one of the most successful in defending itself from the Mongols and the Chinese. China, by contrast, did not even have a name for itself until the nineteenth century; the Han people traditionally called themselves after the dynasty which was in power. Historically, the Vietnamese were the most formidable military society in Asia. In the thirteenth century they had founded the world's first military academy and produced the first military handbook, the *Annam Chi Luoc* (Pike, 1986, p. 10). As tradition had it, 'knowing how to fight the long by the short; the strong by the weak; the great numbers by the small numbers; the large by the small' was a strategy they had practised with success for centuries (Ibid., p. 13).

Whereas the Americans drafted their soldiers (and the draft affected only one in three of those eligible for military service), the North Vietnamese mobilized their entire population. In doing this they were able to overlay a quasi–Marxist message of historical struggle with a teleological goal: the advance to a perfect society. 'Every minute tens of thousands of men die,' remarked Gen Giap. 'Even if they are Vietnamese that doesn't mean much' (Irwin, 1997, p. 232). The Americans tended to interpret such remarks as evidence of callousness, or ideologically induced fanaticism; on other occasions they attributed them to the adherence to a Marxist understanding of history in which human lives mattered little. But such remarks probably owed more to Buddhist fatalism. The struggle with the United States was called the *Dow-Tranh*, a phrase which carried a high emotional charge because of its history. The phrase itself might be new—traced back to the liberation struggle against French rule in the 1930s—but the sentiment was not. The struggle consecrated war as a personal duty and made sense of personal suffering. The individual suffered so that the nation might live. Even the most mundane of sacrifices could contribute to that goal.

In another respect, the decision to fight two wars (an irregular and conventional one) at the same time—to engage in what the Americans called a disynchronic war: a war on two fronts—owed much to Taoism, another ancient Vietnamese belief-system. The United States saw the two conflicts as distinct, the Vietnamese saw them as part of a single struggle. One of the seminal Vietnamese liberation manuals, the *Truong Chinh* (roughly translated: *The Resistance Will Win*), which had first appeared in the mid-1940s, argued for a Taoist yin-yang approach, one which viewed two forces of complementary and contrasting principles as a unitary whole, each making up what the other lacked. The governing principle was to spin out the war, sometimes by emphasizing the conventional, sometimes the guerrilla (Johnson, 1998, p. 92). One may, like Colin Gray, question whether the Vietnamese themselves were always in tune with their own Tao. As Gray comments, Giap's conventional offensives, especially the disastrous Easter offensive of 1972 which the Americans broke with massive airpower (including the B52 used for the first time against an army in the field), revealed an impatience or wish to strike out which played into American hands (Gray, 1991). And one may, like Douglas Pike, argue that at times the Vietnamese seemed to be under the spell of Chinese or Maoist thinking well into the war, often to their own detriment (Pike, 1986, p. 185). But the moral of the story is that their strategic thinking was more in tune with their own tradition, their culture and their implicit religious beliefs.

As Montesquieu understood, there is a major difference between winning a battle and winning a war. Culture matters because it influences the way countries think about war. Clausewitz betrays his European credentials when he writes, 'apart from the short intervals in every campaign during which both sides are on the defensive, every attack which does not lead to peace must necessarily end up as a defence' (Gray, 1991, pp. 92–9). For Americans, winning is often everything. But a counter-insurgency war is more akin to a tough political negotiation than a conventional war. 'Limited wars are intended not to be won, but not to be defeated. The essential is still to be there when the fighting ends.' So wrote the notable French strategist André Beaufre (Coker, 1989, p. 96). The scepticism shown by Beaufre, observes Charles Ackley, clashes, of course, with American ethical traditions which tend to forbid the use of force except for moral or ideological ends. And if we add 'humanitarian' to the list (for Ackley was writing in the 1970s), the logic is even more compelling. After all, how can one settle for anything less than unconditional success? The American people prefer their soldiers to be moral crusaders, not risk managers seeking to contain political damage at an acceptable level. They should never be asked, wrote one political analyst, to provide 'the kind of mercenary professional soldiers' that limited wars require. They should not be asked to engage in long, extended, inconclusive campaigns often marked by inconclusive results (Coker, 1989, p. 47).

This is precisely the challenge the US now faces. In part, this is the consequence of its own military success. Given its overwhelming military superiority it can expect to be engaged asymmetrically not only by non-state actors but also by other states. To quote a contemporary Chinese general: 'War has rules but these rules are set by the West ... if you use these rules the weak countries have no choice. We are a weak country so do we need to fight according to your rules?' (Schwartau, 2000). Expect what others call an 'adaptive response' (a telling Darwinian term) by enemies who understand that the United States continues to attach so much importance to bringing the enemy to battle. In tomorrow's world there are likely to be few battles, decisive or otherwise.

14

WAR AND ETHICS

WHY WE SHOULD RESPECT OUR ENEMIES EVEN IF THEY DON'T RESPECT US (IMMANUEL KANT 1724–1804)

No state at war with another shall permit such acts of hostility as would make mutual confidence impossible during a future time of peace.

(*Perpetual Peace*, 96)

In the introduction to *The Critique of Pure Reason*, Kant complains that he lacks the gift of lucid expression and ventures to hope that others will explain his intentions. As well he might—Kant is a difficult writer. His prose is often opaque. He ushered in a new era: a time when philosophy was claimed by the university and became increasingly inaccessible to the common reader. But his pamphlet *Perpetual Peace* is an easy enough read and it has never been out of print since it was first published.

Kant was also unusual in being a philosophy professor at one of the less prestigious German universities—Königsberg. Citizens of the town used to set their watches by his walks every afternoon—he only failed them twice. The first occasion was on the publication of Rousseau's *Emile* which left him awestruck. The second was the day he heard of the fall of the Bastille (he immediately spoke of it as 'historical sign', pointing to a 'greater moral tendency of mankind') (Habermas, 2006, p. 5). On both occasions he was to be disappointed: *Emile* is not a good book, and the revolution ushered in the Terror. Kant was not politically savvy—he was very much the donnish professor.

But he was also insightful. The Kantian injunction cited above is to do nothing in war that makes peace impossible. It is really at one with his most famous formulation, the Second Categorical Imperative: we are all rational beings and therefore should be treated as ends in ourselves, not merely as means or building blocks to the ends of others. If peace is the only reason for going to war, then we must wage it in a way that does nothing to make it unattainable—by treating our enemies, for example, as a means to a greater end. Kant's views are embodied in the Declaration of the Rights of Man that grounded right behaviour in reason and social contract theory, though we find similar sentiments in Cicero's *De Officiis*.

In Cicero's day, humanity was the prerogative of the aristocracy—when mercy was shown at all it had to be earned, usually in combat. It was rarely shown to commoners (who did not extend it to aristocrats in turn). Mercy was a gift that might be expected but not demanded. It might have a political pay-off but it was largely part of one's existential identify—it often marked a disdain for the world of instrumental ends.

Cicero could have left the argument there—he could have dealt himself out but instead he dealt himself in. In *De Officiis* he leaves the reader in no doubt about his message. 'Let us remember that justice must be maintained even towards the lowliest' (Cicero, 1991, p. 39). He didn't say that cruelty to one's own kind is wrong; he counsels us to avoid being cruel even to the lowliest of our enemies. He accepts the common humanity of both the well-born and the low-born, which was more than they tended to grant each other. He accepted that in war both find themselves in the same community of fate. He was intelligent enough to recognize that restraint from cruelty need not be the product of fellow feeling; it is a demand of war. In warfare men do what they can; in war they do what they must. What is important about Cicero's message is that it is the product of a psychologically more sophisticated sensibility: the recognition that cruelty is counterproductive.

In the essays that constitute his last book, *On Duties*, Cicero sought to apply the tools of Greek philosophy to encourage Romans to live more rational lives. His counsel against cruelty is grounded on the understanding that we have escaped the state of nature into a state of reason. It is our ability to perceive the consequences of our actions that sets us apart from more primitive people. Cruelty always put one at risk of regressing into warfare: as Thucydides had warned, it can deprive people of the ability to satisfy their needs and reduce them to the level of their circumstances. When a soldier is stripped of all his socially acquired virtues and left in a moral vacuum he is in danger of returning to the primal state.

Cicero believed that in earlier times the Romans had practised by instinct what the Greeks had preached but not always practised—like many of his philosophical observations he derived them from earlier Greek authors. He was appalled, for example, that the Athenians should have insisted on cutting off the thumbs of the Aeginetan rowers to prevent them from rowing their triremes. They claimed it was a precautionary measure, 'but nothing cruel is in fact beneficial; for cruelty is extremely hostile to the nature of man'. Cruelty towards our enemies tears away the common fellowship of the human race that the gods themselves established (*On Duties*, 3.28). Respect for the enemy therefore is one of the 'laws' of war. Cruelty, in that sense, is impious and irreverent. It is unnatural (this is what Cicero means by the term) in so far as what makes us human is our 'humanity' (as culture)—our ability to fight wars within rules we ourselves have drawn up. Success in war can only be achieved by acting in conformity with those laws.

His reason for concluding this carries with it a real insight. 'There is no military power so great that it can last for long under the weight of fear' (*On Duties*, 2.26). For fear can beget fearfulness: to inspire fear and appear fearful at the same time is usually ruinous; it is likely to provoke a defeated people to revolt. Even when plundering cities, Cicero advises, it is important that commanders ensure that cruelty is kept within bounds. Perhaps he had in mind the murder of Archimedes by a drunken Roman soldier after Syracuse had fallen (it was Cicero who discovered the great scientist's forgotten tomb on a visit to the city). In fact Cicero is one of the first philosophers to talk of according the enemy rights as part of duties *towards oneself*. Cruelty is a betrayal of that trust.

In short, Kant's injunction is not new. It inheres in the practice of war itself. It is merely expressed in a language with which we are more familiar: that of rights and duties. We situate these rights in conventions, or laws of war. But a 'convention', as the word suggests, is the institutionalization of a common practice, and the practice is independent of its judicial formulation (i.e. enforcement in a court of law). This is clear from Shakespeare's *Henry V* when on the battlefield of Agincourt Fluellen is angered by the massacre of young boys in the baggage train ('this is against all the conventions and laws of war'). So indeed it was. Llewellyn did not see fit to ground this in the idea that the boys have 'rights' which had been violated, or in the hope that the offending force would be brought before a court of law for war crimes.

Henry V first appeared on the London stage in the 1590s, but every generation would have understood—despite the bogus Welsh accent—Fluellen's outrage on hearing of the massacre of the unarmed camp followers. 'Kill the poys and the luggage! 'tis expressly against the laws of arms; 'tis as arrant a piece of knavery, mark you now, as can be offered; in your conscience now, is it not?' (Henry V iv.7, 1–4). Henry reciprocates by carrying out an atrocity of his own: he slaughters the French prisoners of war, but it is a rare departure for him. William Hazlitt thought Shakespeare's king 'an amiable monster' (Bloom, 1999). And so he is. He is icy cold, a man clearly lacking in human warmth. He is a master of words, and a master politician who can bond with his men as he does the night before the battle when he offers them a touch of magic, 'a little bit of Harry in the night'. Part of his 'amiability' is his respect for conventions and practices which (in Keats' words) he does not 'feel in his pulses'. What makes him a monster is that he is willing to waste so many lives to gratify his own ambition within the rules. There is no chivalry in warfare, but there is of course in war which Rousseau, Kant's contemporary, thought it 'barbarous' of his fellow philosophers to have invented.

Let us remind ourselves that Shakespeare's world is not one of rights, and still less is it of legal proscriptions. It is a world in which the common language is that of duty, not in the sense that someone has a right which we have a duty to acknowledge (which is again modern thinking) but in the much stronger sense that no one can have a duty to anyone who cannot owe them a duty in return. It is the language of 'do as one wants to be done by'. We consider we have duties to treat prisoners of war well because if we do not our own may be ill-treated by our enemies. It is that understanding that enables us to escape the state of warfare into the state of war. As a modern thinker, Kant preferred the word 'responsibility': we are responsible for the soldiers we capture, or the women and children who fall into our hands. And that responsibility inheres in the dialectic between war and peace. What is important is not to stop, but to stop short: to stop limited war from becoming unlimited. We owe that responsibility to our ancestors too, for taking us out of the night and giving us our humanity. As usual Mary Midgley puts it very well. What is important is not a string of individual duties to others—Greeks to the Persians, Christians to Muslims or French to Germans. It is the idea that the largest obligation of all is that which we owe to those who gave us our humanity by taking us out of the night. We are part of a great historical stream of effort in which we live and to which we owe loyalty. To return to a state of barbarism would be to dishonour them (Midgley, p. 263).

Since Kant's day that responsibility has extended even further; we now acknowledge not only a debt to the dead, but those who will come after us. We owe future generations a better life, as well as a habitat. The natural world is not ours to trash; it is held in trust during our lifetime. A nuclear war in foreclosing the future would constitute a moral dereliction of duty. The most important injunction of all is our responsibility to ensure that war does not become warfare. Unfortunately, we are always having to re-learn that lesson.

Kant's injunction can be taken independently of his later hopes in *Perpetual Peace* (one of the last works of the waning Enlightenment) (Gay, 1973, p. 405). It was a measure of his confidence in the power of philosophy to instruct us what is in our real interests that he suggested peace would only be attained on a permanent basis if politicians listened to the philosophers—not because they theorize peace, but because they theorize war. In a nod to Hobbes, he concedes that we are violent by nature. Peace has to be 'invented' and it can only be forged once practical men have become convinced that it is not really rational at all. Until that time Reason dictates that we wage war in such a way that we ensure that peace remains within our grasp at all times. The enemy should not feel so embittered as to feel too dishonoured to contemplate it. We should never release passions and hatreds that cannot be contained. In *Perpetual Peace* he sounds an ironic note: of course, 'a war of extermination will permit perpetual peace as it were metaphorically, in the great cemetery of the human race', which recalls to mind his own story of the Dutch innkeeper who put up a sign outside his establishment: 'To Eternal Peace' accompanying the picture of a graveyard.

If war is to be kept within bounds and fought reasonably for reasonable ends, it must be fought by rules which we can reason out, in part, from reading history. In the *Critique of Pure Reason* Kant explained the importance of intelligence—reason approaches nature to learn from it. We do so, not by adopting the passive attitude of a pupil, but by adopting that of a judge who compels a witness to answer questions he himself had formulated (Gay, 1973, p. 8). In this case the question we must ask is this: how best can we obtain a lasting peace?

Kant's answer was in keeping with that of a cosmopolitan European. There is a nice story in Peter Gay's history of the Enlightenment which illustrates how he carried his belief in civility into his life and almost beyond. The week before his death he received a visit from a physician. He rose from his bed to thank him for taking the time to visit him. The doctor tried to persuade his patient to sit down, but Kant would not do so until the doctor had been seated. And then, with some difficulty, he added, 'the feeling of humanity has not yet left me'. The physician, we are told, was almost moved to tears (Gay, 1973, pp. 43–4). But Kant's courtesy was more than an empty formality. It was evidence that in his time civility had become the supreme expression of humanity. So it was natural that he should consider that civility was central to war too: not in terms of chivalry, or the warrior's honour (the code of a Freemasonry), or even in the form of customary conventions that had been a feature of war for centuries. Kant saw civility not as part of the cultural grammar of war but as part of its nature. Its timeless codes and conventions had allowed societies over time to *reason out* what it was prudent to do.

Kant ground his injunction on experience. For we have no way of inferring causal relationships outside experience. We cannot infer from a causal order of nature to a God who is the author of nature. There may well be an intelligent designer at work in the world, but if there is we cannot prove it. We cannot infer from the injunctions of God any moral obligations to behave well. We derive those from the experience of dealing with each other. But Kant then invokes a metaphysical concept: a Categorical Imperative at which point he asks too much of us, and at the same time too little.

He asks too much of us in two respects. The first is the belief in Reason. Reason for Kant is what it was for Plato—they are the two thinkers who saw it as the necessary context of Man's deepest aspirations and ambitions, though Kant also saw it as a mark of our common humanity (a nobler concept than Plato's). This fused at a critical moment with the French Revolution, which he believed had opened a supreme historical window of opportunity for humanity to realize its own freedom in concrete political action—such as the Declaration of the Rights of Man (1789).

Of course today we have far less confidence in reason. We do not spell it with the upper case. And our ability to act unreasonably out of purely rational ends is unlimited, as the revolutionary Terror in France later showed. Ethical rules are a manifestation of the *Zeitgeist*. And the spirit of the times can be murderous, as the poet Yeats recognized in his poem 'The Second Coming' . Its most famous line is 'the centre cannot hold'. But there is another which is even more telling: 'Mere anarchy is loosed upon the world.' What he meant was not disorder or anarchy as such; he meant licensed killing. Twentieth-century states licensed their soldiers to kill in the name of abstract principles, those great 'alibis of aggression', Gay calls them, which allowed them to kill with a good conscience, and to kill on a large scale. One of the books whose insights I find especially invaluable is *The Cultivation of Hatred*, one of the volumes which comprise Peter Gay's monumental study of the bourgeois experience in nineteenth-century Europe. The Victorians engaged in continuous debates about the moral nature of aggression. These were particularly intense when nation clashed with nation, or class with class. The modern age was always trying to master nature, geography or the 'other', and ultimately, of course, 'self'. And it produced alibis of aggression which helped to identify the outsider who was to be bullied, ridiculed or exterminated at will. All 'cultivated' hatred in both senses of the term—they at once fostered and restrained it while providing excuses for natural aggression (Gay, 1993). They also gave hatred a spiritual sanction. Historians have encouraged us to see all the great belief systems of the twentieth century as political religions. De Tocqueville correctly saw the French Revolution as a manifestation of a pernicious 'single religious impulse', a form of religious revivalism. Killing, if sanctioned by God, does not require rules; it is not hedged in by ethical codes, and the same is true when it is sanctioned by History (in the upper case).

In his book on the war in the Caucasus, Tolstoy had shown how quickly civilized men can revert to their natural state, how war can revert very quickly to warfare or indiscriminate violence. In 1942 Ernst Junger in his *Caucasus Notebook* invoked Tolstoy by name, though he attributed the barbarism he witnessed at the front to the new Dark Age in which he lived. 'Things like that belong to the style of the times'(James, 2007, p. 338). *Zeitstil* is the word in German. The point is that barbarism inheres not just in our natures, but in the tendency of war to revert to its origins, especially when discipline breaks down. The state of nature from which we have fled is one to which we can return quickly enough. 'War' is the distance we place not between ourselves and our nature, but between ourselves and the state of nature.

The soldier must feed on war from a distance and the discipline of war (the warrior's honour) is precisely the distance he must maintain.

Unfortunately, the Germans, who were usually scrupulous in adhering to the Geneva Conventions in the west, refused to acknowledge they had any responsibilities in the east where they engaged in a war of extermination against an allegedly barbaric people. And the mentality—the spirit of the time, the *Zeitstil*—was not just a reflection of Nazi indoctrination. It was also to be found in the upper reaches of the German army which prided itself on its ability to retain its honour by wearing a uniform unsullied by national socialism. In the winter of 1941, as the German offensive stalled in front of Moscow, it was decided to let Russian POWs freeze to death by taking away their winter clothing including their overcoats and felt boots. The decision to give them to German soldiers was in defiance of German military law, not to mention the Geneva Conventions. Admiral Canaris, the Head of German Military Intelligence, added in a memorandum on the legality of the war that this was not just a rejection of the Hague and Geneva Conventions, it was a rejection of the entire core of customary law that had defined European behaviour in war for the past two hundred years, including the belief that soldiers who have surrendered have a normative right to life (Kassimeris, 2004, p. 86).

It was, as it happened, a suicidal policy for the Germans to follow and the reason was very pragmatic; there was no need to invoke Categorical Imperatives at all. Some practices (like the Kantian injunction to do nothing that makes peace impossible) are best suited to sustaining war itself as an instrument of politics. Understanding war as a means to peace is the best way of fighting it, which is why the Nazi way of war was ultimately so self-defeating. Two million Soviet POWs had starved to death by 1942 (Harman, 2008, p. 42). Later Russian prisoners were fed and sent to work as slave labour. But the desire to kill and the desire to exploit are irreconcilable when pursued at the same time. Killing through starvation and then working the workers to death (extermination through labour) were irreconcilable ends. One evil negated the other. Killing POWs deterred other Russians—civilians behind the lines—from working with the Nazis against a common enemy: Stalin's regime. The logic of extermination and exploitation, in the end, were mutually exclusive. Hitler's failure was foreordained; it was not historical (all things being equal; after all, he might have succeeded). In the end, it was conceptual (or philosophical); he was bound to fail once he ceased to use war as an instrument of politics (Snyder, 2008, p. 10).

By mistreating Russian POWs, or working them to death, the Germans ensured that war could not be a good practice, as Alasdair MacIntyre would understand the term. This is how he describes it in his seminal book, *After Virtue*:

> Any coherent and complex form of socially established co-operative human activity from which goods internal to that form of activity are realised in the course of trying to achieve those standards of excellence which are appropriate to and partially definitive of that form of activity with the result that human power to achieve excellence and human conception of the ends and goods involved are systematically extended. (MacIntyre, 2002)

There was no potentiality of Nazi war practice: as the war extended it became even more self-defeating. Its logic was simply illogical.

Kant's second error was to make the Categorical Imperative an absolute value. He drew an unhelpful distinction between the first and a hypothetical imperative. The second encourages you to treat prisoners of war well because of what might happen if you do not. This is the hypothetical imperative of prudence. The Categorical Imperative is limited to no such consideration; it is an absolute duty that we owe each other. When we have discerned a Categorical Imperative we discover a rule which admits no exception. It does, of course, have particular uses. The main one is that of individual responsibility. We are agents, not only actors. We are responsible to our conscience for our actions. The Categorical Imperative absolves us of the need to follow orders. But it does not help much in telling us what we should do; it only tells us what we should not. It is problematic in that it detaches the notion of duty from the notion of ends, purposes and needs. We need a more instrumental understanding of ethics. In the end, not only does Kant demand too much of us, he also demands too little.

We need an ends–means ethics which is precisely what the Geneva Conventions provide. War is not a moral activity at all, in fact; it is *ethical*. And it is ethics which distinguishes war from warfare. To be moral, an action must be disinterested, it must be independent of the old legal question, *cui bono*: who benefits? Even to save a life of a companion by throwing oneself on a grenade is not a moral duty: it is an ethical gift. A soldier cannot be court-martialled for not offering it (MacIntyre, 2002, p. 28). Most soldiers for that reason live in a distinctive *ethical* community. Ethics is inherently interested. The ethics of war inheres in that most challenging of questions: how do you get the enemy to surrender or to admit defeat, or even to swallow its shame? Kant's injunction to do nothing in war that puts peace out of reach is not a moral injunction at all: it is a conditional, ethical response.

Of course, all this is problematic for moral philosophers and pacifists who would like to outlaw war. And it is true that the rules of war make it possible for us. The only effective counter to war would be to make it so violent that it became its own deterrent. Gallie calls this the sub-rational option as opposed to the 'super-rational', as when Christian love meets oppression by non-violent means (Gallie, 1978, p. 119). He draws our attention to a passage in Tolstoy's novel *War and Peace*, where we find Prince Andrei on the evening before the battle of Borodino catching a snippet of a conversation between two German staff officers in Russian service, one of whom happens to be Clausewitz. Both are talking about extending the war. Andrei is already sickened by the butchery which he has witnessed at first hand, and is appalled that the rules of war preach chivalry and flags of truce, but do nothing to stop homes from being plundered, or children killed, or foes treated in the most outrageous fashion. 'To hell with all this magnanimity business in warfare', he thinks. 'It boils down to this. We should have done with humbug and let war be war and not a game.' And there's the rub. The laws of war do indeed make it possible, as Rousseau recognized (Gallie, 1978, p. 117).

But the true warrior (one who adheres to the Homeric tradition) has always liked to distinguish himself from other soldiers precisely because he can be relied upon not to kill unethically i.e. under stress, or out of anger, or out of sheer wilfulness. His killing is underwritten by ruthlessness, but that is not to say that killing is wanton. For one American warrior, David Hackworth, precision and restraint are vital:

> I could not tolerate the abuse of civilians, especially not children and women. It was a very personal thing with me ... it went against everything I had been taught. That made my decision to be a sniper. Killing clean shows respect for the enemy, but to kill civilians or to lose control of yourself and your concepts in life in combat is wrong ... that is respect for your enemy ... that is the concept behind the warrior. Kill cleanly, kill quickly, kill efficiently, without malice or brutality. (Goldstein, 2001, p. 159)

Hence the warrior's honour which, given that there are no judges or law courts in the field, has always been the chief medium through which war has been regulated and decency maintained. There is, however, something problematic in Kant's writing. Before the eighteenth century, philosophers believed that ethics was there for a reason—to help us live a good and happy life. The ethical life is a taught life (which is why we need philosophy). Excellence has to be developed and nurtured. Virtue can be taught and encouraged. Indeed, it requires training. It is there to deter bad behaviour and engender good. But it is not there to *impel* people to behave well.

The problem with Kant and the modern age in general is that he was a great legislator. He shared a belief widely held in the west today that war is actually an immoral activity and that the only way to ensure correct behaviour is to legislate for it through conventions and rules. Modern philosophers encourage us to think of morality as a code involving rights and representation which it is the task of philosophers to define. Ethics has become a duty—part of the professional, not the virtuous life. Aristotle, as I have said, set out to make his students better people. Today we find this notion quaint. Goodness is now patrolled, policed and enforced and badness punished in the law courts. This ceases to make war what it was for the ancients: an ethical activity that nurtured good behaviour and even brought it out. Good behaviour was not an instrumental quality, it was the person in the same way that Nietzsche would later argue that bravery is the manifestation of a warrior's goodness or moral worth. Today good behaviour has been instrumentalized as *appropriate* behaviour. So Kant has a lot to answer for by encouraging us to distrust the warrior—to deny him what Emerson called self-trust; today we try to patrol his actions, if not his thoughts.

Emerson's philosophy of self-reliance was at the very core of his thinking. For it was only through self-trust, he insisted, that the best could be expected from a man—or woman. 'Wealth', one of the great essays in *The Conduct of Life*, expresses in a typically American idiom this essential message: 'As long as your genius buys, the investment is safe, though you spend like a monarch.' New powers, innate in the self, will emerge into the light (Bloom, 2002, p. 337). It is a disturbing doctrine for lawyers and moralisers, writes Harold Bloom, not because it is amoral; it is non-moral. Self-trust is a dangerous doctrine because it asks so much of a soldier; it expects him to do the right thing because of what he expects of himself largely as a result of learning the virtuous life through training. It is part of Emersonian transcendentalism: the virtuous life is no different from how it was in Aristotle's day, though our norms are different: how we live the virtuous life has a history too. Emerson's main complaint about trying to regulate virtue was that to have a creed—a set of iron laws and regulations—would deny the human being self-realization. 'As men's prayers are a disease of the will, so are their creeds a disease of the intellect' (Bloom, 2002, p. 341). We must trust in the warrior ethos: we must allow warriors what Emerson called self-trust, not institutional self-regulation. Was Emerson's a personal faith maintained wishfully against the odds? Or was it something that actually inheres in what is useful?

To invoke the language of our own day (which is much less poetic) let me quote the German social scientist Niklas Luhmann, who defines trust as a 'sense of confidence in one's expectations' and views it as an indispensable mechanism for reducing the complexity of modern life. Of course, he adds, distrust works just as well. Hedging in the soldier with rules and regulations; making him answerable to special criminal courts; legislating for the 'warrior's honour', all stem from our distrust of the warrior—our fear that in a crisis self-expectation will not be enough. But, as he also adds, strategies of distrust also leave little time or energy 'to explore and adapt to the environment in an objective and unprejudiced manner' (Luhmann, 1979, p. 72). And it is precisely adaptation—or information processing—which is now so important in war, in the ever more complex, or liquid environment in which armies now deploy.

And this is particularly regrettable because since 9/11 we have been encouraged to see our enemies in terms that make it possible to ill-treat them. For a typical western stereotyping, see Sam Harris' book *The End of Faith: Religious Terror and the Future of Reason*. There is, we are told, a western way of war practised by civilized democracies and there is also a Muslim way of war, 'standing eye-deep in the red barbarity of the Fourteenth Century—a kill-the-children-first approach to war' (Harris, 2004, p. 20). And we ignore the fundamental difference between their violence and ours at our peril. Such works encourage us to externalize the dynamic at the heart of war, the propensity of war to become warfare. Once you externalize violence onto the 'other', every tool and tactic becomes justified, including torture. Once you externalize your own actions as good, and theirs as evil, you find it easier to humiliate them, which may render it, in turn, more difficult for them to come to terms with defeat.

Kant's key insight, that we should respect our enemies, still holds. For he saw that the moment you externalize violence and project it onto the 'other', you may well fail to acknowledge the impulses within yourself that permit you to carry out indefensible acts. In the end—watching at a distance—you end up dismissing Guantanamo Bay and Abu Ghraib or 'extraordinary rendition' as regrettable but inevitable: 'Stuff happens.' Like Junger, we may even comfort ourselves with the thought that 'things like that belong to the style of the times'.

15

WAR AND HISTORY

WHY WAR IS OFTEN 'ETHICAL' (OR PROGRESSIVE) (HEGEL 1770–1831)

To risk one's life is certainly superior to simply fearing death but it is also purely negative and therefore indeterminate and therefore valueless in itself. Only a positive end and content can give significance to such courage. Robbers and murderers whose end is crime, adventurers whose end is a product of their own opinion etc. also have the courage to risk their lives. The principle of the modern world—thought and the universal—has given a higher form to valour, in that its expression seems to be more mechanical and not so much the deed of a particular person as that of a member of a whole. It likewise appears to be directed, not against individual persons, but against a hostile whole in general, so that personal courage appears impersonal. This is why the principle of thought has invented the gun, and this invention, which did not come about by chance, has turned the purely personal form of valour into a more abstract form.

(*The Philosophy of Right*, 328)

There are problems, of course, with Hegel's understanding that war has an 'ethical' (i.e. progressive) dimension because of our knowledge of what happened in the century following his death. Hegel has often had a bad press for that reason. He was a striking example, writes Paul Johnson, of how in the dawning modern age the penman was forming a devastating alliance with the swordsman—a new breed of politicians and generals was coming into existence who had no objection to attaching intellectual horsepower to their gun carriages. Hegel was the first philosopher, he adds, who threw the whole weight of his academic reputation behind the proposal that war had the unqualified sanction of history and that philosophy could be turned into a pseudoscience (Johnson, 1991, p. 822).

In Hegel's day war required of every citizen-soldier not only personal courage but what Hegel called 'the integration with the universal', in which the individual was lost in a larger crowd (the nation) from which as a person he derived his individuality or self-respect. From this modification of courage by the modern principle of thought, Hegel ingeniously, if somewhat implausibly, deduced the invention of the gun which had turned 'a primal form of valour into a more abstract form' (Franco, 1999. pp. 33–4). Ingenious, yes, implausible of course, but Hegel was not writing as a historian. He was writing as a philosopher (albeit one conscious of inventing the philosophy of history as we know it today). The statement, incredible though it may read on the page, is at one with his philosophical assertion that 'self-consciousness achieves its satisfaction only in another's self-consciousness' (Pick, 1993, p. 235).

War, Hegel goes on to say, is an ethical activity because of its origin. In escaping from warfare, we are able to give shape and meaning to history. History itself owes us nothing. And it is mute: it tells us nothing. It is we who speak through it. There are no stories until we decide what is worth telling. There is no plot until we determine the evidence from which stories can be written. Otherwise, there is simply a mass of entangled facts without sense or sequence.

The three stories we have been telling from the beginning, from the days of Heraclitus, are the three elements of Hegel's own master narratives. Master narratives, of course, fall in and out of fashion. Hegel's has not survived the twentieth century, but complexity, cooperation and meaning are themes that war seems to bring out in the history we forge.

War and Complexity. What I find significant in this passage from *The Philosophy of Right* is the understanding that complex societies have continued to evolve into ever-more complex adaptive systems through war. Tribes become cities which, in turn, are transformed into confederations or multi–cultural empires before the emergence of modern states. War has no absolute value, but it sustains those societies, consolidates them, and allows them to move on. It is this ability to survive, however, that we should see as a *means to an end*, not an end in itself. It just so happens that we have achieved such levels of complexity today that war is no longer a necessary or even useful survival mechanism. To put the matter in Hegelian terms, war may have exhausted its historical possibilities. It may have become *zero-sum* for the first time.

War and Cooperation. If complexity is a product of evolution, we must also recognize that the survival of the fittest applies to groups, more than individuals. Survival is a result of greater collaborative effort, including the greatest effort of all before the onset of market capitalism, war-making. An increased survival rate is as much a side-effect of collaboration as its purpose. The collaborative effort of modern states in the present state system means we can no longer afford war—our survival rates, accordingly, have gone up; fewer people than ever die in war (though the same is not necessarily true of the regions of the world which still witness warfare).

War and Meaning. The point about the myth Hegel spun above—namely that guns had by some mysterious transmutation of history confirmed the arrival of a national spirit (as the next stage of complexity) is that it has a unique human appeal. We only understand the world through narrative structures that, like all such structures, have a beginning, middle and an end. In order to experience the pay-off at the end of the story we need to see it as something someone built into the original intention of events. Whether life has meaning is not the point. Our desire to discover it seems to be encoded in human nature, and is manifest even in science. It is hard if not impossible for even the most reductionist of biologists to write accessibly about evolution without indulging in a degree of anthropomorphic purpose. Take terms such as 'advantage', 'survival of the fittest' and 'adapt'. It may be a mix of metaphor and science but can you do science without being metaphorical? Hegel's metaphors were historical. 'I adhere to the view that the World Spirit has given the age marching orders. These orders are being obeyed' (Johnson, 1991, p. 814). Hegel just happened to place History in God's place as the 'intelligent designer'. It really does not matter whether we think there is a designer or even whether there is a design: most of us seek meaning in our lives; it is what makes us distinctive as a species. Cosmologists like Paul Davies think it is natural (i.e. intrinsic) that we think our Universe does indeed have some immanent purposive principle working in it to produce the order and the activity that we see. Such ideas do not suggest there is a designer but they do challenge the Cartesian dogma that there cannot possibly be any purpose outside human life (Davies, 2006).

As human beings we are stimulated far less by the will to know than by the will to understand, and from this the only sciences we admit to be authentic are those which succeed in establishing explanatory relationships between phenomena: in this case between war and history. We all try to understand the world by telling ourselves stories which bear historical interpretations of the times; they are a creation of our need to understand; they are not a product of objective knowledge. We are myth-making machines: a myth is true if it is effective; if it does not give us insight into the deeper meaning of life it has failed (Marxism was often called 'the God that failed'). Myths matter because when they work they force us to change our minds, they give us new hope and compel us to live more fully. Every time we take a step forward we review our mythology and make it speak to new conditions. But human nature has changed remarkably little in the past few thousand years; many of our myths devised in societies very different from our own still address our most essential fears and desires (and many are still tied to war, literally or metaphorically (Armstrong, 2005, p. 11).

Whatever his legacy, Hegel remains one of the greatest of all philosophers: possibly the greatest of the modern age, and what he has to say (though he is very obscure: his prose is a tangled web which even German readers find difficult to disentangle) we should persevere with nevertheless. If war is 'ethical' in a way warfare is not (and such I believe to be the case) we must strip the word of much of its Hegelian baggage, especially its teleological meaning. To claim that war is ethical is also most certainly not to deny its cost—both for the living and the dead; nor is it to deny its violence and futility. To argue that it is ethical is to claim that it is progressive in a way warfare never can be in terms of the three themes I have identified above.

Complexity: To begin with, Hegel grasped the full extent to which our humanity inheres in war. It begins in the great struggle against our animal condition. Instead of a pack in which an alpha male dominates the group, we are a culturally complex species whose humanity lies in our sociability, which inheres in the valuation we have of each other. We fight to get others to recognize our value. And the warrior was for Hegel one of the most valued of all people because he was willing to risk his life, not for material survival, or food, or women (as in Homer's epic poem), but for honour, prestige and reputation, the immaterial factors that define our humanity and which define our ground of freedom. What Hegel grasped is that freedom usually has to be fought for. In the conscript armies at whose head Napoleon marched across Europe, he saw the willingness of a people to sacrifice themselves to realize their freedom. He saw (to cite Engels) history moving from the 'realm of necessity' into the 'realm of freedom'. In war, a state confronts itself as well as the enemy. In that sense, through war, the citizen-soldier discovers he belongs to a nation, a historical unit which had first emerged in medieval Europe in the hundred-year struggle between England and France.

Rather surprisingly, perhaps, the claim can even be found in Karl Popper's *Open Society and its Enemies* which, in all other respects, is unrelenting in its criticism of Hegel's 'system'. In the book Popper dates the democratic leap in fifth-century Athens to its success in war. 'The political and spiritual revolution which had baulked with the breakdown of Greek tribalism reached its climax in the fifth century with the outbreak of the Peloponnesian war.' Athens had embarked on an epoch-making break in which the closed society became an open one: and the key was commerce. At this stage in history, tribal exclusivity and self-suffering were superseded by something else: an empire (Watkins, 1999, pp. 101–3). The navy was the key institution in that development, as Thucydides' 'Archaeology' shows, the short introduction to his *History* in which he gives us a rundown of the development of Greece, seen entirely in terms of the development of naval power. And the *thetes* (the men who rowed the triremes) were at the heart of Athenian democracy (a fact which, as we have seen, Plato so much deplored). This is all strong stuff and, as Watkins claims, there is more than a whiff of Hegelianism in Popper's account. The transition to an open society is clearly for Popper a Hegelian turning point from which there is no going back. And such turning points, far from representing what the philosopher Bradley called 'a ballet dance of bloodless categories', are usually very bloody indeed.

In short, Hegel glimpsed that in human history the propensity for ever-greater complexity inheres in human cooperation. What is Hegel's definition of freedom but interaction with others? For Hegel the nation-state just happened to be the most profound ethical form which in his day cooperation had taken. Freedom, after all, could not be realized unless individuals found freedom in the sense of the whole, in the community in which they lived—the freedom of one was the freedom of all. A socially viable (Hegel's preferred word was 'ethical') state, he wrote, could draw upon a powerful constituting force: 'the consciousness that my interest, both substantive and particular, is contained and preserved in another's interests in the end'. Such a society would be able to realize the common good. In wartime, courage was not a personal but a social attribute because everyone lived in the same community of fate.

What Hegel was claiming was that only a state in which the citizen acknowledges obligations and duties could survive in the modern era. Citizenship must be earned and the responsibilities of each citizen acknowledged. Where rights were claimed in isolation, they would lead to competing claims which would give rise to class conflict or social alienation. Such a state, far from being able to count on the loyalty of its citizens, would become something against which its citizens would make a claim. In that respect, Hegel thought of 'rights' as similar in nature to 'cheques'. The rights a citizen enjoyed had value only if there was money in the bank. This presupposed a society in which everyone was collectively willing to pay the price of the claims made upon them.

We all have capabilities, virtues and talents which require cooperation for their fulfilment, and the nation-state which emerged in late eighteenth-century Europe just happened to be the greatest political unit ever devised in which to channel cooperation and exploit human talent for ends that were deemed consistent with the collective good. People fight for their own private passions and national interests, yet they contribute to the realization of something unintended by anyone. There are several versions of this. Hegel's understanding was based on a philosophy of history which re-valued war in terms of the 'ethical health' of the nation: battle was seen as a sacrament between oneself and the community. A willingness to go to the front may appear senseless to those who acknowledge only the suffering of war, but without such a willingness there can be no love of country, and without love there can be no meaning in a common identity.

There are always other stories, of course, to tell. 'Be my brother or I'll kill you', Chamfort famously satirized the call for fraternity on the lips of the French Revolutionary leaders. And he paid for his witticism, only cheating the guillotine to which he was condemned by taking his own life. The ambitions of the state when harnessed to the revolutionary creed 'liberty, equality and fraternity' knew no bounds. The revolutionaries also called for sacrifices on a scale never asked of a society before. Even so, I think there is a lot to be said for Hegel's position. It would take a pacifist (and a pretty unthinking one) to deny that some wars have not been redeemed by their ethical content. The UK in 1940 is, perhaps, one of the best examples. Another is Athens in the Greco-Persian Wars which confirmed its citizens in their belief that they were a remarkable people who had pulled off a great historical feat, and it was no surprise that from the wars they dated the great historical leap forward that we call the Athenian Enlightenment.

We can always question whether war usually serves an 'ethical' function. We can question whether the survival of the political community—a city-state such as Athens or a nation-state such as UK—was worth it given the loss of life: what was the price of the citizens' sacrament with the nation? The Athenians abandoned their city to be burned down by the Persians; the Russians burned down theirs themselves. Is politics worth so many lives? And what value do we attach to a community's ethical health as opposed to its material existence and the lives and welfare of its citizens? Even Hegel invites us to imagine what would have happened if the Greeks had lost the battle of Salamis. Would it have been so bad for the Athenians? Or for us? Shouldn't our principal responsibility be to ask the unthinkable: can we abolish war?

All of these questions Hegel did not ask for one central reason. One of his most famous sayings is that Owl of Minerva takes flight at dusk; it is a poetic way of explaining that we can only understand our own age when it is coming to an end. Up to and beyond the stage of history through which he was living, war had frequently fulfilled a redemptive function: it had helped forge political society, and a political consciousness. He never suggested these features were permanent; he saw them as historical. We can try to make the future on other terms. The future is not closed, it is open. Our own future, contends René Girard, is going to be more of the same, including complexity, but there will be dialectical turns so astonishing that they are likely to take everyone by surprise (Girard, 2007, p. 261).

We should also recognize that if war like poverty is problematic, yet poverty is an unredeemed evil, whereas war is sometimes a necessary one. If we wish to devalue war—to divest it of its ethical content—we would have to eliminate aspirations to transcendence, claims the Canadian political scientist, Charles Taylor. 'Are we ready for a life of renunciation (are we ready to renounce war as a medium of transcendence)?' (Taylor, 2007, p. 51) 'Or are we willing to go to war for other purposes such as 'exclusive humanism?' (Taylor, 2007, p. 859). The question we must ask is whether at this stage of history war has run its course, or exhausted its historical possibilities? Has it lost its world-historical importance? Has it degenerated into the remnants of war? I shall look at this question when discussing the last of my writers, Werner Heisenberg. For now, let me add that the question may demand to be asked, but it does not demand a single answer.

Cooperation. In terms of Hegel's second claim, let me refer again to the quote at the beginning of the chapter. For the point Hegel was making is that war involves what Jacques Monod called 'the un-wearying, heroic effort of mankind desperately to deny its own contingency' (Midgley, 1985, p. 89). It confronts the individual with death. The fact that we are the only species who know that we are in the world, is the problem. We are the object of our own consciousness. We are at one remove from ourselves. We know we will die. We also know that death is part of the natural order: all things are mutable; they are mortal. But in anticipating death we are observing it. This consciousness in its distance from its own objective existence transcends the natural order. It transforms the nature of our being in the world. Anxiety de-centres us from our own humanity. It is part of our divided self which we can only heal by cooperating with others (Kolakowski, 1989, p. 116).

In teaching us the contingency of life, war instructs us at the same time about the importance of the 'social', the fact that history does not come to an end when we die—we may even be willing to die to allow it to continue on our terms. The most extreme version of this is to be found in *The Philosophy of Right* in which Hegel argues that war mitigates 'the vanity of temporal goods and concerns', the materialism of modern societies. In an (in)famous passage often cited to accuse the author of being a warmonger, we read: 'Just as the blowing of the winds preserves the sea from the foulness that would be the result of prolonged calm, so also corruption in nations would be a product of prolonged, let alone "perpetual", peace.' This thinking is not unique to Hegel. George W. Bush expressed similar thoughts: 'War is terrible, but it brings out, in some ways it touches, the core of Americans who volunteer to go into combat to protect their souls' (Bell, 2007, pp. 315–16).

Robert Kaplan, who served for a time as an embedded journalist with the Marines in Fallujah, adds, 'peaceful times are superficial times. Without great military struggles, we would not be the nation we once were' (Ibid.).

Americans can go back far into their history to derive similar thoughts. In his essay 'The Moral Equivalent of War', William James writes that the American Civil War was an act of re-consecration. 'Ask all our millions, north and south, whether they would vote now (were such a thing possible) to have our war for the Union expunged from history and the record of a peaceful transition to the present time substituted for that of its marches and battles, and probably hardly a handful of eccentrics would say yes. Those ancestors, those memories and legends, are the most ideal part of what *we now own together*, a sacred spiritual possession worth more than all the blood poured out' (James, 1984). The Civil War has indeed been seen in broad brushstroke terms in that it took further, or completed, the revolution that had been inaugurated in 1776. The historian Charles Beard thought the war important enough to merit the description 'the second American Revolution'. What made it an 'ethical activity' is not that it became a great 'spiritual possession', but that it produced social changes that would not, or might not, have come about in any other way. Kant had a similar view of war, except that for him it told a different story: not of freedom becoming conscious of itself, but of peace becoming possible for the first time. In *The Metaphysical Element of Justice*, he wrote that 'the universal and lasting establishment of peace constitutes not merely a part of the whole final purpose and end of the science of right as viewed within the limits of reason' (Temes, 2003, p. 51). There you have it—you can choose between war as a story of freedom evolving, or the triumph of the science of right. Kant might have seen the Civil War as the moment in which the Americans could finally live at peace with themselves.

Interestingly, Hegel himself never identified any particular war as historically redeeming. And he had no interest in forging 'sacred spiritual possessions'—he was interested in how war in general educates us for freedom. James was writing at the end of the nineteenth century, Hegel at the very beginning. Both writers were writing from very different historical vantage points. Both may have been philosophers, but on this occasion James was seeking to distinguish the Civil War from every other conflict which the United States had fought, or probably would fight in the future. Hegel had no interest in any particular war; the general point he was making is that for much of history war has been the medium through which freedom, through fits and starts, has become conscious of itself.

In other words, Hegel did indeed see war as an educative process (in this, as well as the spirit of sacrifice, lies its ethical content)—it promotes cooperation. And there is much to be said for this view. The philosopher Merleau-Ponty portrayed the occupation of France as an educative experience too, which forced the French people to rise to a collective challenge and surmount it. War is the sort of harsh experience that awakens consciousness to new truths. To be sure, one has to buy into Merleau-Ponty's existentialism, then so popular in western philosophical circles. It requires a historical understanding that we have subsequently lost, and it paints the occupation in heroic terms, though in fairness we should add that he made little mention of the Resistance, and had almost nothing to say about the heroism of its members. His 'educative process' was a fair historical representation of what happened because its message was distinctly un-heroic. 'The world is not what I think it is but what I live through', and what we live through we live through with others (Whitehead, 1988, pp. 40–42). The occupation taught one bitter lesson: if we are not careful our own history will be made for us by others. We inherit our social roles; we don't always choose them.

The French, who had been so socially divided before the war, now found that the grounds of their own historicity had changed in ways they found unappealing. Some found themselves labelled 'Aryans', 'Jews' or 'Frenchmen'—and the latter were further subdivided into 'collaborators' or 'members of the Resistance' or just an undistinguished mass. The social polarization which the war had reinforced highlighted the social differences that had existed before the war, and which were deemed to have undermined the war effort. One could go further and make a claim that Merleau-Ponty did not, that History had changed the terms of the debate. 'If a man is to have a history', Sartre wrote in 1952, 'it is necessary that he change, that the world should change him as it is changed, and that he may be changed in turn as he changes the world.' Movement and change were built into Sartre's image of historically conscious Man. 'It was the war which made the obsolete frames of thought explode', he later wrote. Sartre himself emphasized two major features of that change: one which was personal stemmed from his experience as a Prisoner of War; the other which was intellectual derived from his own personal confrontation with history.

As a Prisoner of War he had discovered that the French people would have to forge a life-world of their own if they were to live together harmoniously in peacetime. Only when he found himself interned with his fellow countrymen did he discover a language in which he could break out of the divisive social categories that had paralyzed the French war effort. In the prison camp, he was able to objectify their common predicament and transcend it, in the process discovering what it meant to be French. 'We were never so free as under the German occupation. We had lost our rights and with it the right to speak ... we were deported en masse as workers, Jews, political prisoners.' It just so happened, Germaine Bree points out, that Sartre himself was none of these. Nor was he silent. He wrote three of his most important works, *Flies*, *No Exit* and *Being and Nothingness*, in those years, and it was during the occupation that he first came to prominence as a writer. But he now acknowledged that the survivors needed to identify with those who had fallen victim to the brutality of others (Bree, 1974, p. 164).

Sartre's idea that man is free and defines himself by what he does was one that was widely shared after the war. His philosophy was an invitation to leave the past behind and look to the future. In Sartre's mind, 'every consciousness is consciousness of something'—to be French was to become European. Michel Tournier, one of the greatest of the country's post-war novelists, discovered this for himself when he visited Germany in 1947. In a telling phrase he wrote in his memoirs that 'we had discovered ourselves at last' (Tournier, 1989, p. 71).

Meaning. Finally, to the third of Hegel's claims: the meaning of collective sacrifice. Hegel was spinning a myth when he claimed that history was the story of freedom becoming conscious of itself. No matter how hard we strive for purely rational thought there has always been—and always will be—a reservoir of mythical images which animate us. The meaning of an event is not revealed through its conditions, but because the event may be referred either to the goal at which the historical course aims or to our human destiny, which is either being actualized in history or which demands such actualization. In reality, we are not owed anything by history. Humanity is not true or untrue to itself.

There is no authentic humanity except in our mythical conception of ourselves. War is rooted in myth, not only in rational thought. Each time I demand freedom I reveal the secret of humanity, since I reveal that humanity ought to have freedom. No reading of history can support this belief. It is anchored entirely in the story we tell ourselves about our own history (Kolakowski, 1989, p. 31).

History becomes a mythical court of appeal which ante-dates all historicity and demands that every event should be understood as being in accord or not with a human destiny. Destiny is a cultural construction. Every society at different times in history has its own understanding of what it is. And what is a destiny but the struggle against the indifference of the world to our existence, against that contingency of life that Monod elaborates (Kolakowski, 1989, p. 31).

Myths offer us a social imagery that makes the exercise of power and force comprehensible. It provides a solid sense of meaning which binds people together. Societies that win their wars are those who can make most sense of them. One must be able to situate oneself in history. War can, for example, reinforce a society's belief in itself (and the superiority of its way of life). It can help it rise above its immediate challenges and help it surmount its temporary defeats. Hegel made this view fashionable. He himself happened to be living in the town of Jena when Napoleon passed through in 1806 before defeating the Prussian army in one of his most famous victories the following day. He later wrote in a letter to a friend that he had seen 'the World Spirit riding through the town to a parade'.

Hegel has his critics, but what many tend to forget these days, of course, is that we do not interrogate history with the same enthusiasm we once did; for us everything is historical, but nothing is historic. When criticizing Hegel for excessive historical consciousness we must not forget that philosophy for a time became permeated with historical consciousness. Nietzsche spoke for the whole century when he wrote that what separated his generation from Kant's was that 'in intellectual matters ... we are historical through and through' (Skorupski, 2006, p. 65). When reading Hegel we have to think ourselves back to a time when people accepted that the course of their lives would be determined by history, by public rather than private crises. 'Individual existences will have no interest to me—particularly my own', remarked Victor Serge in his memoirs (Sontag, 2007, p. 77).

We now know that there are no great emancipatory forces (including History) that are working towards some finite end. We know we are not caught up in such forces; we know we cannot excuse the 'inhuman' or unjust—the collateral damage of 'progress'—by incorporating ourselves in such forces; we have lost those alibis of aggression that allowed us to act in good faith. We are burdened with a bad conscience. Today, we no longer tell ourselves Hegelian stories, or glimpse World Spirits, let alone follow world historical figures to our death. The stories we tell ourselves are more modest. But we still continue to tell tales. We tend to see history as a movement not towards progress, but growing complexity. And the more complex the world becomes, the less war has an instrumental purpose. It has become ruinously expensive, systemically disruptive, and at times even suicidal. It unmakes complexity, it doesn't produce it.

All we have left is ethics to tell us what is the right or wrong course of action to pursue. But in returning to ethical first principles we don't have to renounce war or deny that some wars can be 'ethical', although they may not necessarily be redemptive. By ethical I mean that war can advance principles; it can be part of a 'civilizing process' in so far that it can add, not subtract from the complexity of life; it can advance cooperation and still offer a source of meaning. None of these things are true of warfare, which is complicated, not complex; which restricts cooperation to the primary group, and subtracts enemies from humanity in the round; and which is pretty meaningless for all involved. And there is one other reason why we might still find war 'ethical': we still live in a world in which warfare is endemic.

We continue to deny this. We are still listing in the Enlightenment's wake (John Gray). We are still heirs of that progressiv(ism) that told us that war is rapidly exhausting its possibilities. We still think that the marketplace is the medium through which history is now made with its multiple supporting projects like democratic participation, economic interdependence and constructive conflict resolution, a cumulative process which it would be difficult to reverse. Except that it really wouldn't.

Look around you: the world is a fragile place, as is so much of the very real progress that has been made. It is also a fractious place, riven with ethnic tensions and hatreds, tribal animosities and nationalist ambitions. War between the Great Powers may be on the wane (for the moment) but warfare is very much alive—its victims appear on our television screens every other night. As long as we accept that there is no teleological process by which war is programmed to negate itself;

as long as we accept that peace is not a destiny, only an option; as long as we acknowledge the existence of a de-civilizing process at work too, we may still employ war to emancipate ourselves or others. The greater challenge we face is rather different. For most of history we have fought against injustice; in a new century we are likely to be summoned to fight for justice, to institute a just politics, one that finally *does justice* to thought.

16

WAR AND TECHNOLOGY
WHY WEAPONS HAVE A SOCIAL HISTORY
(MARX 1818–83)

Is Achilles possible when powder and shot have been invented? Is *The Iliad* possible at all when the printing press and even printing machines exist? Is it not inevitable that with the emergence of the press, the singing and the talking and the muse cease, that is the conditions for epic poetry disappear?

(The German Ideology, p. 150)

Many of Marx's specific claims have been refuted, but his body of work as a whole has left an indelible mark on modern thought. He is one of the great historical sociologists who tell us that our systems of thought and world views are products of historical forces, and that history itself develops through successive contradictions between historical forces and relations of production. Social forces in history have always been there, we have simply not always recognized them. Sometimes it takes a particular way of thinking to change our attitude. In 1858 Florence Nightingale produced the first coloured pie chart showing the proportion of soldiers killed by disease in the Crimean War, as opposed to those killed in battle. It shocked her fellow Victorians into recognizing a problem as old as war itself: far more soldiers in history have fallen victim to disease than the bullet.

Philosophers encourage us to look at the facts anew, to see the facts differently and thus apprehend reality for the first time. Philosophy makes visible what has always been out there, but what we have not seen before. In forcing us to reconceptualize our world it does, of course, change it because in the process it changes us. Marx taught that war was not a matter of personalities (Achilles, too, should be seen in context). Nor was he the first writer to expose the tendencies that have been observed in the human drama. Instead, he discussed the non-human background forces that are crucial to the shaping of human life. The problem with Marx was that he was a better political economist than he was a philosopher. He imported into philosophy quite unsubstantiated and unsustainable *moral* factors which told his readers what to aim for. To this extent he is in part responsible for some of the ruinous political projects launched in his name that were to lead nowhere at great human cost.

But let us return to the issue in question. By connecting technological conditions to symbolic life and psychological habit, as Marx did in *The German Ideology*, from which I have quoted, he was not only putting forward a taxonomy of culture (Postman, 1993, p. 22). We still divide history into ages defined by the use of weapons: we still divide history into the ages of 'bronze', 'iron' and 'steel', and talk of the 'industrial revolution' or the 'railway age'. But Marx's own taxonomy allows us to capture some critical cultural differences, for example between a tool-bearing culture like that of bronze age Greece and a technological one like our own.

In his introduction to the *Grundrisse* (1857) Marx asked much the same question he had in *The German Ideology*. 'Is the view of nature and of social relations on which the Greek imagination and hence Greek mythology is based possible when [there are] self-acting spindles and railways and locomotives and electrical telegraphs? What chance has Vulcan against Roberts & Co., Jupiter against the lightening rod and Hermes against the *Crédit Mobilier?*' (Baldick, 1990, p. 123). Marx's point was that the Greeks had money but they didn't have capitalism, and capitalism requires constant innovation as a precondition for survival. Accordingly, as he famously wrote, 'all that is solid melts into air, all that is *holy* is profaned'—and what was holy about war was its representation in the epic accounts of great deeds of heroism and sacrifice that bound heroes like Achilles to the community of fellow warriors. In a capitalist world the demand for novelty means that new fashions and ideas become old-fashioned before they can ossify into custom. In the ancient world, by comparison, nothing much changed in terms of production and technique or even technology, and even a poetic genre such as the epic could remain fundamentally unchanged for a thousand years.

WAR AND TECHNOLOGY

As we have seen it was still possible for the old myths to inspire young British officers at Gallipoli to offer up their lives on killing fields that bore the names of the battle sites of the Trojan War. Even today Homer's tale is popular (the young Tom Swofford took it with him to the Gulf) because it tells soldiers that the works and days of men are worth recording and that no catastrophe—not even the burning of Troy—is final. Marx was right to question, however, whether the great myths that give us the illusion of mastering our lives could survive the advent of real mastery over them through industrialization. Later, he acknowledged that the modern age might produce its own mythology. Technology might move into the forefront of the imagination; the new social forces of production might generate myths of their own to fill the vacuum left by the destruction of the old beliefs. In correspondence with a friend he suggested that the modern age might even multiply them (Baldick, 1990, p. 123). But he also feared that the new myths would be life-denying, not life-affirming. Technological progress, he warned, might endow material forces with intellectual life and transform human life into the material force out of which history could be made (Baldick, 1990, p. 140).

Marx was touching upon the relationship between our humanity and the tools (including weapons) we invent. He was wrong about Achilles and the printing press. What inheres in the nature of war is technology and technique; this is what makes war different from warfare where weapons (spears, clubs or today's machetes and kalashnikovs) are crude; they do not extend the range of human ambition, only the scale of destruction. In war we are the weapons and machines we construct and deploy in battle; the relationship is a symbiotic one.

The tools that Achilles used (such as the famous shield forged by the god Hephaestus which Alexander was shown on his way into Asia) centred humanity in its own story and forged a unique frame of mind, what Bernard Knox calls 'the heroic temper'. The heroic temper later posed a problem for a democracy. The key challenge for Plato, as we have seen, was how to tame Achilles and domesticate the warrior spirit. But the point was that technical developments in war did not threaten the humanist tradition.

Take another great epic poem, the *Song of Roland*, one of the many *romances de geste* which like *The Iliad* were intended to be declaimed, or rather chanted from castle to castle. There is nothing more heroic even in *The Iliad* than Roland's refusal to summon help and blow the famous horn and thus save his life and that of his friends. Achilles and Roland worshipped different gods and served different world views. But the great tradition survived, in part because the tools of war did not change: the spears and shields and swords that Roland used would have been familiar to Homer's heroes. Even a tool, of course, can threaten to undermine a traditional belief or world view. The example most often cited takes us back to the *Song of Roland*—it is the invention of the stirrup. The stirrup made it possible to fight on horseback and thus enhanced the power of the knights and to some extent changed the nature of feudal society. But, in the end, it did not change society that much. If anything, it reinforced the Great Tradition of the aristocratic warrior. It helped disguise the sheer brutality of war by making possible in peacetime ritualized jousts and tournaments, the crucial training ground for the knights' preparation for war. By the eleventh century when *The Song of Roland* was composed, the image of the mounted knight had become a universal stock trope. With gunpowder and the printing press everything changed. This was Marx's point. Weapons gave way to technology. History ushered in the *technological* age.

The character of war changed once again. It prompted many writers before Marx to ask the same question: could the old myths long survive? Take the poet Byron in his uncompleted poem *Don Juan*. 'But now instead of slaying Priam's son/we only see and talk of escalade/ bombs, drums, guns, bastons, batteries, bayonets, bullets/hard words which stick in the soft Muses' gullets' (Manguel, 2007, p. 143). War was becoming indebted more and more to what Thomas Carlyle called 'the true deity: mechanism'. Was Achilles possible in an age in which in one day alone (the first day of the Somme), 20,000 British soldiers marched to their death? Or when during the American Civil War in one engagement, the siege of Petersburg, an entire unit (the First Maine) lost 630 men out of 900 in the first seven minutes of an attack?

Marx's genius was to recognize that it is in the nature of war *we are what we build*. In *The German Ideology* he tells us that we begin to distinguish ourselves from other animals as soon as we begin to produce the means of our own subsistence. 'As individuals express their life, so they are. What they are, therefore, coincides with their production.' Man is indeed a rational being but his reason is actualized in productive activity.

To be worked to death in the industrial factories of the nineteenth century was, in his eyes, no different from slavery, and if anything the former was worse (there were no social welfare nets, no cradle-to-grave systems there as there were on the southern plantations). But this is where he just happened to be wrong. There is a significant difference which he refused to acknowledge. No Northern wage labourer was especially happy with his lot but his rebellious stirrings were easily contained. Industrial capitalism may well have dehumanized the workforce by turning workers into 'hands' but it also humanized them by turning them into consumers. In the South slaves simply did not accept their condition. Although the occasional rebellion was successfully suppressed, far more insidious in the long term was the day to day resistance which weakened the Southern economy to such an extent that according to some historians America's slaves effectively brought about their own liberation (Ashworth, 2008). Aristotle imagined a spinning-wheel that could operate on its own—one that did not need human labour, but he dismissed the idea almost at once because he could not imagine a world without slavery. We can—it is called progress, and it is real enough.

Marx was on much stronger ground when he saw the machines of his own age as a form of 'dead labour'. Take the machine gun which put to death labour that had been necessary before its invention (it called for no skill on the part of the operator). And the labour that was put to death by it on the other side now numbered in the tens of thousands. Guns, like everything else, writes John Ellis in the gem of a little book, *The Social History of the Machine Gun*, have a social history like the rest of us (Ellis, 1976, p. 9). The history of technology is part and parcel of social history in general, and the last chapter of his book sets out his case particularly vividly. As Ellis writes, the nineteenth-century Europeans thought that the machine gun, precisely because it encapsulated the principle of serialization, was the product of a rational culture—those who did not have it by definition could not build it. The logic of the machine gun was very simple and it was stated pithily by G.E. Moore, the Cambridge philosopher who taught Keynes. *We* are more advanced than they because we can kill them faster than they can kill us (Midgley, 2006, p. 246).

European societies employed the machine gun in the last and most frenetic phase of European imperialism to get non-western societies to 'see reason'—to see the benefit of European rule. They were anxious to persuade native societies to act more 'reasonably' and they were quite willing to punish them if they proved wilful. There is one essential explanation for why the people of Pondoland in Eastern Cape decided not to fight the British, and allowed themselves to be annexed to South Africa in the 1890s without a fight. Cecil Rhodes mowed down a mealy field with machine guns in front of the Paramount Chief and his councillors and explained that they would suffer the same fate if they did not submit. And so they submitted as did many other colonial peoples who, even if they did not suffer directly themselves, saw their neighbours suffer and chose to submit before they experienced the worst (Low, 1973, p. 22). One could take the argument even further: either the world is one in which there are limits to human reason, at which point there are sanctions against indulging in human impulses and ambitions, or it is a place where reason is so untrammelled and unlimited and the strong (or reasonable) are the more civilized that the latter can be confident in the exercise of power. And one is never more powerful than when winning an argument, or depriving the weak (as did Rhodes) of even the satisfaction of being right.

Of course in 1914–18 the British were to suffer the same fate: the majority of casualties on the Somme were accounted for by German machine guns (the cracking of the machine guns reminded the poet Edmund Blunden of the screeching of 'steam being blown off by a hundred engines') (Ellis, 1976, p. 138). It was a telling metaphor for the British army's first introduction to industrialized war. This continued apace after World War One. Weapons designers were engineers or statisticians who concerned themselves not with death but 'lethal area estimates' and 'kill probabilities', as well as 'sensitivity and compatibility studies'—not the data for a dating agency but procedures for making sure that a given bomb could be used in a given airplane (Kassimeris, 2006, p. 29). In C.P. Snow's classic account of intrigues in Whitehall during World War Two, we learn of the bitter arguments over the strategic bombing of Germany between those for whom bombing has become a matter of faith and those who doubt whether any country can be bombed to the peace table. The disputes are not about the ethics of bombing but the statistical probabilities of success: 'In private we made bitter jokes of a losing side. "There are the Fermi–Dirac statistics," we said. "The Einstein–Bose statistics. And the new Cherwell non-quantitative statistics." And we told stories of a man who added up two and two and made four.' (Gratzen, 1989, p. 405)

The archetypal example of emotional distancing is the story of the navigator of the *Enola Gay*, the plane which dropped the first atomic bomb. He claimed to have 'come off the mission, had a bite and a few beers and hit the sack, and had not lost a night's sleep over the bomb in 40 years' (Kassimeris, 2006, p. 23). In *Dr Strangelove*, the ultimate movie version of nuclear war. Kubrick's masterstroke (writes J.G. Ballard) is to tilt the dramatic action of the film so that the audience's sympathies slide across the value scale and eventually lie with the machines of destruction—the B52s with their sleek A-bombs and their brave but baffled crews (Ballard, 1997, pp. 18–19). The question then the film raises is whether by externalizing technology we lose ourselves as the 'subject' of our culture, and therefore the subject of myth. Atomic bombs have a social history too, and so do the robots we are planning to send into battle in the not too distant future. If we are what we build, are we programming ourselves out of war? One day soon will we be asked to see war from the machine's point of view?

'The essence of technology is not technological.' (Heidegger, *The Question Concerning Technology*, 1949)

Marx had been aware of a new challenge that the industrial revolution had raised: the world was beginning to change within an individual lifetime. Thinking about the future—especially whether the nature of war might change—had become a response to a demand of the times: the need to think through individual survival. It was another philosopher a century later in the shadow of the atomic bomb who took Marx's critique much further.

Martin Heidegger (1889–1976) is one of the most difficult of philosophers. His language is tortuously opaque. The obscurity of his thought, his leviathan sentences and atrocious grammar, the very density of his thinking are all a very real problem for his readers. Gunther Grass's pastiche of Heidegger's metaphysics, *The Dog Years*, is a telling indictment of the damage that obscurity of language did to German thinking in the course of the twentieth century. Even more daunting is what Heidegger did not say: his notorious silences (his great silence after the Holocaust and the refusal to discuss or even face up to his own flirtation with Nazism). More daunting still is the great challenge he set all of us towards the end of his life. For it may well be, he warned, that we have not yet begun to know how to think adequately. Perhaps Rousseau was right after all: if we had done so, we might not have invented war.

There is another problem in citing Heidegger, which is why I have concealed him in this section on Marx. In one of his many books on the art of the novel, Milan Kundera recalls a line by the philosopher Friedrich Schlegel written in the last years of the eighteenth century: 'The French Revolution, Goethe's *Wilhelm Meister* and Fichte's *Epistemology* are the most important trends of our era' (Kundera, 2007, p. 159). Placing a novel and a work of philosophy in the same set of political events as the French Revolution shows what Europe was in modern times. It is difficult to imagine, he adds, that thirty years ago he or anyone else would have written: 'Decolonization, Heidegger's critique of technology and Fellini's films embody the most important trends of our era.' This way of thinking has gone—it is no longer in tune with the spirit of the times. Who would dare to associate a work of philosophy (or a novel) with the collapse of Communism in 1989? It is not that works of such importance do not exist, or that we have lost the capacity to recognize them. These questions have no meaning. The west no longer looks for its teleology in the mirror of philosophy as it once did.

Kundera is a valuable witness, however, to the fact that Heidegger's critique of technology is one of the last seminal philosophical texts which had an impact on our thinking. For it was he who introduced the word 'technology' into common usage. Before that, the 'practical arts' or 'applied sciences' or 'engineering' were commonly used to designate what is now called 'technology'. Nor had philosophers really asked themselves before about the relationship between human nature and technology except (as had Marx) in terms of culture—the idea that behaviour is transmitted by learning rather than acquired by inheritance. Humans learn, they told us (i.e. they have more culture than other species and a superior culture at that). It is true that other animals (chimpanzees) use what appear to be tools, but there is no real evidence that young chimps are taught to use them. There is no real evidence of cultural transmission. They merely copy others or figure it out for themselves. As Hobbes says, what makes us human is education. We are taught our humanity, and it begins very early in our development. For culture there must be instruction, and institutional learning and above all knowledge: the recognition that accumulated and transmitted learning makes life richer and better in terms of survival rates (we have the Maxim gun, after all, and they do not) (Allen, 2004, p. 211).

Humans are the only ones to have reason (that means the ability to transcend instinct and cooperate for a purpose). Other species can reason out problems (basic) and even invent tools (equally basic), but we invent tools for a widening spectrum of purposes. We invented two revolutionary weapons to increase our own strength—the spear throwing stick (the first lever) and the bow (the first motor). What makes a tool a human implement is that it has no biological purpose; we don't need it for our basic survival, but we do for our advancement. This is why inventions are copied, reproduced and frequently improved upon, and sometimes even replaced by something better. All of this requires us to make human life other than it is (i.e. to improve it).

Imagination is shared by other species too—chimpanzees can draw what they see every day, but they do not fast forward. The human imagination is very different. Take the very first cave paintings. They are not a representation so much as an appearance, a stepping back from reality, the ability to overview it from a distance. Cave paintings were the first expression of the power of anticipation, of the forward looking imagination. They telescoped the mind from what is seen to what can be inferred or conjectured; the cave-dwellers who painted the walls of the cave also forged the weapons to hunt the animals they depicted. In these paintings the hunters made themselves familiar with the challenges to come and thus equipped themselves with the courage to meet them (Bronowski, 1974, p. 54).

Heidegger recognized the purely instrumental definition of technology: as equipment, or the tool or the machine for a purposive end. But he also added, and it is one of his most important insights, that *the essence of technology is not technological*. Its 'essence' is how it changes our relationship with the world as well as our relationship to ourselves. It gets us to see the world around us very differently. And an essence is something that every being has: it is that by virtue of which a being or thing counts as a being or thing of that kind. It is why philosophers since Aristotle have tried to define the essence of humanity: is it speech, is it reason, or is it, as Marx insisted, labour? Marx was indebted to Schopenhauer, who in *The World as Will and Representation* had claimed that what defines our humanity is the work we do, since whenever we are not asleep we are always at work. 'A mind that is vividly aroused by willing … is incapable of comprehending the purely objective nature (the being-in-itself) of things' (Schopenhauer, 381). We see only what refers back to the will or our purpose, and one of the examples Schopenhauer offers is that of a general who, far from seeing the beauty in a landscape, sees only a battlefield. In other words, there is a tendency for all objective nature to be re-ordered in our minds, at least into a resource for our subjective will.

Heidegger meant a number of other things by the word 'essence'. I have mentioned one: the what, or *quidditas*: everything has a 'whatness' that enables us to say that something is different from something else. But another definition is 'enabling': the condition of its own possibility. The visual field is a condition of possibility which makes it possible for us to see a visual object. Heidegger added a third definition—the ground of enabling, or that in which a given mode of existence attains. In his 1949 essay, 'The Question Concerning Technology', he discusses the third definition at length.

Technology is not an artefact, it is a way of thinking about the world and our place in it. The Greeks had a more harmonious relationship with nature than we do. Consider, Heidegger invites us, an old wooden bridge that lets a river run its preordained course while we cross it in safety, compared with a modern hydroelectric dam that turns the river into a resource to be used as we wish. Or consider an ancient woodcutter who takes only the wood he needs and allows the rest of the forest to remain intact, compared with a modern timber company that cuts down an entire forest and replaces it with exotic pines whose acid needles prevent anything else from growing (Young, 2001, p. 38). The modern world view is one that sees technology as life-changing. The Greeks did not.

One explanation is that the Greeks did not have clocks. We moderns do, and the clockwork mechanism encourages us to see the world itself as a machine that can be taken apart and reassembled at will. It is this understanding that makes modern science possible. What interested Heidegger most, however, was not modern technology itself, although he considered it more violent than the ancient: a bulldozer can do far more damage than a spade. Ultimately it is the use to which we put it that constitutes our relationship with the world. What is the ground (Heidegger asks) to the violence we do to the world, the violence of a nuclear war or the everyday violence we do to nature.

For Heidegger modern war as reified at Hiroshima represented the complete triumph of technical instrumental reason. Science encourages us to see nature and humanity as a standing reserve or resource, and, of course, the problem with all resources is that they are to be used, and frequently used up. In the late modern era the will to power had become the standard of all human conduct. The total rationality of means had been accompanied by the total irrationality of ends, and that included using human beings as a perfectible resource in an attempt to refashion human nature. Stalin significantly called Marxists the 'engineers of the human soul'.

Let us return to Ellis' *Social History of the Machine Gun* where we find violence in service to those wants, especially in the case of the mad land grab which marked the last phase of European expansion—the scramble for Africa. The violence inherent in modern war inheres not so much in the material, the gunpowder itself, as in the technique, the serialization of death—together with other inventions which had amplified our vulgar wants, such as mass production and productivity. The machine gunner requires very little training, and if securely dug in, has little need of courage. Violence also inheres in the modern mindset: knowledge is power. It makes happen. It forces others to see reason, or to behave more reasonably. Once you think of yourself as more reasonable or rational than your enemy, you will see the world and war itself anew. Heidegger says, 'He who ... knows what is, knows what he will in the midst of what is' (Young, 2001, p. 40). This gnomic utterance conveys his fundamental thought: how you see things is how you act. The character of a culture's 'horizon of disclosure' is the essence of technology. War became more 'rational'—i.e. open to statistical analysis. All that happened, of course, as Heidegger observed, was that the machine instead of becoming our slave became our master. The total wars of the twentieth century, both of which he survived, were the nearest equivalent to the vision of war for war's sake. In a nuclear conflict it would have been realized very soon. In J.G. Ballard's telling formulation, our ability to make war on the earth from space was 'the first demonstration, arranged for our benefit by the machine, of our own dispensability as a species' (Ballard, 1997, p. 280).

Were they writing today, Heidegger and Marx would recognize that our relationship to technology has changed once again. Marx knew that in the period up to the industrial revolution technological change was so slow that no one would significantly notice it within their lifetime. The printing press probably was the single most radical change of the sixteenth century. With the invention of the steam engine this changed, and it has been changing ever since. Complexity as the convergence of invention, communications and progress doubles every ten years. Current rates of doubling mean that there was more change in the 1990s than in the previous ninety years (Singer, 2009). We don't know where this is leading, but we may intuit (and many do) that the changing relationship between ourselves and the machines/tools we use may change the nature of war.

The technologies we construct for war are frequently hailed as 'revolutionary'. Revolution means a radical change, but it also refers to the movement around a fixed course that returns always to a starting point. Each definition of the world can be applied here. As Marx and Heidegger both appreciated, the new technologies of the modern era had the capacity to bring about radical change and even single-handedly to change the character of war, and this is likely to continue indefinitely. But each time the character of war changes it brings us back to its nature—to such familiar features as its uncertainty and unpredictability; to the play of chance; and the importance of the human factor. Marx was the first to raise a more fundamental question—would technology change the nature of war especially with regard to myth making at its heart. Robotics, I hazard, does indeed raise this question, but we have no conclusive answer yet.

The real challenge will come when robots have to make value judgements (which is how decisions are derived). At the moment, robots are engaged in sequential programming: processing data step by step. Human beings, by contrast, engage in parallel processing. They can process different sequences at once which allows real-time thoughts, real-time memories, sensations and deductions. On the day that robots can engage in parallel processing then the nature of war really will have changed, both instrumentally and existentially, and metaphysically as well, for their use in war will render obsolete the concept of sacrifice. Should we allow the humanity of our species to be displaced by the needs of efficiency and utility? We have long held that success or failure in war should be related to our own virtues: courage, endurance, perseverance, all of which are deeply rooted in human nature. A more accurate claim would be that success or failure is rooted in the difference between our ideals and our reality, and our capacity to act as moral beings.

So, even if the Achilles myth does not survive, the core of the myth—the need to take responsibility for our actions—probably will. We are the technology we use, and this will probably not change in the near future. The information that computers process is the information *we* want to obtain. We cannot programme a computer, for example, to notice what it has not been programmed to notice. We programme the computer for purposes of our own, not the computer's. One day we might give robots a conscience, as they are attempting to do at Georgia MIT, but ethical programming is our own. Robots are programmed to do what we want or require of them, and to do so we hope with due regard to the rights we accord ourselves, including our enemies. For a robot to function autonomously, we would have to give it purpose of its own, but for that we would have to give it feelings as well. Everything we know of consciousness is that it is embodied—natural selection gave us feelings as well as capacities to act upon them. Without feelings we would not have ambition. Our distant ancestors evolved a neural machinery little by little, and the tools it has provided us have helped us transform the world. A machine could not be endowed with consciousness unless it were to undergo the same evolution. We could, perhaps, programme it to evolve, but why would we want to? What would be the point of subcontracting our purposes to others? The essence to all of us is our individual uniqueness: we are all very different. That uniqueness is given expression by its embodiment, which we have enhanced over time through the tools we use. Achilles will continue to inspire tomorrow's warriors, even in the world of star troopers, as long (that is) as we wish to retain human agency.

17

WAR AND CULTURE

WHY WAR HAS ITS OWN 'CULTURAL GRAMMAR' (ENGELS 1820–95)

Napoleon wrote [about] the combat between French cavalry, who were bad riders but disciplined, and Mameluks in Egypt, who were the best horsemen of the time but undisciplined, as follows: 'Two Mameluks were undoubtedly more than a match for three Frenchmen. A hundred Mameluks were equal to a hundred Frenchmen; three hundred Frenchmen could generally beat three Mameluks, and a thousand Frenchmen invariably defeated fifteen hundred Mameluks.'

(Rees, *The Algebra of Revolution*, p. 117)

In *Anti–Dühring* Engels develops some of the themes that both he and Marx had set out in *The German Ideology*, the first recognizably Marxist work. The book is important because it takes as a critical insight and theme that we produce ourselves through labour. We have neither a fixed nor unchallenged nature which is either biological (today we would say genetic) or spiritual. There is instead a dialectically conceived relation between our nature as determined by our conditions of life and the practical transformation of those conditions (Marx, 1996, p. 21). It follows that one cannot speak of humanity as such except at a highly abstract level. History is made by people who have specific needs and problems that are shaped by a particular condition of life. They are products of their circumstances, but they can also change their circumstances if they recognize the fact in time.

Engels claimed that material factors in war are important: all theories, forms of consciousness, religions and morals arise from the mode of production. He highlights Clausewitz's claim (a writer whom he much admired): every era fights wars in its own fashion. Hence his short but brilliant sketch of the history of war from classical times to the present, involving the Nomads (Tartars); the city-states of the ancient world; the feudal kingdoms of medieval Europe; the eighteenth-century European states that were usually in a perpetual state of war with each other; and the embryonic nation-states of his own day. It follows that for Clausewitz, as indeed for Engels, everything must be studied within its own social context.

Take one of the great mysteries of war: numbers. Numbers do make a difference. Military historians are often impressed by how small numbers in armies can often prevail against larger ones; an army that is severely outnumbered can sometimes emerge the victor. In such cases winning involves turning quantity into quality. The Mongols overcame considerably higher than a two to one inferiority in numbers as they conquered a large part of the known world. The key to their success was the application of a Napoleonic formula, centuries before it was formulated. The strength of an army, like the quantity of motion in mechanics, is esteemed by the mass multiplied by the velocity, and the Mongols achieved this by moving at twice the speed of their opponents (Chambers, 1979, p. 65). They not only practised war differently, they thought about it differently: in terms of the economy of force, unity of command, the capacity to concentrate. All these features which appeared in nineteenth-century manuals on war had been known to the Mongols seven hundred years earlier. But we are dealing, of course, with a pre-modern, nomadic people, not a modern state, and that made all the difference. The Mongol commanders who had invaded Europe, and were probably only a few years away from reaching the Atlantic coast, were bound by tradition to return home for the election of a new Khan when the old one died (like Attila from over-drinking). The invasion of Europe was postponed—as it turned out, indefinitely.

In short, Engels was the first major thinker to apply a systematic Marxist analysis to war. It is expressed in a famous letter to Marx twenty years earlier. 'Among other things, I am now reading Clausewitz's *On War*. A strange way of philosophizing but very good on its subject. On the question whether war can be called an art or a science, the answer given is that war is most like trade' (Pick, 1993, p. 48). War is a currency, and like a currency it can be debased. It is debased when it reverts to warfare because it shows no transformative 'value'; it is revalued when it promotes what Engels understood to be progress. And the medium of valuation is culture, which invades our being and changes us radically: it is the most 'ingressive' transformative summons available to human experiencing'. It is ingressive because it fashions the myths by which we live, those that tell us, in effect, to change our life (Steiner, 1990, pp. 142–3).

Adopting the perspective of a nineteenth-century European, Engels was thinking exclusively in terms of western culture, and progress as a 'myth' distinctive to the western world. Thus in *Anti–Dühring* (1878) he tells us that the introduction of firearms revolutionized the waging of war. It promoted state formation and put power in the hands of the burghers in the cities. Progress, in this case, had been painfully slow: it took three hundred years before the flintlock musket gave the infantry a distinct advantage, but that, in turn, gave western armies an edge over all others. The American and French revolutions changed the way the west thought about war in terms of mobilizing human capital by allowing it to marry capitalism to the exercise of military power.

Of course, the Engels quote above begs almost as many questions as there are answers. Is there a 'way of warfare' distinctive to a culture as some historians argue? Is there still a distinctly western one, or is there now merely an 'American' one? And what, if anything, is distinctive about it? And what, for that matter, is a 'way of war' (for there are no ways of warfare: warfare is colourless—it has no 'character' of its own that can readily be discerned).

A 'way of war' is a set of attitudes towards war which is culturally conditioned, or framed. Attitudes, we are told by philosophers, are structured arrangements of feelings; they involve thought and they generate rules. Every organization, business and even university cultivates attitudes in those who work for it or those it trains. In *Homo Ludens* the Dutch historian Huizinga quotes a Dutch industrialist to the effect that two attitudes dominated business, defined by which side of the business an employee found himself on. The technicians tried to produce so much that the sales department could never hope to sell everything in stock; the sales department tried to sell so much that the technicians could never keep pace with demand. He had always regarded business as a game whose purpose was to inculcate attitudes to be fostered in the next generation of businessmen (Midgley, 2003, p. 161).

The same could be said of war: two sides are engaged in the same business, but see their role-play as different. Unlike a business, the success of one precludes the success of the other, and the business cannot turn a profit for everyone. The American anthropologist Ruth Benedict wrote about the conquest of the Americas:

> War may be as it was among the Aztecs, a way of getting captives for the religious sacrifices. Since the Spaniards fought to kill, according to Aztec standards they broke the rules of the game. The Aztecs fell back in dismay and Cortes walked as victor into the capital. (Midgley, 2003, p. 171)

In other words, the difference between warfare and war is that the latter is ritualized, and culture determines what the rituals (or rules) are. In the case of the Aztecs, Benedict was being grossly simplistic. They did not go under without a fight, and they adapted to the Spaniards as far as they could (they were defeated in the end as much by disease as by bullets). And historians are now inclined to attribute the Spanish success not to the fact that they found themselves fighting a bronze age culture so much as to their own willingness to adapt—instead of fighting by their own rules (as they would have done back home) they took part in a Meso-American style of war, giving their own allies who did most of the fighting a decisive advantage in the form of guns, horses and dogs which the Indians did not have. In much the same way the US left most of the ground fighting against the Taliban to the Northern Alliance in 2001, tipping the balance in favour of their allies by providing them with massive air support. We should recognize, writes Midgley, that the restraining rules are not irrational or foreign to the needs and emotions involved in war. They are simply the shape that the activity takes. The point I am making is this: there seems to be a profound and complex need for war in all human societies and at all times. It is because the need is real that war has a nature; it is because it is complex that it reflects the culture engaged in it. Which is only to say that what is universal as a need is experienced differently: every war has its own cultural grammar which expresses the needs and emotions of the two (or more) sides taking part. Those from the same culture will play by the same rules (or try to change them usually only in duress, and often too late). When war pits two different cultures against each other, there will be a clash of styles—the ultimate 'culture shock'.

It is fairly telling that the west has been supreme in war for the past 200 years, and was supreme for a time long before that, when Greek armies were led by Alexander the Great and the Roman legions by a succession of highly professional commanders. In his book *Why the West has Won* (the American title *Culture and Carnage* is much more vivid) Davis Hanson tells us just how lethal the western way of warfare was—he shows us Alexander destroying an empire of 70 million with an army of less than 40,000 men; Cortes wreaking havoc on an imperial people of 2 million in less than two years; the Americans in the Tet Offensive in Vietnam (1968) 'wasting' 40,000 Viet Cong soldiers for the loss of only 2,500 men. These military successes, Hanson tells us, had little to do with morality or intelligence and everything to do with superior military capacity, which owed everything, in turn, to culture.

For Hanson the Greeks introduced three concepts into war that in Engels' terms enabled it to translate quantity into quality. One is the decisive battle which is distinguished by the overwhelming use of force at a critical moment. In the *Third Philippic*, Demosthenes bemoaned the fact that of all the arts the Greeks had taken the art of war in a new direction—decisiveness. And decisiveness required shock battle. In his third victory at the Granicus River Alexander had at his disposal shock troops who could hack their way through the line. The Persians were a mixed mob of barbarians. Some threw javelins, other stones, and only a few used real weapons (the description is that of the historian Curtius)—i.e. weapons used face to face at close quarters (Hanson, 2002, p. 93). Alexander knew his enemy. The Persian army was strong only in numbers. It could not handle shock combat; he knew it would buckle under pressure, and he knew the tactics to adopt: cut through the front line and then aim for the king, Darius. Once he fled from the battlefield, as he did soon enough, he knew the Persian army would disintegrate. The willingness to risk all in one encounter has distinguished much of western military history, from the Greek phalanx meeting the Persians in hand-to-hand combat to the German blitzkrieg of World War Two and more recently America's striking 'Shock and Awe' campaign in Iraq.

Secondly, Hanson claims, the west has managed to field armies with a high degree of *primary group cohesion*. The idea of the army as a collective hero can be traced to the writings of Plato in the *Laches*. Here, too, we may be able to trace a linear progression from the Republican armies of Rome, which could often field citizens for seventeen years at a time (the longest rate of mobilization of any society in history), to the US army whose primary group cohesion gives it a cutting edge: the degree of attachment soldiers have to their comrades, their unit, and their country (Wong, 2002, p. 21). And finally there is the use of technology as a force multiplier, especially since 1870 when western technological superiority first became pronounced. The essence of technology, Heidegger tells us, is not technological. The essence is how we see it and use it, and the purposes it serves. Both are conditioned by cultural factors. For Hanson, 'scientific method, unfettered research and capitalist production', which he claims all first developed in the west, explain why western societies have enjoyed such a decisive technological lead (Hanson, 2002, p. 360).

So much for the western way of war, as Hanson describes it. And to be fair to him it is a much more complex picture than I have sketched. He does not maintain, for example, that the west has always been superior to other cultures. He concedes that it has often suffered defeat. What is he is arguing is that its cultural preferences have given it a greater margin of error over its enemies.

To sum up, Hanson takes the Greeks to have 'invented' a way of warfare still practised in the west. In taking the American people into the War on Terror George Bush still saw fit to cite the ancient Greeks as one of the sources of his own political vision. Perhaps this is going back too far in history. To compete successfully a society has to be organized, and it is here that time and again the west has been afforded a critical advantage. What Hanson and others identify as a western tradition involves a large degree of social power. The key, writes Stephen Toulmin, was the invention of discipline. It is a word which we associate with another: drill which makes obedience automatic and self-control in the presence of danger a habit. War involves role specialization, each with its own drills and techniques. Specialists arise in different fields; institutions become more efficient. Discipline-based professions arise that foster the concept of professionalism. Drill was first introduced into European arms in the 1590s by such military leaders as Maurice of Nassau. But the idea that an army is not a rabble but a multitude of individuals organized to work together in time soon caught on. The Dutch were the first to introduce a systematic method of training, to set up military academies whose staffs taught standardized procedures as a drill which students had to perform step by step in one, and only one, correct way (Toulmin, 2000).

If there is an identifiable and distinctive western way of war, therefore, we may be on safer ground tracing it back to the seventeenth century's dialogue with the ancient world. For the disciplines the Europeans invented encouraged them to adopt a rigorously *instrumental* way of reasoning. And one of the areas which instrumental rationality tends to 'bracket off' from consideration is ethics. Even Max Weber made a case for handling problems in a 'value-neutral way', as if one could speak of social knowledge as 'scientific'. Ethical concerns were often lost sight of, so much so that the Europeans came near to destroying themselves in the mid twentieth century as a result of the ruthless application of instrumental rationality to the practice of war. As Clausewitz remarked, if war had become more 'civilized', that was because science opened up opportunities for restraint. But society certainly didn't become any nicer. As more social energies were released, the strong were supplied with more legitimate reasons to justify their actions.

There are still dangers, however, in suggesting that there is a specific western way of war. Let me highlight two. It has long been a feature of western thinking to see the world in terms of binary opposites: solid and liquid; truth and lies; the body and soul; white and black (both literally and metaphorically); male and female. One side is considered privileged (or right); the other side unprivileged (or wrong). What is important about this system of binary opposites is that it is ontological. It is deemed to underpin a different way of thinking, acting and feeling. So that in opposition to a western way of war there must be a non-western which is representative of a different mentality.

The oriental mind, remarked John Foster Dulles, 'is more devious than the occidental' (Dower, 1986, p. 310). This is a typical example of what the late Edward Said called 'orientalism'. Said argued that a large mass of writers had accepted the basic distinction between east and west as the starting point for elaborate theories concerning the orient, its people, customs and 'mentalities'. Said concluded that European culture had gained in strength and identity by setting itself against the orient as a sort of surrogate 'self'—the orient had helped to define the west as its contrasting idea and experience. This tends to encourage ethnic and racial stereotyping.

Nearly fifty years later John Keegan, writing in the immediate wake of 9/11, concluded:

A harsh, instantaneous attack may be the response most likely to impress the Islamic mind. Surprise has traditionally been a favoured Islamic military method. The use of overwhelming force is, however, alien to the Islamic military method....Westerners fight face to face, in stand-up battle, and go on until one side or the other gives in. They choose the crudest weapons available and use them with appalling violence, but observe what, to non-westerners may well seem curious rules of honour. Orientals, by contrast, shrink from pitched battle, which they often deride as a sort of game, preferring ambush, surprise, treachery and deceit as the best way to overcome an enemy.... Relentlessness as opposed to surprise and sensation, is the Western way of warfare. It is deeply injurious to the Oriental style and rhetoric of war-making. Oriental war-makers, today's terrorists, expect ambushes and raids to destabilise their opponents, allowing them to win further victories by horrifying outrages at a later stage. Westerners have learned, by harsh experience, that the proper response is not to take fright but to marshal their forces, to launch massive retaliation and to persist relentlessly until the raiders have either been eliminated or so appalled by the violence inflicted that they relapse into inactivity. (Keegan, 2001)

At the end of this passage this usually perceptive author insisted that he was not caricaturing Afghans, Arabs or Chechens as particularly devious or underhand, but, in effect, this is exactly what he was doing. Indeed, he went on to add that the war against terrorism belonged to a much older conflict between settled, creative productive westerners and predatory, destructive orientals.

Now what Engels did not claim is that societies or civilizations have distinctive mentalities. When we talk of a mentality being different from our own, we should ask first whether cultures have mentalities, any more than do the people we associate with every day? Doesn't the appeal to a distinct mentality simply re-describe the phenomenon we find puzzling? Does it, in fact, explain anything at all? Or should we seek explanations for why different cultures think about war differently, not in mentalities but in styles of enquiry or the questions they ask? And the question non-western societies have asked increasingly since 1870 is how they can resist the west, given its decisive advantage in technology.

Thus Paul Bracken accounts for Vietnamese tactics in the Vietnam war in terms of a cultural preference for indirect warfare (Bracken, 2000). But given that the two occasions on which the Vietnamese engaged the United States in open battle they lost decisively, it can be argued that they employed a guerrilla strategy because it was the only effective response to American military power. In the Easter Offensive in 1972 they lost 100,000 men in the space of six weeks largely to air assault—this was the first time the USAF used its B52s to attack an army in the field, rather than level a city. In other words, guerrilla warfare may not necessarily be a cultural preference so much as a political necessity. The Vietnamese were faced with the same conundrum they had been forced to address in the thirteenth century when the Mongols had overrun the country. Then they had abandoned their cities and taken to the hills. Instead of conceding defeat they had waged a guerrilla war and finally driven out the invaders.

Let me return to the question of mentalities. For the very term suggests that we are born with different abilities. We are not. What we have are different capabilities, and culture, of course, determines whether we are allowed to cultivate our abilities or not—in Engels' phrase to turn quantity into quality. Different cultures also channel their abilities in different directions. In terms of the nation state, for example, the west created a political unit that was able to mobilize more of its citizens more effectively than practically any other in history.

But once we start talking in terms of capabilities we find that certain western societies including the strongest, the United States, sometimes do not realize their full potential. In our post-modern times western societies are more risk-averse than ever. Western armies don't always (à la Keegan) fight 'face to face', in stand-up battle. In recent years the non-western world has chosen to target this predisposition to be risk-averse. The American military pull-out from Beirut in the early 1980s and from Mogadishu ten years later have become in the Arab world symbolic of how it is possible for the weak to prevail using its own cultural capital—suicide bombers (Beirut, 1983/Iraq after 2004) or heavily armed militias (Mogadishu, 1993). Whether they will always prevail is not the point. War, as Clausewitz reminds us, is an interactive process, and the very disparity of western military power over others—its ability to take apart a society in three weeks but not police it effectively afterwards—doesn't always produce an endgame so much as a determination to play the game by different rules.

The second problem with defining a specific western way of war is more germane to my principal theme. It encourages us to essentialize western culture. It is a perverse form of occidentalism. The truth is that there have been different political cultures within western society which have pursued different ways of war. We would expect nothing less given that the west was largely at war with itself for the last 500 years.

A striking example is Nazi Germany, which also managed to translate quantity into quality but in ways that were often at odds with

Hanson's 'western way of war'. Its close combat record was far superior to its enemies. Writing in the 1970s, Colonel Trevor Dupuy claimed that it had been 20 per cent more effective than the Allies in both world wars. 'In other words 100 Germans in combat units were the equivalent of about 120 British or American troops in combat units and equivalent to about 250 Russians in combat units' (Dupuy, p. 281). The point he was making was not that the average German soldier was two and a half times brighter than the average Russian, but that put in a unit his productivity was much greater. What is perhaps even more striking, Germany was far more advanced than the United States in military technology. It invented the first jet aeroplane, the first ballistic missile, the world's first cruise missile and even a prototype intercontinental bomber which flew 26 miles east of New York in the last months of the war. It is only the fact that it was ultimately unsuccessful that allows us to ignore it entirely. But its very defeat begs an important question. Nazi Germany's abilities were as great as those of its western enemies, the United States and the United Kingdom. But its capabilities in the end were far less impressive because they were shaped by a peculiar political culture. Nazism was an example of what historians call 'reactionary modernism', the belief that willpower alone could transcend material conditions. The upshot was its first significant defeat, the Battle of Britain.

In 1940 the RAF was run by professionals who had spent years mastering their profession. The Luftwaffe's High Command was run by a swashbuckling adventurer (Goering) and a Key Commander (Kesselring) who had been trained as an artillery man and who had spent only one third of the time in the air compared with his principal opponent, Dowding. By 1940, the British had also carefully prepared a system which applied modern technology, including radar, to war in the air. The Germans, by contrast, largely improvised their attack and did not fully exploit the technology at their disposal, including radar. In addition, the British worked as teams and played down individual efforts whatever the public love affair at the time with the air aces. German pilots, by comparison, were actually encouraged to think of themselves as knights of the air (Bungay, 2000, p. 395).

One example was Lieutenant Hans-Otto Lessing who wrote home to his parents in the summer of 1940 that the previous day he had registered his fifth kill. No one did he hold in higher regard than his commander, who had already registered twenty. And he admired his enemy, the British, as well, particularly one Hurricane pilot who had 'played a game' with thirty Messerschmitts without himself getting into danger. As he told his parents, he was having the time of his life: 'I would not swap places with a king. Peace is going to be very boring after this' (Bungay, 2000). He never had a chance to find out; the following day he was shot down over the Channel. The letter—and there are many more like it—give an insight into the peculiar warrior ethos of the Luftwaffe. For many pilots war was indeed a game. Many were interested in scores rather than the final outcome. Each wanted to out-do the other. The Luftwaffe, indeed, went out of its way to encourage 'score-chasing' by individual pilots. It played up the warrior's honour, the existential status of its pilots. By contrast, the RAF refused to celebrate its own air aces officially throughout the war and cooperated only reluctantly with press interest in their life stories.

On the eastern front, by contrast, war soon became a grim Darwinian struggle that offered only one choice: that of killing or being killed. In the east the Germans replaced material strength and rational planning, which had served them so well in the western campaign of 1940, with an amoral, ruthless, fanatical view of war, with a nihilistic element at its centre: the celebration of death. In an attempt to overcome the hopelessness of the situation, battle was glorified as the real, supreme essence of 'being'. After its defeat at Stalingrad, the army reverted to the infantry tactics of the Great War, digging in, fighting for every inch of ground, refusing to admit defeat. It fought all the way back to Berlin. It is this emphasis on the existential element to the neglect of the instrumental that leads Omer Bartov to talk of the de-modernization of the German army in the east (Bartov, 1991, pp. 13–28). War was transformed in the process into warfare.

And that is the chief challenge that faces the west today. Its enemies will not face it on—but off—the conventional battlefield where the existential dimension is now to be found. De-modernizing the battlefield is the main way by which warriors, terrorists or others can attempt to counter the west's technological and organizational advantage, plus its attempt to bring war into the post-modern era. They may not succeed, of course, any more than the Germans, but it is sobering to remind ourselves of the cost the Germans were willing to incur even after it had become painfully clear that the war was lost. The statistics tell their own grim story. Before the July plot in July 1944, 2.8 million German soldiers were killed in battle; an additional 4.8 million died after it as war in the east came to resemble Hobbes' state of nature. If a society can call on an equal level of sacrifice it will give the west a run for its money. Culture matters as much as ever. It still gives war its distinctive 'cultural grammar'.

18

WAR AND THE WARRIOR
WHY THE WARRIOR IS A HUMAN TYPE
(NIETZSCHE 1844–1900)

I see many soldiers: would that I saw many warriors! 'Uniform' one calls what they wear: would that what it conceals were not uniform!
You should have eyes that always seek an enemy—your enemy. And some of you hate at first sight. Your enemy you shall seek, your war you shall wage—for your thoughts. And if your thought be vanquished, then you honestly should find cause for triumph in that....
You say that it is the good war that hallows every war? I say unto you: it's the good war that hallows any cause....
You may only have enemies whom you hate, not enemies you despise. You must be proud of your enemy: then the successes of your enemy are your successes too.

(Nietzsche, 'On War and Warriors', *Also Sprach Zarathustra*)

'Don't read books' is one of the last entries in Nietzsche's notebooks (Calasso, *The 49 Steps*, p. 30). Hitler went into battle with a book by Schopenhauer, not Nietzsche, in his knapsack, but Nietzsche moulded the opinion of a generation of young Germans who went to war twice in the course of the twentieth century. He was a dangerous writer, not least because his aristocratic impulses set him at odds with the democratic age. Throughout his life he held to his opinion that the masses were beyond redemption. 'Not to the people let Zarathustra speak ... To lure many away from the herd, therefore I come' (McIntyre, 1998, p. 118).

Liberal philosophers still don't like him for that reason. Richard Rorty used to argue that if we don't find *Zarathustra* amusing we clearly don't have a sense of the absurd. Chesterton agreed: too much depth concealed too little real thinking. The Germans, commented another English writer, Aldous Huxley, dived deeper than anyone else and came up muddier, and there are still those who blame Nietzsche for both World Wars. But *Zarathustra* (though a youthful work) is certainly a heartfelt one: it is Nietzsche's deepest testament, and in its pages we find words penned about one of the most profound realities of war: the possibilities of transcendence. It is a product of a period of crisis in Nietzsche's life (he tells us this himself in his autobiographical work, *Ecce Homo*). In that book Nietzsche calls *Zarathustra* 'a type, a physiological presupposition of what is good health', a lodestar for those yet to come, 'a premature, born yet undemonstrated future' (Ansell-Pearson, 2005, p. 85).

The problem is that once you have read Nietzsche, you cannot unread him. He gets into the imagination. He is one of the great prose writers in German, a language worth learning to read him in the original. He made vivid his own concepts in a way few other philosophers have done. Take 'the will to power' which was seized upon by artists very quickly. Indeed, for some time after his death Nietzsche himself was seen in Germany and outside more as a literary figure than a philosopher. His greatest influence in the early part of the last century was not on fellow philosophers, but authors like André Gide and Robert Musil and Gottfried Benn, and Andrei Bely in Russia, not to mention Bernard Shaw and D.H. Lawrence in England. His influence on art persists to this day. We find a distorted embodiment of his philosophy in Cormac McCarthy's novel *Blood Meridian* (1985) in the person of one of the great diabolic characters in late-twentieth-century fiction, Judge Holden. What the great literary figures offer us through fiction is a chance to know heroes better than they know themselves. Holden is actually based on a true filibuster who massacred and scalped Indians in post-civil war America. (He is one of two great proto-Nietzschean figures in American literature: the other being General Cummings whom we have already encountered.) The judge, however, is quite different from the cynical Cummings. He is War Incarnate. 'War is God', he claims because it is the supreme expression of the ego, of the game of will against will. 'The way of the world', he declaims:

is to bloom and flower and die, but in the affairs of men there is no waning and the noon of his expression signals the onset of night. His spirit is exhausted at the peak of his achievement. His meridian is at once the darkening and the evening of his day. He loves games? Let him play for stakes. (Bloom, 1999, p. 437)

What apparently grounds the widespread respect for war is the understanding that the warrior is both honourable and well-intentioned; he is a man (nearly always a man) trying to lead a morally good life, earnest in his desire not to act either unlawfully or illegitimately. None of these is true of Judge Holden who, Bloom adds, is a 'theoretician of war everlasting'. To use my language, he is a theoretician, in other words, of warfare.

By the time it opens the US had attained the frontier and re-ordered it, and conjured war out of warfare. But the Judge is an authentic warrior from a primal past: a warrior not of war, but of warfare. 'Whoever would seek out his history through what unravelling of loins and ledger books at the shore of a void without terminus or origin.' He represents *our* origins: that is the point of the story.

This is the nature of war whose stake is at once the game and the authority and the justification. Seen so, war is the truest form of divination. It is the testing of one's will and the will of another within that larger will which because it binds them is therefore forced to select. War is the ultimate game because war is at last a forcing of the unity of existence. (Bloom, *How to Read and Why*, pp. 254–63)

In the book, the gang become outlaws when the authorities no longer need their services. They break back into the disorder from which they have come. The novel ends with the Judge performing an obscene dance of death (the rest of the gang having been killed), but then we know by the end that Holden is immortal. The last words he speaks are those of an age in which the warrior was not tamed or domesticated:

As war becomes dishonoured and its nobility called into question, those honourable men who recognize the sanctity of blood will become excluded from the dance which is the warrior's right, and thereby will the dance become a false dance and the dancers false dancers.

Warfare, the author reminds us, remains alive in all of us ready to break out at any time.

There are some elective affinities between Nietzsche's heroes and McCarthy's judge, but in the end the red judge is not a Nietzschean figure: he reflects warfare not war because he has too much wilfulness, and not enough will. Read on one level, Zarathustra can be seen as calling war the supreme game for the true warrior. If we fight hard we enhance life. Elsewhere he designates bravery as goodness, a virtue in itself: it is the game that matters not the result. And the great Dutch historian, Johan Huizinga, has a chapter on the game of war in his book, *Homo Ludens*. This is not Nietzsche's point of departure, however. The warrior, he tells us, is a human type who finds his humanity in war, and war will not end until such time as it no longer affords the warrior a chance to be himself. The existential realm of war marks out the private space of the warrior. It is that realm where a soldier confronts his own mortality; it is also that realm that makes him a moral agent in the eyes of the society that sends him out to do battle in its name. Warriors are to be found both in warfare and war; but in the former their humanity is expressed very differently.

It is transcendence that is so hallowing: it makes sacrifice sacred. I have cited at the beginning of this chapter a passage from William Kaufmann's translation of *Zarathustra* (still my favourite, perhaps out of loyalty to a man who spent much of his life trying to rehabilitate Nietzsche's reputation in the English-speaking world). The section *On War and Warriors* is a lament for a dying breed. Nietzsche feared that the existential dimension of war which had enabled humanity to transcend warfare by making it a contest of excellence was being progressively hollowed out as the nation-state intruded more and more into private life. Nietzsche grasped that in an age of democracy and mass politics the warrior as a human type was under threat for the first time. Mass culture was beginning to deny everyone their own 'private space'.

How could a warrior respect another across national boundaries when nation-states encouraged their citizens to demonize their enemies in generic terms: by class, nation or even race—in those great 'alibis of aggression' that allowed states to kill millions with a good conscience. None of this was for the true warrior, Nietzsche insisted. The warrior may hate his enemies but he should never despise them. At time he may even be proud of them—indeed their defeat means nothing if it is not honestly obtained. An enemy's success can be yours also: there is no shame in being defeated by an enemy whose fighting skills one admires.

War, for the true warrior, should be personally redemptive but redemption was being nationalized as well. Soldiers were being asked to fight for causes; the warrior ultimately fights for himself. Not for Nietzsche an age of nationalism and its conscript soldiers. 'I see many soldiers: would that I saw many warriors... "Uniform" one calls what they wear, would that what it conceals was not uniform!' In an explicit break with the ideal of the conscript, Nietzsche goes on to say that the warrior is not interested in peace; he is not interested even in winning. One can still triumph in defeat by fighting well; this will determine how it is remembered by others or even if it is remembered at all. And the true warrior has no interest in a long or risk-free life. 'Your love of life shall be love of your highest hope; and your highest hope shall be the highest thought of life. Your highest thought, however, you should receive as a command from me—and it is: man is something that should be overcome. Thus live your life of obedience and war. What matters long life? What warrior wants to be spared?' (Kaufmann, 1968, p. 160). Try, if one can, to ignore the overblown romanticism and even the philosophy of 'overcoming' which was Nietzsche's trademark. *Zarathustra's* command is to live life, not squander it, and the battlefield can provide that moment of transcendence when heroes become 'themselves' for the first (and often last) time.

Now, even a conscripted soldier can find war personally redeeming: it is the myth of redemption which helps sustain war itself. In his fascinating oral history of World War Two, Studs Turkel recounts many stories of men who found that their experience either in the European or the Pacific theatres had been the most significant time of their lives. Everything else had paled into insignificance. Turkel told the psychiatrist Oliver Sacks that he had met thousands of men who felt they had been 'marking time' since their demobilization (Sacks, 1985, pp. 30–31). Veterans often remember war (strange for those who have not fought it), fondly for the friendships forged, for the intensity of battle which they were lucky of course to survive, and above all for the intense moral certainties, especially engendered in a 'good' war such as World War Two. Some soldiers go to the worst battlefields in the world, but come back more alive than they had been before they had set out. Take James Salter's reminiscences about flying an F-86 and engaging in dog-fights over the Yalu River. He recounts his baptism of fire. 'It had been a great voyage', he says of his time in the Air Force. 'The voyage probably of my life.' Everything that followed afterwards was anti–climactic (Alvarez, 2007, p. 117).

But there is a critical difference between a rush of adrenalin or an intense experience in battle or the forging of deep friendships with other soldiers and the element of transcendence which makes a warrior. The latter is the nearest we actually get to Nietzsche's myth of 'self-overcoming'. It is at one with what *Zarathustra* teaches that what is great about man is that he is a bridge and not a goal; the task of human existence is to become more human. The human is a 'fragment, riddle and the dreadful chance'; it is material to be worked upon which is why the warrior has to put himself constantly to the test. There is a phrase in *Zarathustra* which captures transcendence in battle. 'Into every abyss I shall bear the blessing of my affirmation' (Nietzsche, *Zarathustra,* Section 6). 'When I close my eyes,' wrote Ernst Junger, that most emeritus of German warriors, 'I sometimes see a dark landscape in the background … I recognize myself as a tiny figure, as if drawn with a piece of chalk. This is my outpost, right next to nothingness—down there in the abyss I am fighting for myself' (Steiner, 1983, p. ix).

The word 'abyss'—French allows the epithet *'abyssal'* and its nominal use—George Steiner reminds us, is vitally ambiguous. 'There is the threat of deconstruction but also the intimation of a great calm, of a tide whose return will cleanse matter of the separation, of the violence inherent in making' (Steiner, 1983, p. 27). The point of the abyss is that it is psychological. 'Who among the philosophers before me has been a psychologist?' Nietzsche asked in *Ecce Homo* ('Why I am destiny'). He glimpsed that the true subject of philosophy had become the self.

Nietzsche's existential heroes are forever pushing back the boundaries of the world and finding themselves on the brink of an eternal truth, or are lost in contemplation of the emptiness at the heart of things. That is the problem with transcendence: it can represent an epiphany for some, and a crisis of faith for others. The monster you fear most may well be you: those who look in to the abyss long enough, Nietzsche warns, may soon find the abyss staring into them.

One writer (with Tennyson's famous poem in mind) calls it the 'Ulysses factor': we all have a need to roam, but we became interested in the inner journey to that 'undiscovered country', our own psyche at precisely the time we had mapped out the rest of the world (Alvarez, 2007, p. 91). It might even be suggested—to take the argument further than perhaps it permits—that in discovering ourselves (our inner experience), we have made the quest for the outer world redundant. In descending into the nightmare world of the *Heart of Darkness*, the madness that he has witnessed at first hand, Marlow tells us that when he was a child he had a passion for maps, especially the blank spaces on the Earth. Whenever one looked particularly inviting he would put his finger on it and say, 'When I grow up, I will go there.' The North Pole was one such place—but he tells us he will not be going there now. 'The glamour is off.' The glory of war has not been much talked about since 1915 but we still watch war movies. Young men are still inspired by what they think to be glamorous (a better word than 'glorious', which really has lost its shine). There is no glamour in warfare but there is in war—as long as it continues to demand warriors.

Perhaps the most revealing warrior of all was Ernst Junger (1896–1998) who won the Iron Cross in January 1917 and the highest German award for valour, the *Croix pour le Mérite* the following year. By the close of the war he had been wounded at least fourteen times—not counting the 'trifles', as he put it: ricochets and grazes (Junger, 2004, p. 288). Despite the anonymous battlefield, he found himself targeted at least eleven times, surviving each experience. I doubt whether any other warrior in the twentieth century had an equally distinguished record, and I am pretty sure that none had a better.

For Junger, war was almost entirely an existential experience, as one account of a raid on a French trench makes clear:

These moments of nocturnal prowling leave an indelible impression. Eyes and ears are tensed to the maximum, the rustling approach of strange feet in the tall grass an unutterable menacing thing. Your breath comes in shallow bursts; you have to force yourself to stifle any panting or wheezing. There is a little mechanical click as the safety-catch of your pistol is taken off; the sound cuts through your nerves. Your teeth are grinding on the fuse-pin of the hand-grenade. The encounter will be short and murderous. You tremble with two contradictory impulses: the heightened awareness of the huntsman, and the terror of the quarry. You are a world to yourself, saturated with the appalling aura of the savage landscape. (Junger, 2004, p. 183)

In one of those raids, Junger was one of only three men out of the original fourteen who managed to make it back to their own lines.

Let me quote another revealing passage which describes a moment when he was wounded in the chest. 'As I came down heavily on the bottom of the trench, I was convinced it was all over. Strangely, that moment is one of the very few in my life of which I am able to say they were truly happy. I understood, as a flash of lightning, the true inner purpose of my life' (Junger, 2004, p. 373). He doesn't actually tell us what the purpose is. He is striking a Nietzschean pose: it is the aphorism that is important. For one of the major themes of Junger's reflections on war is that the experience itself generates meaning, it is transfiguring as well as transforming. 'What is important is not what we fight for, but how we fight', he concluded in *Battle as Inner Experience*, in a passage that could have been lifted from *Zarathustra*.

As Andreas Huyssen reminds us, this does not demand any intersubjective relationship with the enemy, it is entirely self-referential—it represents an existential wager which dresses up combat in quasi–metaphysical terms. In an essay entitled 'The Will' written in 1926, Junger insisted, 'we must believe in a higher meaning than the one we are able to give to events, and we must believe in a higher destiny within which that we believe we determine is being fulfilled' (Huyssen, 1995, p. 379). He believed very much in what he called the 'front experience'—it transformed him. The trouble is it transformed many others, including Hitler, the man he claimed to despise most. Hitler too offered the German people a unique destiny. His quest for meaning gelled with that of a nation that also was trying to find what Junger called 'new, deeper puzzles' in its own nihilistic (or apparently meaningless) experiences.

There was, of course, a critical difference between Junger and the Nazis, if we wish to recognize it (and many for perfectly good reasons do not). Junger himself never bought into the culture of sacrifice which became central to the destiny the Nazis promised the German people—it was, after all, their capacity for sacrifice which in Hitler's mind made the Aryan race superior to every other. Compare Junger's attitude with that of one of his *pour le Mérite* colleagues, Fedor von Bock, who became a Field Marshall on the eastern front in World War Two. Bock told his soldiers that there was no greater honour than dying for the Fatherland ('Our profession should always be crowned by heroic death in battle') (*Time* Magazine, 21 September 1942). Junger, by comparison, was interested in affirming his life through combat, not bringing it to an early end. Ironically, he lived to be over a hundred.

What we are discussing here is what Charles Taylor calls 'external transcendence' (Taylor, 2007, p. 630). War calls forth suffering, courage and nobility; it helps us transcend our material circumstances. If this is the case there probably isn't a 'moral equivalent' to war (as William James had hoped). Junger found transcendent meaning in World War One in a way he could not find in the Second. He did not succumb to the Hitler myth, although, as we have seen, in the horrors of the eastern front he regretfully saw only 'the style of the times' from which he felt that the German army could remain personally aloof. The 'style of the times' was a phrase hardly adequate to the war's horrors, but it is highly revealing nonetheless. No one can fail to see that in Junger's writings war functions much more like a religion, a promise of meaning of earthly existence as well as a form of redemption. Yet it asks in the end too much of us, for this is salvation by faith, not good works. And it is by its works that we in the west judge the value of war today.

The word 'style' is revealing for another reason. It conveys a certain aesthetic of its own, in this case 'wonder'. Theodore Nadelson says those who have seen combat remain attached to its 'arresting elements, to its wonder' (Nadelson, 2005, p. 112). By 'wonder' he means a changed state of mind provoked by an encounter which shifts the usual and expected into something dramatic, dazzling, even bewildering. Wonder occurs when the normal plane of existence is lifted and we glimpse a new reality behind appearance. Alan Sager, a young American volunteer fighting in the French Foreign Legion in World War One, wrote to his mother in the third month of the war (October 1914): 'Every moment here is worth weeks of ordinary *experience* ... This will spoil one for another kind of life.' Sager was killed in the first wave of men who went over the top at the Somme two years later. It was a fate he practically invited. In a letter to a friend a few weeks before the battle, he confided, 'I'm glad to be going in the first wave. If you are in this thing, it's best to be in to the limit. And this is the supreme experience' (Holmes, 1994, p. 271).

The Russian writer Mikhail Bakhtin captures the essence of this in the wider field of aesthetics. He devised a new concept, the chronotype, which literally means 'space-time', and expresses the inseparability of space and of time in the novel. 'Characteristically, it is not private life that is subjected to and interpreted in the light of social and political events, but rather the other way around—social and political events gain meaning in the novel only thanks to their connection with private life. And such events were illuminated in the novel only so far as they relate to private fate: that essence is purely social, and political events remain outside the novel' (Bakhtin, 1998, p. 100).

Translated into our own field of enquiry, one could contend that in moments of intense combat the social and political reality of war is translated for the individual soldier into the here and now. But some such moments are vastly more important than others—and it is those moments that can be said to constitute 'chronotypes'. In literature, the important moments are those of encounter, epiphany and metamorphosis. They are the 'turning points' in a hero's life. They 'depict only the exceptional, utterly unusual moments in a man's life, moments that are very short compared to the whole length of the human life. But these moments shape the definitive image of the man, his essence as well as the nature of his entire subsequent life' (Henriksen).

What makes many suspicious of warriors, of course, is that by definition the moment of awakening cannot be shared with others. More disturbing still, the use of aesthetic categories tends to translate war into an aesthetic experience—the sublime of destruction. It is real enough but we should never justify war by reference to an aesthetic peculiar to itself. For to do so encourages a sort of detachment from the meaning of war. Indeed, what many of us find repugnant in Junger's writing is the fact that he is very much an observer. In *Phaedrus*, Plato says, 'An artist's eye must feed on beauty from a distance and the discipline of art is precisely the distance which he must maintain' (Mazzeo, 1967, p. 157). Junger was far too distant. What one critic calls the 'the tone of ironical pessimism' which pervades his World War One writings is that of a man above the struggle, a narrator, largely untouched by what he saw around him (Steiner, 1983, p. ix). It is always the *other* person who is dead, the *other* soldier who is caught on the wire, the *other* whom Junger observes with such meticulous detachment.

Frequently in his diaries and journals he refers to himself in the third person, as an outsider looking on. In a diary entry for April 1946, he congratulated himself on his restrained recording of violent acts, for his finely honed talent for appreciating them in terms that were essentially aesthetic—in other words, for his ability to transcend the suffering of *others*. He found a bombing raid on a Renault works outside Paris in March 1941 particularly disappointing. The entire spectacle he thought had been rather tawdry, or worse still rather melodramatic. 'Seen from my quarter', he recalls after noting in passing that several thousand workers had been killed in the raid and several thousand more wounded, 'the affair looked rather like stage lighting in a shadowed theatre' (Steiner, 1983).

The inevitable conclusion we may draw from Junger's own need for transcendence, his need to get in touch with a higher reality, is that the rest of mankind does not really count for very much. These days warriors have to be more circumspect. Our own view of transcendence has changed. We have now a public space emptied of any reference to ultimate reality (Taylor, 2007, p. 2). Our consideration is for a rational world in which we can appreciate reality in terms of the greatest benefit to the greatest number, or for a cosmopolitan internationalism, the new spirit of the age that puts us in touch with what is ultimately important: our own humanity. What is interesting in all this is not the devaluation of war, so much as revaluation of peace. Peace has been emptied out of any metaphysical or extra human content. In Charles Taylor's words this outcome may even be said, perhaps, to represent the final triumph of secularism. Secularization demands (in his own words) that war cannot be part of 'lived experience'. It cannot fulfil any reality greater than itself. It cannot be about human overcoming, it must be about human being. And war certainly cannot be what it was for the Nazis, an attempt to translate 'being' into authenticity.

Junger was representative of a very different world view. It is not just that even the exponents of war no longer invoke the same principles (Taylor, 2007, pp. 13–14). All beliefs are held within the context we take for granted. We now draw distinctions as Junger did not, between natural and supernatural, immanent and transcendent. Hiving off the immanent from the transcendent is a mark of our age. We are a long way from Nietzsche's warrior in recognizing as we must that there is nothing higher than human fulfilment. There is no 'becoming' that involves being put in touch with some Platonic Form, or God or History or Being. We live in a world of self-sufficient humanism which accepts no goals beyond human fulfilment, and no allegiance to anything beyond it (Taylor, 2007, p. 18). This does not invalidate, however, Nietzsche's belief that the nature of war is distinctive from warfare, and what is distinctive is an existential dimension which is the warrior's and ours by association—for the moment at least, we still listen (even thrill) to the stories of the warrior's deeds.

But we now translate the warrior's experience into a different language. We encourage our own warriors to put existence before essence. Some readers will recognize this as an echo of Albert Camus' famous plea at the end of World War Two to put survival before the wish to forge a better world. In an atomic age it was the urgent demand of the times. Today our warriors are asked to kill those who would deny others the right to life whether on the killing fields of Rwanda or the ethnic killing grounds of the Balkans. Our warriors are sanctioned to kill so that others may live; they are sent off to do battle with enemies who would deny the right to life to other people. And more importantly, of course, they are asked to die for the same ends. None of which is the same as killing or dying to make one's own life worthwhile. The warrior remains a human type, but his humanity is extended to an imagined community larger than the nation—the human community, the realization of Rousseau's vision that one cannot be a good citizen knowing that others are oppressed. Indeed, this cosmopolitan vision may be the only way in which warriors can write themselves into the imagination of the rest of us as they continue the age-old struggle to reconcile their instinct for survival with their sense of honour.

19

WAR AND THE FUTURE

WHY WAR IS NOT A SCIENCE (HEISENBERG 1901–76)

What we establish mathematically is objective fact only in small part. In larger part, it is a survey of possibilities.

(Heisenberg, *Dilactica*, 1948)

'War is a great and profound subject which concerns the philosopher as much as the general', claimed Joseph de Maistre (Bell, 2007, p. 52). In the course of the twentieth century, scientists also came to realize that they could no longer adopt an Olympian detachment; they were responsible for their own inventions—they too were challenged to think philosophically. Like many shotgun weddings, that between science and philosophy has had its high and low points. Some great philosophers have been great scientists too: Aristotle, Descartes and Leibnitz come to mind. Some have even made use of scientific work in their philosophical enquiries. And then there is a tradition going back to Galileo and Darwin by which scientists had dabbled with philosophy, and Heisenberg is one of their number. We can say he was forced to turn philosopher by the impact of modern science in its application to war, just as war forced the first historians to philosophize too, including Tacitus whom Gibbon famously called 'the philosopher's historian' (Gay, 1972, p. 30).

Philosophy has even given birth to a number of sciences, such as psychology and cognitive science. Philosophical speculation provides the appropriate methods of asking and answering science's questions (in the case of physics by empirical and mathematical means). One might, writes Grayling, argue that philosophy brings itself into question by finding the right way to deal with its questions so that independent trains of enquiry take over and produce concrete results (Grayling, 2009, p. 265). But it can't do this for war. Philosophy has never allowed military science to become an independent area of enquiry, nor could it—because if we were ever able to make war an independent enquiry (an enquiry independent of philosophy) the independent enquirers would have to confront philosophy all over again at the limits of their advance.

Philosophy, Aristotle reminds us, is born of wonder that we are able to ask questions of existence. Instead of taking the world around us for granted, we seek ultimate causes or try to penetrate a larger reality behind the world we perceive with our senses. Wonder also means bewilderment, because to philosophize is to allow oneself to be bemused (Patocka, 1996, p. xvi). It demands that we carry on a constant conversation with ourselves and others. To problematize life, to find it bewildering, is to acknowledge the variety we find within the unity.

And the A-bomb made war more problematic than ever before. The two bombs dropped on Japan in 1945 were the product of an age that had believed in its hubris that there were no barriers to scientific investigation. Ibsen once remarked that on the ruins of all civilizations one would find the inscription, 'he did not dare' (Holub, 1990, pp. 50–51). But daring too much, venturing into the unknown, taking a great leap into the dark, threatened to bring civilization to an end. In science the action often precedes the comprehension—of no other invention was this more true than the research on the atomic bomb. There were some members of Oppenheimer's team in the New Mexico desert on the day of the first nuclear test who even feared that it might trigger off a chain reaction that would destroy the world. The species had gone from accounting for its existence by inventing all all-inventing God to perfecting the means of self-destruction as a paradoxical proof of its own omnipotence. The impulse to create had become pregnant with the impulse to destroy.

These were desperate times. In 1947 the US Joint Chiefs of Staff asked the Atomic Energy Authority for a programme of bomb production capable within a few years of 'killing a nation'. The deadline which they set expired two years before Heisenberg delivered the Gifford Lectures from which I have quoted above (Kassimeris, 2006,

p. 56). It was an age when Herman Kahn began theorizing about how thermonuclear weapons might be used effectively, offering his sponsors at the RAND Corporation what one British politician called a 'Sears Roebuck catalogue of nuclear options' (Healey, 1989, p. 247). At times, the atomic age really did seem to bear out Camus' despairing conclusion that 'the only serious philosophical question is that of suicide'.

Heisenberg, one of the great physicists of his age, was invited by the University of St Andrews to deliver the Gifford Lectures in 1955–6. They were subsequently published as *Physics and Philosophy* and have remained in print ever since. Heisenberg reminded his audience that the invention of thermonuclear weapons had changed the political structure of the world. He himself had been involved in the Nazi nuclear programme—to what extent is still a matter of conjecture, though the issue is discussed in Michael Frayn's play *Copenhagen* (1998). What made Heisenberg an acute observer of his times was that he refused to fall in with the popular fallacy that the atomic age had rendered war obsolete. He considered this much too optimistic a conclusion. On the contrary, the absurdity of nuclear war made war on a smaller scale much more likely:

> Any nation—or political group which is convinced of its historical and moral right to enforce some change to the present situation—will feel that the use of conventional arms for this purpose will not involve any great risks; they will assume that the other side will certainly not have recourse to the nuclear weapons since the other side, being historically and morally wrong in this issue, will not take the chance of war on a large scale. (Heisenberg, 1989, p. 179)

It was the absolute 'totalitarian' certainty of belief that Heisenberg thought more dangerous than the actual weapons the superpowers continued to develop and deploy. We must, he told the students, realize that what looks historically or morally right to one side may look wrong to the other. The only way out was for everyone to show greater tolerance of each other's ideological positions. Indeed, quantum science had shown that a complete picture of reality is not to be had. In the world of politics this meant that no one had access to absolute truth.

The best philosophers have always insisted that they have no access to the truth because they cannot reveal it (if it is there to be revealed). They cannot even have the consolation of religion, which allows its devotees to apprehend truths through faith. They can only tease out the truth as it appears to them (and us at particular times). 'Philosophy comes to consist in an invitation, a path, a point of access' into the truth, writes Alain Badiou (Badiou, 2008, pp. 15–16). Whenever philosophers have claimed access to the truth (whenever they have attempted like Marx to turn philosophy into a science) the outcome has ended in disaster. And although Marx cannot be blamed for the errors or even crimes committed in his name after his death, he lent himself to the distortion of his own philosophical enquiry by claiming a privileged access to the meaning of history. (Nietzsche's fate also reveals we have responsibility not only for what we say, but how we say it.)

It is an ethical demand in philosophy, adds Badiou, to conserve *polemos* (or the dialectical conflict) in order to avoid *stasis* (Badiou, 2008, p. 19). For it is the conflict of ideas, dreams, aspirations and ambitions that makes up the glorious and yet daunting complexity of life. It is pointless to try to end conflict by realizing truth in time, rather than eternity. To realize it in time, he adds, would be to foreclose any further development of ourselves, any future 'becoming'. The future is open-ended; because it is, what we must do is channel conflict into different ends. War doesn't have to be the only, or even major, way of resolving disputes and differences of opinion. There's no determinism here. We could even go out of the war business if we ever collectively chose to do so.

In the quantum world probabilities, wave functions and quanta all involve radically new ways of seeing reality. What Heisenberg was suggesting was that the measure of humanity in the nuclear age was the willingness to accept that truth is subjective. What is true for us is not necessarily true for other people. All the historical truths of the last century were all-pervasive because they were considered to be, in turn, subsets of the biggest historical myth of all—progress. Heisenberg argued passionately that the stories we tell ourselves are important: they change the world just as the world, when it changes, changes us. So we should be careful about the stories we tell ourselves and others. Reductionism is dangerous because there is no way of ordering the world politically any more than there is of ordering history. Historians, for the most part, like philosophers, have gone from trying to order life to studying it in all its complexity.

Heisenberg's greatest contribution to the new science remains the Indeterminacy Principle which maintains that an electron cannot have a world-defined position and a world-defined momentum in the absence of an actual observation of either its position or its momentum. One cannot usefully talk about what an electron is doing between observations because it is the observation alone that creates the reality of the electron. The electron possesses both wave-like and particle-like aspects, either of which can be manifested, but neither of which has any meaning in the absence of a specific experimental context. Any talk of what is really going on is just an attempt to infuse the quantum world with a spurious concreteness for the ease of our own imagination (Davies, 1989, p. 10).

As Heisenberg insisted, 'what we observe is not nature itself, but nature exposed in our method of questioning'. Just as we cannot have access to a larger truth beyond experience, so it is clear that our powers of empirical perception, like our powers of pure logical conception, are both incapable of making sense of reality as a whole. It is not that there is no such 'wholeness' to grasp; it is that there is no 'objective reality' that runs its course regardless of our interest in it. The distinctions between objective and subjective are no longer fixed. We are what we observe: the world is what we make of it. We cannot, in other words, distinguish ideas (forms) from a real world constantly in flux which copies them, because those changing realities can only be understood through the ideas. Heisenberg's exit strategy was modern and it owed everything to western science, which postulated an immanent (not transcendent) order in nature which could be understood and explained in its own terms. Quantum physics forces us back on ourselves, which is where the invention of philosophy began.

Heisenberg's universe is radical for that reason. The Indeterminacy Principle can be rephrased thus: the external world contributes to the content of experience, but the mind regulates the form those experiences must take. Thus there can be no conclusive or final interpretation of experience. The world is, as Heraclitus claimed, in constant flux—the persistent shape and identity of oceans and rivers are maintained by the endless flux of the particles that arrange themselves to compose them. In other words, there are no fixed things, no fully specifiable entities, because the constituents of the things we take for granted (such as the oceans and rivers) can never be precisely and completely determined. Which is why you cannot have causality as we have traditionally understood it. A cause cannot lead to a predictable effect. And war is notoriously unpredictable, particularly in its consequences. We can never eliminate collateral damage; the stronger does not always succeed in imposing its will (quality is not always translated into quality); war can degenerate into a political warfare quickly enough.

Quantum mechanics echoes what Heraclitus intuited: the random is neither a construct nor a form of exclusion (Frayn, p. 80). It arises naturally from the fact of observation. The only predictions we can make are probabilistic ones. As Frayn adds, indeterminacy is not confined to the world of sub-atomic particles. Some of the practical implications in other fields have turned out to be significant. For most of us, the anomalies of life are so small as to be meaningless. In war they are all too real. Those anomalies have substance, like Pascal's Rules, only in the context of human thought and purpose, both of which will determine their significance or meaning. Which brings us back to where we began, to Heraclitus. The complexity which war promotes makes it ever more complex. Understanding the 'rules' will only change that to the extent that it changes our attitudes to war itself.

There is a parallel here, writes Frayn, with the indeterminacy of particles, and the indeterminacy of our experience of war, of course, prevents it shaping our knowledge and behaviour no more than the indeterminacy of particles prevents them determining the physical structure and chemical behaviour (Frayn, 2008, p. 392). Indeterminacy does not change the reality of war: some win, some lose. As Donald Rumsfeld might add, history happens (but not, as he himself experienced in Iraq, in ways that any of us can necessarily predict in advance). 'Shock and awe' was not, as the term suggested, cause and effect. The Iraqis may have been shocked, but in the event they were not awed.

Heisenberg's universe challenges (as he himself wrote) the great nineteenth-century philosophical ideas of Hegel and Marx and their uncompromising beliefs and certainties. In the eyes of the physicist they rely far too much on the mechanical concept of causality, especially its Kantian a priori character. Quantum mechanism is a statistical theory (Davies, 1989, p. 5). It can make definite predictions about the ensemble of identical systems, but generally it cannot tell us anything definite about an individual system. And where it differs significantly from other statistical theories, such as weather forecasting or economics, is that the chance element is inherent in the nature of the quantum system and not merely arises from our limited grasp of all the variables that affect the system.

Of course we mustn't make the mistake of confusing categories. Human beings are not electrons. They are self-conscious beings who are able to establish connections with others like themselves on the basis of calculations of self-interest or empathy. The problem with

Hobbes' account of the state of nature is that it is too atomistic; humans are not like atoms colliding with other atoms. In reality they are not individuals but social beings that only survive by coalescing, cooperating and conjoining with others like themselves.

The pre-Socratics may have been depressed by the awareness of the brevity and triviality of human life, but they were also inspired by its unfolding potential. Heisenberg thought Heraclitus had been right to regard fire as the basic element of that potentiality, employed as a metaphor (Heisenberg, 1989, p. 50). The difficulty of reconciling the idea of one fundamental principle with an infinite variety of phenomena had been solved by recognizing that the strife of the opposite is really a harmony. The world is so complex—it presents such an infinite variety of things and events, colours and sounds—that in order to understand it we have to introduce some kind of order, and order means some kind of unity. It is the 'tension of opposites' that constitutes the unity of the One. From this springs the belief that there is one fundamental principle: change. 'We must know that war is common to all and strife is justice and that all things come into being and pass away through strife' (Heraclitus) (Warren, 2007, p. 51).

But change is not a material cause. It is represented in Heraclitus' philosophy by fire as the basic element which is both matter and a moving force. For fire is dynamic—it transforms fuel into heat and light. It is an obvious choice for a writer who thought the universe was in constant flux. 'All things are repayment for fire, and fire for all things just as goods are for gold, and gold for goods' (Warren, 2007, p. 65). There is an exchange value here, but you can only exchange valuables if there is a marketplace in which goods can be traded. There is an economy of violence, too, in the world, but not in the state of nature, the cosmic night.

Heisenberg took this idea into the quantum world by replacing the word 'fire' with the word 'energy'. Energy is the ultimate convertible currency. The formula $E=mc^2$ tells us that energy can be turned into matter and vice versa. Heisenberg also had a mathematical formula. Energy can be changed into motion, light and heat. We know that mass and energy are essentially the same concept, that all elementary particles consist of energy, and that energy is the essential property or substance of the world. Energy is the primary cause of all change. More recently some writers have claimed that it is information, not energy or fire, that is the chief motivating force of the universe:

Information is ... the material of which all the elementary particles, all atoms and therefore all things in general are made and at the same time information is also that which is moved ... Information can be transformed into movement, heat, light and tension. Information can be regarded as the cause of all change in the world. (Siegfried, 2000, p. 8)

This viewpoint, concedes the author, is much further than many scientists would be prepared to go, but the information processing model does not invalidate the old one: it complements Heisenberg's model as his own complemented Heraclitus'. It offers a different way of understanding the same thing; what powers complexity.

Soldiers may not yet be information processors but many spend a large part of their time on simulation and VR systems that take them away from the world of experience and embed them in a world of information. As they know more about the world in terms of information, so they may know less about war as lived experience. And yet the world manifestly has not done away with war and possibly never will. For that reason it is all the more incumbent upon the societies that wish to remain in the game to understand what Pascal called the 'rules'. But the rules are becoming increasingly difficult to apply. Even great powers are finding it difficult to translate a tactical success into a conclusive political outcome.

And Heisenberg provides one explanation. We may know the forces in the atomic nucleus that are responsible for the emission of alpha-particles, but this knowledge contains uncertainty brought about by the interaction between the nucleus and the rest of the world. If we wanted to know why the alpha-particle was emitted at a particular time, we would have to know the microscopic structure of the whole world, including ourselves, and that is impossible. Causation in the quantum world is no longer mechanical. This makes it difficult to buy in fully to a *rule-based* system including war.

As Alan Beyerchen writes, just as in most other activities, in war too the 'authoritative guide' for western thinking has been that of linearity. By this he means the idea of proportionality or constant returns to scale (in terms of output versus input) and additivity (the whole is equal to the sum of its parts). Now we are finding counter-intuitively that life is distinctly non-linear. 'Small' causes can have disproportionately large consequences, while the 'parts' of human society and the international system cannot be readily compartmentalized owing to the strength of the synergies between them. This can largely be attributed to the influence of human factors on causal relationships and interactions. History, psychology and culture multiply or diminish causal effects as well as engendering a synthesis between entities. The sum of the parts does not always equal the whole. Feedback loops (based on indeterminacy and 'trigger effects') often ensure that the interactions between cause and effect are mutually constitutive (Beyerchen, 1992–3, p. 61).

I suspect that Heisenberg would have been unimpressed by our deep interest in predictive computer modelling and war gaming programmes. For they won't help make war any more predictable either. The constitutive algorithms, comprising the various possible tactical situations like player actions and eventual end-game scenarios, are all developed by human programmers and thus are constrained by the limits of their imagination, their cognitive ability and their susceptibility to cognitive dissonance.

None of this is to devalue the 'rules' I have sought to identify in this book. It is however a reason to drop the term, and embrace my preferred term, 'regularities'. Quantum science does not deal in prediction—though it does allow probabilities to be specified precisely, as Paul Davies writes in an introduction to the Penguin version of Heisenberg's book. In such a complex universe, relationships count most. We define important factors not with regard to an 'essence' but connections with other factors. As Heisenberg writes, just as no fact can stand alone apart from its association with other facts, so modern physics now divides the world, not into different groups of objects, but different groups of connections. Our chief intellectual concern is not grasping objects as a form of knowledge but our relationship with other people and the natural world. Modern physics now admits that many important factors in the universe may not be open to clear definitions; all that scientists can do is to define them with respect to their connections. And the main point about connections is that they are complex as opposed to complicated (Lukacs, 2006, p. 66). So too is war: it is what distinguishes it most from warfare.

Rousseau revisited

Given that the philosophers invented war, why has philosophy not received its full due? Why have philosophers been ignored so often by the rest of us (especially in the military)? It is not just the language they use, for until the eighteenth century it was readily accessible to any intelligent person. And writing about war, philosophers tended to eschew metaphysics and address real problems in a very practical language. The problem actually lies with philosophy itself.

First, the great philosophers, when writing about war, were conditioned by the issues of their own time (by its character). Take the three-dimensional nature of war, which Plato explains as essential to its nature. He was interested in the 'Achilles problem', which *The Republic* is designed to solve. To do that, he had to ban the poets (the very group that idealized the warriors, and made them fit subjects for emulation). Plato rejected Homer because he thought Achilles, though undeniably brave, was unfit to be a role model for a citizen. He therefore tried to suppress the existential element of war (another reason why he also attacked the way in which the great poets had stimulated warriors over the centuries to try to re-enact Achilles' deeds). We will not grasp what motivated him to do this, if we see *The Iliad* only as a poem. We should think of it instead more as the Bible—a book of social etiquette which told its readers how they should behave. We find repeated references to what is 'proper' or 'fitting'.

Machiavelli's dislike of the existential element of war was informed by a different fear, that of mercenaries. If we think of mercenaries only in terms of members of private security companies today, or the French Foreign Legion, or going back further in time to the Hessian soldiers serving the British in the American Revolutionary war, we will not appreciate his real concern. Mercenaries were the terrorists of their age who were quite prepared to turn on their masters and compromise their interests whenever they were not paid. Even pirates who hired themselves out when countries went to war against each other engaged in extraordinary acts of terror, such as the sacking of Panama City in 1690. Machiavelli was anxious to suppress the appetites; 'civic militarism' had little time for the existential dimension.

Secondly, distortions in emphasis were compounded by another factor. Philosophers, in writing about war, tended to begin philosophizing from the point of view of their own philosophical concerns. Plato had a particular interest in *praxis* and, particularly towards the end of his life, in the philosopher-king. Marx's writings on war are more important than they have been given credit for, for his concerns were largely how industrialization and mechanization were changing the nature of war. The machine, he wrote, never creates value, but merely transforms its own value to the product. In the case of war, the machine had called into question not only the role of the warrior on the battlefield, but even the prospect of writing about war in epic terms. Was Achilles possible in an age of gunpowder, he asks. He correctly predicted, as it happened, the demise of the epic poem, though he had to await the real industrialization of warfare in 1915 for its eventual demise. And industrialization did not arrive with the introduction of factories, it arose out of the measurement of work. It is when a job can be measured, when you hitch a man to a job, when you can measure his output, that you have modern industrialization. The warrior's output was measured, too, in a product: firepower.

Beyond cultural bias and personal idiosyncrasy, philosophers in writing about war have added a third factor which inheres to the character of western philosophy itself. It is highly polemical. It is, in every sense of the word, agonistic. Philosophers are always arguing for the one true position, whether Plato, Machiavelli or Marx. Plato had it in for the arts because the great heroes and characters of literature were flawed human beings, and because they brought out the worst in spectators. There is a telling anecdote in *The Republic* about a man called Leontius who was walking along the north wall of Athens when he came across a group of dead prisoners who had just been executed for crime. He wanted to look at them, but also felt disgust. He walked away and then came back, his eyes wide open. 'Look for yourselves, you evil wretches' (he said, addressing his eyes). 'Take your fill of this beautiful sight.' Yes, there is an aesthetics of violence, as Nietzsche and others understood. Even death can be 'beautiful'. It can certainly move us. For Aristotle, by contrast, the arts were vital to the instrumental world—theatre was vital to Athenian democracy. On the stage the citizen saw re-enacted the drama of his own political life, and was therefore better informed not only of his condition, but also his responsibilities as a citizen. For Aristotle, art and politics were joined at the hip.

Machiavelli's concerns were similarly polemical. Not all mercenaries turned on their paymasters, or wrecked cities; many were a great deal more instrumental in their purposes than he suggested. Indeed, the examples he gives us are striking precisely because the men he paints seem to have no existential interest in war, and are certainly not willing to make sacrifices, or put their lives on the line for anyone.

For all three reasons I have chosen in this book to take a comprehensive, and therefore inclusive, approach to the subject. It is one that ranges across centuries and transcends historical interests and philosophical schools of thought, while reflecting, as it must, the interests of the schools at the time. For philosophy has its own dialectics. Philosophers interact too with the world, and the history they and others make, and each of the philosophers I cite were influenced by the changing character of war, which fed back, often quite noticeably, into their work. What is striking about the fifteen authors I have invoked in this work is that they found themselves on the inside of the history they were trying to comprehend. In that sense, the rules they imparted about war were not like the laws of physics that exist prior to our own existence on the planet. Philosophy is more like psychology and economics; such sciences also propose laws, but they only appear with, and are dependent upon, our own observation.

As Matthew Arnold claimed, for the creation of any masterpiece, two powers must combine—the power of the author and the power of the moment, and one is not enough without the other. The moment in question was that great 'mind event' (the term is W.H. Auden's), the French Revolution, though to speak of the power of the moment is not to gainsay the power of the writer. Most of my selected authors lived in interesting times. Heraclitus found himself writing in a period of social conflict in the Greek city-states, which eventually drove him into exile (the world of the city-states was a giant laboratory in which we see many of our own contemporary practices reflected back, including 'regime change'—social conflicts within the city walls were fuelled by outside powers who sought to support or overthrow from within democratic or oligarchic regimes). In the wake of the defeat of Athens, Plato turned to philosophy to make what sense he could of its predicament, and the madness which had condemned its greatest philosopher—Socrates—to death for impiety. He left as a result the first complete corpus of philosophical works, which in time became the foundation of the western philosophical canon. Hobbes was writing at a time not just of civil war at home, but of what some historians identify as a 'general crisis' that engulfed all the monarchies of western Europe and transformed competitiveness back into competition—or back into the state of nature from which most seventeenth-century Europeans thought they had escaped.

Marx and Engels, for their part, were aware that the Industrial Revolution had made technology the determining factor in war. 'We see ... that the now *objective* existence of industry has become the open book of the human consciousness, human psychology perceived in sensory terms' (Sebald, 2005, p. 98). Nietzsche was all too aware that the conscript armies of his own day would be unleashed in a ruinous world war. He wrote that he had to escape to the mountains to avoid the 'silent rage' he would experience if he were to make an 'eye witness to the politics' of his own age (Nietzsche, 2001, p. 339). Heisenberg and his generation did not live long enough to witness the nuclear endgame to which the pursuit of grand politics eventually gave rise.

Is there a general lesson to be drawn from this book? If there is one it is this. As Heisenberg astutely outlined, what today we would call the process of globalization has not, alas, brought conflict to an end. Paradoxically (and war inheres in paradoxes of all kinds, as I have tried to illustrate in this work), the very fact that so much of the world finds itself mired in a state of nature—that warfare (not war) would seem to be the norm in contemporary international affairs—makes it all the more important that the rest of the world adhere to the rules (the practices and conventions that philosophers over the centuries have invoked to differentiate war from warfare). If we ignore the Kantian imperatives, we end up with Guantanamo Bay, or extraordinary rendition; if we ignore St Augustine's insight that peace is a contested concept, we are likely to conclude that the peace for which we are fighting is an incontestable good—that our peace should be everyone else's. Too often in today's fight against terrorism, we also ignore Aristotle's admonition that war must remain a political activity, not a moral crusade against a concept—terrorism.

In writing this book, I was influenced to a large extent by the problems and challenges that face the west today. But I have also put pen to paper with the near future in mind as well. Pick up any book on contemporary war and you will find reflections on the future (robotics promises to take us into and across the next frontier; mercenaries seem to have been re-invented as private security companies). The constant 'restlessness of technology' (the phrase is Hans Jonas') is always promising to deliver something not only innovative, but revolutionary; we are told we live in a permanently revolutionary age—hence the American military's fascination with all things technological. It would be wrong, nevertheless, to think that any of these developments are likely to be revolutionary enough to change the nature of war itself. Try though we will, we will never transform war into a science with bind-ing rules. We will deal only with those regularities that, in their very paradoxical nature, we will continue to find frustrating.

I expect that this book will upset many readers, including philosophers who will object to my handling of philosophy. Some will find fault with my own reading of particular works which has been influenced by certain writers—Gadamer on Heraclitus, Stanley Rosen on Plato etc. Others who engage in narrow textual analysis will find fault with its broad eclectic sweep. Militarists, too, may find it too abstract, or removed from the realities that they face every day. One recalls the story of the philosopher Musonius Rufus who, Tacitus tells us, was afforded a rare opportunity as a philosopher to address the troops on the frontier. It was not a great success. He was ridiculed and jostled, and would have been trampled on (Tacitus tells us) if he had not 'listened to the warnings of the quieter soldiers and the threats of others, and given up his untimely wisdom'. Many philosophers have thought their words of wisdom wasted on the military, which is a pity. Aristotle did not. He gave Alexander the Great an annotated version of *The Iliad* which he took with him on his campaigns; its loss is one that we should regret, for it might have given us a further insight into the mind of one of the greatest of all philosophers.

And there will be those horrified by the general thesis of this book. There will be some who will not want to draw a distinction between war and warfare, indeed who feel that the very attempt perpetuates conflict. There will be those who, like Rousseau, think it is incumbent upon us to think of ways of abolishing war, not finessing it. But the great philosophers have tried to find the rules of war not because of their interest in war, but because of their pronounced interest in life. For most the brutality and evil of war has been real enough; few have been cheerleaders. Unlike Musonius Rufus, fewer still have been given the opportunity to address soldiers in the field in the expectation of being listened to. It is their intellectual detachment which has allowed them to see war in all its forms and colours. Contrary to Rousseau's claim, few ever mistook discussion for the thing itself. The history of war offers a sobering lesson. We do not know better, and frequently we do not know more. Instead, we have to relearn again and again the lessons that were imparted centuries ago. In the end, it is our failures, not successes, that force us back to our books.

BIBLIOGRAPHY

Ackroyd, Peter, *Albion: The Origins of the English Imagination* (London: Chatto and Windus, 2002).
Allen, Barry, *Knowledge and Civilisation* (Boulder: Westview Books, 2004).
Alvarez, Al, *Risky Business* (London: Bloomsbury, 2007).
Angelo, Sydney, *Machiavelli* (London: Paladin, 1969).
Ansell-Pearson, Keith, *How to Read Nietzsche* (London: Granta, 2005).
Aristotle, *The Poetics* (trans. Stephen Halliwell) (Chapel Hill: University of North Carolina Press, 1987).
Armstrong, Karen, *The History of God* (London: Vintage, 1999). *A Short History of Myth* (Edinburgh: Canongate, 2005).
Aron, Raymond, *18 Lectures on Industrial Society* (London: Weidenfeld and Nicolson, 1970).
Ashworth, John, *Capitalism in the Ante Bellum Republic, Volume 2, The Coming of the Civil War 1950–61* (Cambridge: Cambridge University Press, 2008).
Auerbach, Erich, *Mimesis: Representations of Reality in Western Literature* (New York: Garden City, 1953).
Augustine (ed. R.W. Dyson), *The City of God against the Pagans* (Cambridge: Cambridge University Press, 1998).
Aurelius, Marcus, *The Meditations* (London: Dent, 1968).
Bacevich, Andrew, 'Illusions of Managing History: the enduring relevance of Reinhold Niebuhr', *Historically Speaking*, 10:3, January-February 2008.
Badiou, Alain, *Infinite Thought: Truth and the Return of Philosophy* (trans./ed. Oliver Feltham and Justin Clemens) (London: Continuum, 2006), *Conditions* (London: Continuum, 2008).
Baldick, Chris, *In Frankenstein's Shadow: Myths, Monstrosity, and Nineteenth-Century Writing* (Oxford: Clarendon Press, 1990).
Ballard, J.G. *A User's Guide to the Millennium* (London: Flamingo, 1997) *Miracles of Life: An Autobiography* (London: Harper, 2008).
Balzac, Honoré de (ed.), *Napoleon: Aphorisms and Thoughts* (London: Oneworld Classics, 2008).

BIBLIOGRAPHY

Bartov, Omer, *Hitler's Army in the Third Reich* (Oxford: Oxford University Press, 1991).

Bauman, Zygmunt, *Does Ethics have a Chance in a World of Consumers?* (Cambridge: Harvard University Press, 2008).

Bayerchen, Alan, 'Non-linearity and the unpredictability of war', *International Security*, 17:3 (Winter 1992).

Beer, Francis and de Landtscheer, Christ'l (eds) *Metaphorical World Politics* (East Lansing: Michigan State University Press, 2004).

Bell, Daniel, *The End of Ideology* (Cambridge: Harvard University Press, 2000).

Bell, David, *The First Total War: Napoleon's Europe and the Birth of Modern Warfare* (London: Bloomsbury, 2007).

Benedict, Ruth, *Patterns of Culture* (London: Routledge, 1935).

Bernstein, Richard, *Philosophical Profiles: Essays in a Pragmatic Mode* (Oxford: Blackwell, 1986).

Bessell, Richard, *Nazism and War* (London: Phoenix, 2004).

Blackburn, Simon, *Plato's Republic: A Biography* (London: Atlantic, 2006).

Blainey, Geoffrey, *The Causes of War* (London: Macmillan, 1973).

Blanning, T.C.W., *The French Revolutionary Wars 1787–1802* (London: Edward Arnold, 1996).

Bloom, Harold, *Shakespeare: The Invention of the Human* (London: Fourth Estate,1999), *Genius* (London: Fourth Estate, 2002).

Bobbit, Philip, *Shield of Achilles War, Peace and the Course of History* (London: Allen Lane, 2002), *Terror and Consent: The Wars for the Twenty-First Century* (London: Allen Lane, 2008).

Boehmer, Elleke, *Colonial and Postcolonial Literature* (London: Opus, 1995).

Booker, Christopher, *The Seven Basic Plots: Why We Tell Stories* (London: Continuum, 2004).

Bourke, Joanna, *An Intimate History of Killing: Face to Face Killing in 20th Century Warfare* (London: Granta, 1999), 'Barbarization v. Civilization in time of war' in George Kassimeris, *The Barbarization of Warfare* (London: C. Hurst & Co., 2006).

Bracken, Paul, *Fire in the East: the Rise of Asian Military Power and the Second Nuclear Age* (London: Harper Collins, 1999).

Bree, Germaine, *Camus and Sartre: Crisis and Commitment* (London: Calder and Boyars, 1974).

Brodsky, Joseph, *Less than One: Selected Essays* (London: Penguin, 1987).

Brunt, P.A., 'Thucydides the compassionate historian' in Albert Fell (ed.), *History and Historians* (London: Oliver and Boyd, 1968).

Buchanan, Mark, *Small Worlds: Uncovering Nature's Hidden Networks* (London: Phoenix, 2002).

Bungay, Stephen, *The Most Dangerous Enemy: A History of the Battle of Britain* (London: Aurum Press, 2000).

BIBLIOGRAPHY

Burgess, Anthony (trans. and adapted), *Sophocles: Oedipus Rex* (Minnesota: University of Minnesota Press, 1972).
Burrow, John, *A History of Histories* (London: Allen Lane, 2007).
Calasso, Roberto and Shepley, John, *The 49 Steps* (London: Random House, 2002).
Campbell, Joseph, *The Hero with a Thousand Faces* (Princeton: Princeton University Press, 1963).
Caputo, Philip, *A Rumour of War* (London: Macmllan, 1978).
Carr, E.H., *What is History?* (London: Penguin, 1971).
Cartledge, Paul, *The Greeks: A Portrait of Self and Others* (Oxford: Oxford University Press, 2002).
Chambers, James, *The Devil's Horsemen: The Mongol Invasion of Europe* (London: Phoenix, 1979).
Clastres, Pierre, *Society Against the State* (Cambridge: Zone Books, 1974).
Clausewitz, Carl von, *On War* (trans. Peter Paret/Michael Howard) (Princeton: Princeton University Press, 1976).
Coker, Christopher, *The Future of War: The re-enchantment of war in the 21st century* (Oxford: Basil Blackwell, 2005).
Collingwood R.G., *The Idea of History* (Oxford: Oxford University Press, 1970).
Craig, Leon, *The War Lover: A Study of Plato's Republic* (Toronto: University of Toronto Press, 1994).
Critchley, Simon, *The Book of Dead Philosophers* (London: Granta, 2008).
David, Saul, *Victoria's Wars* (London: Penguin, 2006).
Davies, Paul, *Introduction to Heisenberg, Physics and Philosophy* (London: Penguin, 1989), *The Goldilocks Enigma: Why is the Universe just right for life?* (London: Penguin, 2006).
Davis, Mike, *Planet of Slums* (London: Verso, 2006).
Dawkins, Richard, *The Selfish Gene* (Oxford: Oxford University Press, 1976).
Delgado, James, *Khubilai Khan's Lost Fleet* (London: Bodley Head, 2009).
Dennett, Daniel, *Darwin's Dangerous Idea* (London: Penguin, 1996), *Breaking the Spell: Religion as a Natural Phenomenon* (London: Penguin, 2006).
Doctorow, E.L. *City of God* (New York: Little, Brown, 2000), *Creationists: Essays* (New York: Random House, 2007).
Dodds, E.R., *The Greeks and the Irrational* (Berkeley: University of California Press, 1971), 'Plato and the Irrational Soul' in Gregory Vlastos (ed.), *Plato II: Ethics, Politics, Philosophy* (London: Macmillan, 1971).
Dower, John, *War Without Mercy* (New York: Pantheon, 1986), *Embracing Defeat: Japan in the Aftermath of World War II* (London: Penguin, 1999).
Dupuy, Trevor, *Understanding War: History and Theory of Combat* (New York: Pen & Sword Books Ltd, 1987).
Ehrenreich, Barbara, *Blood Rites: Origins and History of the Passions of War* (London: Virago, 1997).

BIBLIOGRAPHY

Eliot, Thomas, *The Use of Poetry and the Use of Criticism* (London: Faber & Faber, 1964).
Ellis, John, *The Social History of the Machine Gun* (London: Pimlico, 1976).
Engels, Frederick, *Anti–Dühring* (Leipzig, 1878).
Euben, Peter, *Platonic Noise* (Princeton, NJ: Princeton University Press, 2003).
Feldman, Allen, *Formations of Violence* (London: Politico, 1991).
Ferguson, Adam, *An Essay on the History of Civil Society* (Farnborough: Gregg, 1969).
Ferguson, Nial, *Colossus: The Rise and Fall of the American Empire* (London: Penguin, 2004).
Ferrarin, Alfredo, *Hegel and Aristotle* (Cambridge: Cambridge University Press, 2001).
Ferrill, Arthur, *The Fall of the Roman Empire: The Military Explanation* (London: Thames and Hudson, 1986).
Finkielkraut, Alain, *In the Name of Humanity: Reflections on the Twentieth Century* (London: Pimlico, 2001).
Ford, Dennis, *The Search for Meaning: A Short History* (Berkeley, California: University of California Press, 2007).
Franco, Paul, *Hegel's Philosophy of Freedom* (New Haven: Yale University Press, 1999).
Frayn, Michael, *Copenhagen* (London: Methuen, 1998), *The Human Touch: Our Part in the Creation of the Universe* (London: Faber & Faber, 2008).
Freeman, Charles, *AD 381: Heretics, Pagans and the Christian State* (London: Pimlico, 2008).
Frisch, Max, *Sketchbook 1946–1949* (New York: Harcourt Brace, 1983).
Froese, Katrin, *Rousseau and Nietzsche: Towards an Aesthetic Morality* (New York: Lexington, 2001).
Fukuyama, Francis, *The End of History and the Last Man* (New York: Free Press, 1992).
Gadamer, Hans-Georg, *Truth and Method,Dialogue and Dialectic: Eight Hermeneutical Studies on Plato* (New Haven: Yale University Press, 1980), *Literature and Philosophy in Dialogue: Essays in German Literary Theory* (Albany: State University of New York Press, 1994), *The Beginning of Philosophy* (New York: Continuum, 1998), *The Beginning of Knowledge* (New York: Continuum, 2001), *A Century of Philosophy: A Conversation with Riccardo Dottori* (New York: Continuum, 2006).
Gallie, W.B., *Philosophy and Historical Understanding* (London: Chatto & Windus, 2004), *Philosophers of War: Kant, Clausewitz, Marx, Engels and Tolstoy* (Cambridge: Cambridge University Press, 1978), *Understanding War* (London: Routledge, 1991).
Gauchet, Marcel, *The Disenchantment of the World: A Political History of Religion* (Princeton, NJ: Princeton University Press, 1998).
Gay, Peter, *The Enlightenment: An Interpretation, Volume I: The Rise of Modern Paganism* (London: Wildwood House, 1973), *Volume II: The Science of*

BIBLIOGRAPHY

Freedom (London: Wildwood House, 1973), *The Bourgeois Experience: From Victoria to Freud, Volume III: The Cultivation of Hatred* (New York: Norton, 1993).

Gillespie, Michael, *Hegel, Heidegger and the Ground of History* (Chicago: University of Chicago Press, 1984).

Girard, René, *Evolution and Conversion: Dialogues of the Origins of Culture* (London: Continuum, 2007).

Goldstein, Joshua, *War and Gender: How Gender Shapes the War System and Vice Versa* (Cambridge: Cambridge University Press, 2001).

Gottlieb, Anthony, *The Dream of Reason: A History of Philosophy from the Greeks to the Renaissance* (London: Allen Lane, 2000).

Gottschall, Jonathan, *The Rape of Troy: Evolution, Violence and the World of Homer* (Cambridge: Cambridge University Press, 2008).

Gratzen, Walter (ed.), *Longman Literary Companion to Science* (London: Longman, 1989).

Gray, Colin, *Modern Strategy* (Oxford: Oxford University Press, 1991).

Gray, Jesse Glenn, *The Warriors: Reflections on Men in Battle* (Lincoln: University of Nebraska Press, 1959).

Grayling, A.C., *Liberty in the Age of Terror* (London: Bloomsbury, 2009).

Greene, Brian, *The Elegant Universe: Superstrings, Hidden Dimensions and the Quest for the Ultimate Theory* (London: Vintage, 2000).

Greenfield, Susan, *The Quest for Identity in the 21st Century* (London: Sceptre, 2008).

Habermas, Jurgen, *The Divided West* (Cambridge: Polity, 2006).

Halberstam, David, *The Coldest Winter: America and the Korean War* (London: Macmillan, 2008).

Hanson, Victor Davis, *The Western Way of Warfare: Infantry Battles in Classical Greece* (Oxford: Oxford University Press, 1989), 'Socrates Dies at Delium' in Cowley, Robert, *More What If?* (London: Macmillan, 2001), *Why the West has Won* (New York: Doubleday, 2002), *A War Like No Other* (London: Methuen, 2006).

Harman, David, 'History's New Pessimists', *Prospect*, July 2008.

Harris, Marvin, *Cannibals and Kings: the Origins of Cultures* (London: Collins, 1978), *Cows, Pigs, Wars and Witches: The Riddle of Culture* (New York: Vintage, 1989).

Harris, Sam, *The End of Faith: Religion, Terror and the Future of Reason* (New York: Norton, 2004).

Hayman, Ronald, *Nietzsche: A Critical Life* (London: Phoenix, 1995).

Haythornwaite, Paul, *Hard to Kill: Famous Napoleonic Battles* (London: Cassell, 1996).

Hazlitt, William, *Selected Writings* (Oxford: Oxford University Press, 1991).

Healey, Denis, *The Time of My Life* (London: Michael Joseph, 1989).

Hegel, Friedrich, *Elements of the Philosophy of Right* (Allen W. Wood, ed.) (Cambridge: Cambridge University Press, 2008).

Heisenberg, Werner, *Physics and Philosophy* (London: Penguin, 1989).

BIBLIOGRAPHY

Herzog, Tobey, *Vietnam War Stories: Innocence Lost* (London: Routledge, 1992).
Hill, Christopher, *Society and Puritanism* (London: Panther, 1969).
Hillsman, James, *A Terrible Love of War* (London: Penguin, 2004).
Hinsley, F.H., *Power and the Pursuit of Peace: Theory and Practice in the History of Relations Between States* (Cambridge: Cambridge University Press, 1967).
Hobbes, Thomas, *The Leviathan* (London: Penguin, 1971).
Holmes, Richard, *Firing Line* (London: Pimlico, 1994).
Holub, Miroslav, *The Dimension of the Present Moment* (London: Faber & Faber, 1990).
Howard, Michael, *The Invention of Peace: Reflections on War and International Order* (London: Profile, 2000), *Liberation or Catastrophe: Reflections on the History of the 20th Century* (London: Continuum, 2007).
Huizinga, Johan, *Homo Ludens* (Amsterdam: Amsterdam University Press, 1938).
Huxley, Aldous, *Texts and Pretexts* (London: Grafton, 1986).
Huyssen, Andreas, *Twilight Memories: Marking Time in a Culture of Amnesia* (London: Routledge, 1995).
Ignatieff, Michael, *Empire Lite* (New York: Vintage, 2004).
Iriye, Akira, 'War is Peace, Peace is War' in Nobutoshi Haghihara/Philip Windsor (eds), *Experiencing the Twentieth Century* (Tokyo: University of Tokyo Press, 1985).
Irwin, Alistair, 'The Buffalo Thorn: The Nature of the Future Battlefield' in Holden Reid Bryan (ed.), *Military Power: Land Warfare in Theory and Practice* (London: Frank Cass, 1997).
Jaeger, Mary, *Archimedes and the Roman Imagination* (University of Michigan Press, 2009).
James, Clive, *Cultural Amnesia* (London: Picador, 2007), *Revolt of the Pendulum: Essays 2005-8* (London: Picador, 2009).
James, William, *Essential Writings* (ed. Bruce Wilshire) (Albany, New York: State University of New York Press, 1984).
Jarvie, Ian (ed.), *Popper's Open Society After 50 Years: The Continuing Relevance of Karl Popper* (London: Routledge, 2003).
Johnson, Paul, *The Birth of the Modern: World Society 1815-1830* (London: Weidenfeld & Nicolson, 1991).
Johnson, Ray, 'War, Culture and the Interpretation of History: the Vietnam War Reconsidered', *Small Wars and Insurgencies*, 9:2, 1998.
Jones, James, *The Thin Red Line* (New York: Dell, 1998).
Junger, Ernst, *Storm of Steel*,(trans. Michael Hoffman) (London: Penguin, 2004).
Kaplan, Fred, *The Wizards of Armageddon* (New York: Simon & Schuster, 1983).
Kassimeris, George, *The Barbarization of Warfare* (London: C. Hurst & Co., 2006).

BIBLIOGRAPHY

Kateb, George, *Hannah Arendt: Politics, Conscience, Evil* (Totowa: Roman & Allenhead, 1984).

Kaufmann, William, *The Portable Nietzsche* (London: Penguin, 1968).

Keane, John, *Reflections on Violence* (London: Verso, 1996).

Kearney, H.F., 'Scientists and Society' in Ives, E.W., *The English Revolution, 1600–1660* (London: Edward Arnold, 1971).

Keegan, John, *A History of Warfare* (London: Pimlico, 1996), 'In This War of Civilisation, the West will Prevail', *Daily Telegraph*, 8 October 2001, *Churchill* (London: Phoenix, 2002), *Times Literary Supplement*, 18 July 2008.

Kelly, Raymond, *Warrior Societies and the Origins of War* (Ann Arbor: University of Michigan Press, 2000).

Keynes, John, *Essays in Biography* (New York: Norton, 1951).

King, Winter, 'Illegal settlements', *Harvard Law Review*, 44:2, September 2003.

Klein, C.Y., 'Long Defence: Victory without Compliance', *Competitive Strategy*, 15:3, July–September 1996.

Knox, Bernard, *Essays: Ancient and Modern* (Baltimore: Johns Hopkins, 1989).

Kolakowski, Leszek, *The Presence of Myth* (Chicago: Chicago University Press, 1989).

Koselleck, Reinhart, *Futures Past: On the Semantics of Historical Time* (New York: Columbia University Press, 2004).

Kundera, Milan, *The Curtain: An Essay in Seven Parts* (London: Faber & Faber, 2007).

Laidi, Zaki, *A World Without Meaning: Crisis of Meaning in International Politics* (London: Routledge, 1998).

Lakoff, George and Johnson, Mark, *Metaphors We Live By* (Chicago: Chicago University Press, 2003).

Lane-Fox, Robin, *The Classical World: An Epic History from Homer to Hadrian* (London: Allen Lane, 2005), *Travelling Heroes: Greeks and their Myths in the Epic Age of Homer* (London: Allen Lane, 2008).

Lear, Jonathan, *Happiness, Death and the Remainder* (Cambridge, Mass.: Harvard University Press, 2000).

Lebow, Ned, *A Cultural Theory of International Relations* (Cambridge: Cambridge University Press, 2008).

Levin, Michael, *J.S. Mill on Civilisation and Barbarism* (London: Routledge, 2004).

Lichtenberg, Georg (trans. R.J. Hollingdale), *The Waste Book* (New York: New York Review Book, 1990).

Lloyd, G.E., *Demystifying Mentalities* (Cambridge: Cambridge University Press, 1990).

Locke, John, *Political Essays* (ed. Mark Goldie) (Cambridge: Cambridge University Press, 1997).

BIBLIOGRAPHY

Losurdo, Domenico, *Heidegger and the Ideology of War: Community, Death and the West* (New York: Humanity Books, 2001).

Luhmann, Niklas, *Observations on Modernity* (Palo Alto: Stanford University Press, 1998), *Trust and Power* (Chichester: John Wiley, 1979).

Lukacs, John, *Remembered Past: On History, Historians and Historical Knowledge: A Reader* (ed. Mark Malvasi) (New York: ISI Books, 2005).

Lynch, Christopher, Introduction to Machiavelli, *The Art of War* (Chicago: Chicago University Press, 2003).

MacIntyre, Alasdair, *A Short History of Ethics* (London: Routledge, 1998), *After Virtue: A Study of Universal Theory* (London: Duckworth, 2002).

Machiavelli, Niccolo, *The Prince* (Chicago: Chicago University Press, 1998), *The Art of War* (Chicago: Chicago University Press, 2003).

Macpherson, C.B., *The Political Theory of Possessive Individualism* (Oxford: Clarendon Press, 1962).

Mailer, Norman, *The Naked and the Dead* (London: Flamingo, 1992).

Mandel, Robert, *The Meaning of Military Victory* (Boulder: Lynne Rienner, 2006).

Manguel, Alberto, *A Reading Diary* (Edinburgh: Canongate, 2005), *The Library At Night* (New Haven: Yale University Press, 2006), *Homer's The Iliad and The Odyssey: A Biography* (New York: Atlantic Books, 2007).

Marshall-Cornwall, James, *Napoleon* (London: Batsford, 1967).

Marx, Karl, *The German Ideology* (ed. C.J. Arthur) (London: Lawrence & Wishart, 1996).

Marx, Karl, *The Grundrisse: Foundations of the Critique of Political Economy* (trans. Martin Nicolaus) (London: Penguin, 1973).

Maslow, Abraham, *Motivation and Personality* (New York: Harper & Row, 1970).

Mason, Philip, *A Matter of Honour* (London: Jonathan Cape, 1974).

Masters, Alexander, 'Eternal flames', *Times Literary Supplement*, 18 June 2004.

Mazzeo, Josef, *Renaissance and Revolution, the Remaking of European Thought* (London: Methuen, 1967).

McGrath, Alister E., *Dawkins' God: Genes, Memes and the Meaning of Life* (Oxford: Blackwell, 2005).

McNeill, J. and McNeill, William, *The Human Web: A Bird's Eye View of World History* (New York: Norton, 2003).

Mead, Walter Russell, *God and Gold: Britain, America and the Making of the Modern World* (New York: Atlantic, 2007).

Midgley, Mary, *Evolution as a Religion: Strange Hopes and Even Stranger Fears* (London: Routledge, 1985), *Science and Poetry, Heart and Mind* (London: Routledge, 2003), *The Myths We Live By* (London: Routledge, 2004), *Beast and Man: The Root of Human Nature* (London: Routledge, 2006).

Montesquieu, *The Spirit of the Laws* (eds Anne Cohler, Basil Miller, Harold Stone) (Cambridge: Cambridge University Press, 2008).

Moorhead, John, *The Roman Empire Divided* (London: Longman, 2001).

BIBLIOGRAPHY

Morford, Mark, *The Roman Philosophers* (London: Routledge, 2002).
Morrison, Ken, *Marx, Durkheim, Weber* (London: Sage, 1995).
Moskos, Charles (ed.) *The Post-Modern Military: Armed Forces after the Cold War* (Oxford: Oxford University Press, 2000).
Munkler, Herfried, *New Wars* (Cambridge: Polity, 2005).
Murdoch, Iris, *The Fire and the Sun: Why Plato Banished the Poets* (London: Penguin, 1977), *Metaphysics as a Guide to Morals* (London: Penguin, 1992).
Nelis, Jan, 'Modernist Neo-Classicism and Antiquity in the Political Religion of Nazism', *Totalitarian Movements in Political Religions*, 9:4, December 2008.
Nietzsche, Friedrich, *The Gay Science* (ed. Bernard Williams, trans. J. Nauckhoff) (Cambridge: Cambridge University Press, 2001), *On the Genealogy of Morality*, (ed. Keith Ansell-Pearson, trans. C. Diethe) (Cambridge: Cambridge University Press, 1995), 'Homer's Contest' in Kaufmann, William (ed.), *The Portable Nietzsche* (London: Penguin, 1968), *Human, All Too Human* (ed. R.J. Hollingdale) (Cambridge: Cambridge University Press, 1986), *Thus Spoke Zarathustra* (trans. Adrian Del Caro) (Cambridge: Cambridge University Press, 2006), 'What I owe to the Greeks', *Twilight of the Idols* (trans. R.J. Hollingdale) (London: Penguin, 1990).
Nuttall, A.D., *Shakespeare: Thinker* (New Haven: Yale University Press, 2007).
Ober, Joseph, *Democracy and Knowledge: Innovation and Learning in Classical Athens* (Princeton: Princeton University Press, 2008).
O'Donnell, James, *Augustine: A New Biography* (New York: Harper Collins, 2005).
Opel, J.R. 'Vengeance and Civility: a New Look at Early American Statecraft' in *Journal of the Historical Society* 8:1, March 2008.
Origo, Iris, *The Vagabond Path* (London: Chatto & Windus, 1972).
O'Rourke, Patrick, *Peace Kills: America's Fun New Imperialism* (London: Picador, 2005).
Paret, Peter and Moran, Daniel (eds), *Carl von Clausewitz: Two Letters on Strategy* (Ft Leavenworth: US Army Command & General Staff College, 1984).
Parker, Geoffrey, *Empire, War and Faith in Early Modern Europe* (London: Penguin, 2002).
Parkin, Russell (ed.), *Warfighting and Ethics* (Canberra: Land Warfare Studies Centre, 2005).
Patočka, Jan, *Theoretical Essays in the Philosophy of History* (Chicago: Open Court, 1996), *Plato and Europe* (Palo Alto: Stanford University Press, 2002).
Percy, Sarah, *Mercenaries: The History of the Norm in International Relations* (Oxford: Oxford University Press, 2007).
Pick, Daniel, *War Machine: The Rationalisation of Slaughter in the Modern Age* (New Haven: Yale University Press, 1993).

BIBLIOGRAPHY

Pike, Douglas, *PAVN: the People's Army of Vietnam* (Novato, California: Presidio Press, 1986).

Pinker, Steven, *The Blank Slate: The Modern Denial of Human Nature* (London: Allen Lane, 2001), *The Stuff of Thought: Language as a Window into Human Nature* (London: Penguin, 2007).

Plato, *Ion* (trans. Benjamin Jowett) in *Selected Dialogues of Plato* (New York: Modern Library, 2001), *The Republic* (trans. Francis Cornford) (Oxford: Oxford University Press, 1971), *Complete Works* (ed. John M Cooper) (Indianapolis: Hackett Publishing, 1997).

Plutarch, *Essays* (trans. Robin Waterfield) (London: Penguin, 1992).

Popper, Karl, *The Open Society and Its Enemies, Volume I: Plato* (London: Routledge, 1972), *The Open Society and Its Enemies, Volume II: Hegel and Marx* (London: Routledge, 1972), A *World of Propensities* (Bristol: Thoemnes, 1990), *Conjectures and Refutations: The Growth of Scientific Knowledge* (London: Routledge, 2002).

Postman, Neil, *Technopoly: The Surrender of Culture to Technology* (New York: Vintage, 1993).

Raphael, Frederick, *Some Talk of Alexander* (London: Thames and Hudson, 2006).

Rees, John, *The Algebra of Revolution: The Dialectic and the Classical Marxist Tradition* (London: Routledge, 1998).

Ricks, Thomas, *Fiasco: The American Military Adventure in Iraq* (London: Allan Lane, 2006).

Roberts, Adam, *Science Fiction* (London: Routledge, 2000).

Rorty, Richard, *Contingency, Irony and Solidarity* (Cambridge: Cambridge University Press, 1989).

Rosen, Stanley *Plato's Republic: a study* (New Haven: Yale University Press, 2005).

Rousseau, Jean-Jacques, 'State of War, 1755' in Chris Brown, Terry Nardin, Nick Rengger (eds), *International Relations in Political Thought: Texts from the Ancient Greeks to the First World War* (Cambridge: Cambridge University Press, 2002).

Rowland, David, *The Stress of Battle: Quantifying Human Performance in Combat* (London: Stationery Office, 2006).

Sacks, Jonathan, *The Man Who Mistook His Wife For a Hat* (London: Picador, 1985).

Sandler, Stanley, 'The First Casualty: Germ Warfare, Brainwashing and Other Myths About the Korean War', *Times Literary Supplement*, 16 June 2000.

Sandywell, Barry, *The Beginning of European Theorising: Reflexivity and the Archaic Age* (London: Routledge, 1996).

Schopenhauer, *The World as Will and Representation* (New York: Harper & Row, 1968).

Schwartau, W., 'Asymmetrical Adversaries', *Orbis*, 44:2, Spring 2000.

Scruton, Roger, *An Intelligent Person's Guide to Philosophy* (London: Duckworth, 1996).

BIBLIOGRAPHY

Sebald, W.G., *Campo Santo* (London: Hamish Hamilton, 2005).
Sebastian, Tim, 'Russia Fights on the Page as well as on the Front Line', *Evening Standard*, 12 August 2008.
Sennett, Richard, *Respect: The Formation of Character in an Age of Inequality*, (London: Penguin, 2003), *The Corrosion of Character* (New York: Norton, 1998).
Shankman, Steven and Durrant, Stephen, *The Siren and the Sage: Knowledge and Wisdom in Ancient Greece and China* (London: Cassell, 2000).
Shay, Jonathan, *Achilles in Vietnam and the Undoing of Character* (New York: Simon & Schuster, 2004).
Shipley, Graham and Rich, John (eds), *War and Society in the Roman World* (London: Routledge 1993), *War and Society in the Greek World* (London: Routledge, 1993).
Sidebottom, Harry, 'Philosophers' Attitudes to War' in G. Shipley and J. Rich, *War in Society and the Roman World* (London: Routledge, 1993).
Siegfried, Tom, *The Bit and the Pendulum: From Quantum Computing to M Theory*, (New York: John Wiley, 2000).
Skorupski, John, *Why Read Mill Today?* (London: Routledge, 2006).
Slim, Hugo, *Killing Civilians: Method, Madness and Morality in War* (New York: Columbia, 2008).
Snyder, Timothy, 'Dialectic of Death', *Times Literary Supplement*, 15 August 2008.
Sontag, Susan, *At the Same Time: Essays and Speeches* (London: Penguin, 2007).
Sorensen, Roy, *A Brief History of the Paradox: Philosophy and the Labyrinths of the Mind* (Oxford: Oxford University Press, 2005).
Spengler, Oswald, *The Decline of the West* (Oxford: Oxford University Press, 1991).
Steiner, George, *Introduction to Ernst Junger, The Marble Cliffs* (London: Penguin, 1983), *Real Presences* (London: Faber & Faber, 1990), *Grammars of Creation* (London: Faber & Faber, 2001), *My Unwritten Book*, (London, Weidenfeld, 2008).
Stewart, Jon, *The Hegel Myths and Legends* (Evanston: Northwestern University Press, 1996).
Strathern, Unna, *A Brief History of the Future* (London: Constable & Robinson, 2007).
Summers, Harry, *On Strategy: A Critical Analysis of the Vietnam War* (Novato: Presidio, 1995).
Surowiecki, James, *The Wisdom of Crowds* (New York: Anchor, 2005).
Swofford, Tom, *Jarhead: A Marine's Chronicle of the Gulf War* (New York: Scrivener, 2003).
Tacitus, *Histories* (Oxford: Oxford University Press, 1997).
Taylor, Charles, *A Secular Age* (Cambridge: Harvard University Press, 2007).

BIBLIOGRAPHY

Temes, Peter, *The Just War: An American Reflection on the Morality of War* (Chicago: Ivan R. Dee, 2003).

Thucydides, *A History of the Peloponnesian War* (trans. Rex Warner) (London: Penguin, 1972), *On Justice, Power and Human Nature: Selections From the History of the Peloponnesian War* (trans. Paul Woodruff) (Indianapolis: Hackett, 1993).

Tidrick, Kathryn, *Empire and the English National Character* (London: I.B. Tauris, 1990).

Toulmin, Stephen, *Return to Reason* (Cambridge: Harvard University Press, 2001).

Tournier, Michel, *The Wind Spirit* (London: Collins, 1989).

Trittle, Laurence, *From Melos to My Lai: War and Survival* (London: Routledge, 2000).

Trouillot, Michel-Rolph, *Global Transformations: Anthropology and the Modern World* (New York: Palgrave Macmillan, 2003).

Turley, William, *The Second Indo-China War: A Short Political History, 1954–75* (Boulder: Westview Press, 1986).

Twain, Mark, *A Connecticut Yankee in King Arthur's Court* (New York: Norton, 1982).

van Creveld, Martin, *On Future War* (London: Brassey's, 1991), 'War' in Cowley, Robin and Parker, Geoffrey (eds), *Osprey Companion to Military History* (Oxford: Osprey, 1996).

Vattimo, Gianni, *The Transparent Society* (Cambridge: Polity, 2005).

Vernant, Jean-Pierre, *The Origins of Greek Thought* (New York: Cornell University Press, 1982).

Virilio, Paul, *Pure War* (London: Semiotext, 1997).

Voltaire (ed. John Iverson), *Philosophical Dictionary* (New York: Barnes & Noble, 2006).

Walzer, Michael, *Arguing About War* (New Haven: Yale University Press, 2004).

Warren, James, *PreSocratics* (Durham: Acumen, 2007).

Warrington-Ingram, R.P., *Sophocles: Interpretation* (Cambridge: Cambridge University Press, 1980).

Watkins, John, 'A Whiff of Hegel in The Open Society' in Ian Jarvie and Sandra Pralong, *Popper's Open Society after 50 years* (London: Routledge, 1999).

Watson, Adam, *The Modern Mind: An Intellectual History of the 20th Century* (London: HarperCollins Perennial, 2002).

White, Stuart, *Equality* (Cambridge: Polity, 2007).

Whitehead, Kerry, *Merleau-Ponty and the Foundation of Existential Politics* (Princeton, NJ: Princeton University Press, 1988).

Williams, Bernard, *Shame and Necessity* (Berkeley: University of California Press, 1994).

Wilson, Edward O., *Consilience* (New York: Alfred A. Knopf, 1998), *On Human Nature* (Cambridge: Harvard University Press, 2004).

BIBLIOGRAPHY

Windsor, Philip, 'Cultural Dialogue in Human Rights' in Windsor, Philip, *The End of the Century: The Future and the Past* (Tokyo: Kodansha Institute, 1995).

Wittgenstein, Ludwig, *Philosophical Investigations* (Oxford: Blackwell, 1974).

Wong, Leonard, *Why They Fight: Combat Motivation in the Iraq War*, US Army War College, Strategic Studies Institute (Carlisle: July 2002), available on: http://www.carlislearmy.mil/ssi/pubs/whyfight/whyfight.pdf.

Wood, James, *How Fiction Works* (London: Jonathan Cape, 2008).

Wood, Michael, *In the Footsteps of Alexander the Great* (London: BBC Worldwide, 2001).

Woolf, Greg, 'Roman Peace' in Rich, John and Shipley, Graham, *War and Society in the Roman World* (London: Routledge, 1993).

Wright, Robert, *Nonzero: The Logic of Human Destiny* (London: Vintage, 2001).

Young, Julian, *Heidegger's Later Philosophy* (New York: Cambridge University Press, 2001) 359 Barbarous Philosophers—full.doc 359.

INDEX

Aeschylus: *Oresteia*, 16; *Prometheus Bound*, 17
Alcibiades, 72; and Nikias, 64, 69; debate with Thucydides, 73; Sicilian Expedition, 113, 165; Siege of Potidaea, 85; student of Socrates, 65, 85
Alighieri, Dante: view of war, 121
Al-Qaeda: and Iraq, 123
Arendt, Hannah, 59
Aristotle, 40, 58, 68, 113, 157, 189, 245–6, 255; and Heraclitus, 19, 48; and Machiavelli, Niccolo, 139; and Renaissance, 142; and Thucydides, 70; Athenian Lyceum, 107; *Eudemian Ethics*, 114; language of, 53, 107, 112; *Nichomachean Ethics*, 25, 108; navy of, 86; *Poetics*, 48, 72; *The Ethics*, 108; The *Politics*, 28–9, 86–7, 108–9, 113, 115; view of Athens Assembly, 86; view of war, 111, 116, 133
Athens, 69, 71, 79, 255; ambassadors of, 74; and Cicero, 181; and Plato, 79, 165, 197; and Thucydides, 71; assembly of, 72, 86; condemned Socrates to death, 165; conflict with Sparta, 23, 68, 72, 157, 164; democracy of, 114, 163, 197, 255; economic strength of, 114; fall of, 72, 256; Greco-Persian Wars, 199; Lyceum, 107; naval supremacy of, 115; port of Piraeus, 78; Theseus, 65
Augustine, 135, 257; background of, 131–2; *The City of God*, 130, 133, 137; *The Confessions*, 133; view of Roman Empire, 130, 132
Aurelius, Marcus: background of, 120; *Meditations*, 120

Bentham, Jeremy: view of warfare, 29
Bonaparte, Napoleon, 222; defeat of Prussian army (1806), 204; failures of, 164; invasion of Russia (1812), 27, 175; military of, 197; wars of, 7, 160
Bush, George W., 34, 121, 123, 137, 200, 226; administration of, 69, 75, 122–3; Invasion of Iraq (2003), 75

Caractacus: defeat of, 117
China: and Second World War, 7; influence in Vietnam War (1959–75), 178
Christianity, 23, 38, 131–2, 182; and New Zealand, 158; and Roman Empire, 129–30; Bible, 154, 254; internal conflicts of, 157; Old Testament, 51; persecution of, 118
Cicero: *De Officiis*, 180; *On Duties*, 180–1; view of Athens, 181

273

INDEX

Clausewitz, Carl von, 85, 87–8, 159, 171, 188; and Engels, Friedrich, 222; and Invasion of Russia (1812), 27; and Europe, 178; and Montesquieu, Charles de, 174; criticisms of, 14; *On War*, 11–12, 81, 86–7, 101, 122, 222, 227, 229
Cold War, 38–9, 134, 167; and *1984*, 36; and Kissinger, Henry, 36, 166; and USA, 121, 166
Crimean War (1853–56): Nightingale, Florence, 207

Darwin, Charles, 97, 245; Natural Selection, 155; *The Descent of Man*, 20; theories of, 98

Engels, Friedrich, 228; and Marx, Karl, 34, 174; and Clausewitz, Carl von, 222; *Anti–Dühring*, 221, 223; *The German Ideology*, 174, 221; view of technology, 256; view of war, 221, 223, 256
England: Luddites, 33
Enlightenment, 3, 11, 55 174, 205; and Montesquieu, Charles de, 30; and Rousseau, Jean-Jacques, 148; *philosophes*, 8, 173
Epictetus: Stoic, 117
Euripides: *Ion*, 54, 88–9; *Sisyphus*, 16; *Supplicants*, 65
Europe, 4; and Clausewitz, Carl von, 178; and Kant, Immanuel, 26, 157, 184; ruling classes of, 143, 222; wars of, 3, 25, 56, 144, 205, 222

Fascism, 34: Social Darwinism, 34; view of peace, 136
First World War (1914–18), 135, 240, 242; and France, 241; and Germany, 173; and Russia, 166; and UK, 212; Battle of the Somme (1916), 241; Great Powers, 156; outbreak of, 166; Treaty of Versailles, 135; trench warfare of, 239–40; USA entry into (1917), 136
France: and Germany, 183; and First World War (1914–18), 241; and Second World War (1939–45), 202–3; Foreign Legion, 241, 254; *Declaration of the Rights of Man* (1789), 180, 184; Resistance, 202; Revolution (1789–99), 5–6, 184, 198, 214, 256
Freud, Sigmund: *Civilisation and its Discontents*, 110

Geneva Convention, 186
Germany: and First World War (1914–18), 173; and France, 183; and Second World War (1939–45), 164, 173, 186–7, 232; Luftwaffe, 230–1; Nazism, 34, 57, 136, 160, 187, 229–30, 240, 243
Gide, André: and Sartre, Jean-Paul, 33; and USSR, 32–3

Hegel, Georg Wilhelm Friedrich, 55, 85, 162, 195–7, 203; and Heisenberg, Werner, 250; essence of being, 125; influence on Popper, Karl, 197; Owl of Minerva, 91, 199; spirit of, 103; *The Philosophy of Right*, 194, 200; view of war, 13, 193–4, 196, 198, 200–2; writings of, 5, 30
Heidegger, Martin: and Heraclitus, 13, 214; and Patočka, Jan, 59; language of, 213; silence over Nazism, 213; *The Question Concerning Technology*, 216; view of technology, 215, 217–18; view of war, 217
Heisenberg, Werner, 248; and Hegel, Georg Wilhelm Friedrich, 250; and Heraclitus, 251; and

INDEX

Marx, Karl, 250; death of, 257; Gifford Lectures, 246–7; Indeterminacy Principle, 248–9; quantum physics, 249, 251, 253; view of war, 253

Heraclitus, 18, 39–40, 50–1, 54–6, 58, 60, 62, 194, 250, 256, 258; and Aristotle, 19, 48; and Heidegger, Martin, 13; and Heisenberg, Werner, 251;and Hesiod, 52; and Nietzsche, Friedrich, 18; and Plato, 13; and Rousseau, Jean-Jacques, 40; and Socrates, 43, 47–8; background of, 48; exile of, 18; language, 12; view of war, 50, 63

Herodotus, 71; and Thucydides, 58, 67, 163; *Histories*, 15; Battle of Thermopylae, 93; theogony of, 52–3

Hesiod, 16, 31: and Heraclitus, 52; myths, 52–3; poetry of, 44

Hitler, Adolf, 133, 160, 240–1; failures of, 164, 186–7; influenced by Schopenhauer, Arthur, 233

Hobbes, Thomas, 16, 40–1, 153–4, 158, 165, 167, 169, 256; and Kant, Immanuel, 183; *Leviathan*, 154–5, 163; state of nature, 4, 103, 113, 124, 145, 165, 214, 233, 251; translation of *History of the Peloponnesian War*, 66, 164; view of war, 26–8, 156, 161, 168

Homer, 94, 143, 188; criticisms of, 20, 91, 165–6; *The Iliad*, 15, 17, 19, 23, 90–1, 100, 114, 196–7, 209, 258; view of warfare, 79, 96–7; view of underworld, 83; writing style of, 91

Iraq: Abu Ghraib, 191; and Al-Qaeda, 123; Invasion of (2003), 65, 70, 74–5, 126, 137;

Fallujah, 122–4; 'Shock and Awe', 225, 250

Israel: hostility towards 105

Japan; and Second World War, 7, 61, 134, 167, 171; Samurai ethos, 167

Johnson, Lyndon B.: government of, 75

Kant, Immanuel, 28, 40, 44, 61, 91, 105, 183–4, 188–90, 250; and Europe, 26, 157, 184; and Hobbes, Thomas, 183; and Nietzsche, Friedrich, 204; and Rousseau, Jean-Jacques, 182; and Trotsky, Leon, 35; Categorical imperative, 187, 257; death of, 184; 'hidden plan', 55; *Perpetual Peace*, 179, 183; The *Critique of Pure Reason*, 179, 183; The *Metaphysical Element of Justice*, 201

Kissinger, Henry: and Cold War, 36, 166

Korean War (1950–53): Chinese entry into, 74–5

Lenin, Vladimir, 136

Locke, John: *Second Tract on Government*, 33–4

Machiavelli, Niccolo, 40, 149–51, 155, 255; and Aristotle, 139; and Renaissance, 141–3, 148; background of, 140; Medici, 140; *The Discourses*, 24, 146–7; *The Prince*, 25, 139, 143, 145; view of war, 141–5, 147, 254

Marx, Karl, 9, 29 40, 135–6, 177, 207, 222, 248, 255; and Engels, Friedrich, 34, 174; and Heisenberg, Werner, 250; debt to Schopenhauer, Arthur, 215; introduction to *Grundrisse*, 208;

INDEX

The *German Ideology*, 174, 207–8, 210, 221; view of technology, 211, 213–14, 217–18, 256; view of war, 208–10, 254, 256

More, Thomas: *Utopia*, 144

Montesquieu, Charles de, 169, 176; and Clausewitz, Carl von, 174; and de Tocqueville, Alexis, 171; and Enlightenment, 30; and *The Spirit of Laws*, 30, 74, 174; view of war, 173

New Zealand: and Christianity, 158; Maoris, 158

Nietzsche, Friedrich, 7, 12, 16, 31, 131, 163, 234–5, 240, 248, 255; and Heraclitus, 18; and Kant, Immanuel, 204; and Pascal, Blaise, 38; and Thucydides, 66; death of, 234; *Ecce Homo*, 234, 238; Homer's Contest, 14, 17; *Human, All Too Human*, 15; influence of, 233; ostracism, 58; On War and Warriors, 236–7; view of war, 243, 257; The *Birth of Tragedy*, 14; *The Genealogy of Morals*, 18, 61; *Zarathustra*, 107

Nikias, 69; and Alcibiades, 64, 69; and *Laches*, 64; and *History of the Peloponnesian War*, 72; negotiated peace treaty with Sparta, 64

Nixon, Richard M., 166

Odysseus, 83

Orwell, George: *1984*, 35–6, 136–7; and Spanish Civil War (1936–39), 32; *Homage to Catalonia*, 32

Pascal, Blaise, 42, 252; and Nietzsche, Friedrich, 38; and Voltaire, 38; *Pensées*, 38

Patočka, Jan; background of, 58; student of Heidegger, Martin, 59; view of war, 59

Peloponnesian War, 29, 64, 66, 68, 75, 197; challenges of, 78

Pericles: strategy of, 114–15

Plato, 20, 39, 43, 65, 79, 90, 92, 165, 184, 209, 242, 258; and Heraclitus, 13; and Renaissance, 142; and Socrates, 64, 78, 81, 95; and Thucydides, 66, 78; argument with Protagoras, 84; criticisms of Homer, 91, 163; dialogues of, 78, 107; *Ion*, 94; *Laches*, 64, 225; Sophists, 54; The *Laws*, 15, 17, 81, 86, 91; *The Phadeus*, 94; *The Republic*, 24, 31–2, 42, 77–8, 80–2, 84, 90, 94–5, 132, 146, 254–5; view of Athens, 79, 165, 197; view of war, 28, 49, 79, 83, 97, 147, 254

Polybius: fall of Carthage, 74

Popper, Karl, 84, 170–1; *A World of Propensities*, 172; and Hegel, Georg Wilhelm Friedrich, 197; *Conjectures and Refutations*, 18; *The Open Society and its Enemies*, 18, 197

Powell, Colin: and Thucydides, 63; Invasion of Iraq (2003), 65, 70

Protagoras, 90: argument with Plato, 84

Renaissance, 140–2; and Aristotle, 142; and Machiavelli, Niccolo, 141–3, 148; and Plato, 142

Roman Empire, 118; and Christianity, 129–30; armies of, 225; *Pax Romana*, 119, 121; successes of, 122

Roosevelt, Franklin D.: New Deal of, 124

Rousseau, Jean-Jacques, 3–5, 11, 41–2, 244, 258; and Enlightenment, 148; and Kant, Immanuel, 182; criticism of Heraclitus, 40; criticisms of, 15; *Discourse on Inequality*, 5; *Discourse on*

INDEX

Political Economy, 147; *Emile*, 179; views on war, 8–9, 159, 182, 188, 213
Rumsfeld, Donald, 121, 250
Russia, 150, 170, 199; Moscow, 174; and First World War (1914–18), 166; invaded by Bonaparte, Napoleon (1812), 27, 175; military actions of, 175; October Revolution (1917), 160; Tsars of, 175

Sartre, Jean-Paul: *Being and Nothingness*, 203; criticism of Gide, André, 33; *Flies*, 203; image of man, 202; *No Exit*, 203; POW, 202–3
Schopenhauer, Arthur; and Hitler, Adolf, 233; and Marx, Karl, 215
Second World War (1939–45), 7, 18, 61, 94, 212, 237, 243; and China, 7; and France, 202–3; and Germany, 164, 173, 232; and UK, 199, 230; and USSR, 35, 160; blitzkrieg, 225; Easter Front, 240; end of, 126, 134, 246; German losses, 35; Japan, 7, 61, 134, 167, 171, 216, 246; Nuremburg Trials, 135; Operation Barbarossa, 160, 175, 186, 231; outbreak of, 166; Pacific Theatre of, 94, 237; Pearl Harbour Attack, 70; POWs, 186–7
Seneca: Stoic, 121
Seven Years War (1756–63), 6
Shakespeare, William, 96, 113–14; and Trojan War, 111, 114; characters of, 96, 166, 182; *Coriolanus*, 96; *Henry V*, 83, 181–2; language of, 112; *The Life and Death of King John*, 166; *Troilus and Cressida*, 111–12
Socrates, 11, 23, 84, 251; and Heraclitus, 43, 47–8; and *Ion*, 90; and Plato, 64, 78, 81, 95; and *The Laws*, 81; condemned to death by Athens, 165; siege of Potidaea, 85; teacher of Alcibiades, 65, 85
Soviet Union (USSR), 160, 186; and Gide, André, 32–3; and Second World War 91939–45), 160; fall of, (1989) 214; government of, 175; ideology of, 62; Operation Barbarossa, 73, 160, 175; POWs, 186–7; Red Army, 35, 230
Spanish Civil War (1936–39): and Orwell, George, 32
Sparta: and Nikias, 64; and Thucydides, 26, 71; conflict with Athens, 23, 68, 72, 157, 164; defeat at Thermopylae, 20, 93; decline of, 115; failure of, 70, 115–16; military of, 19, 115; navy of, 115
Stoicism, 120; and Epictetus, 117; and Seneca, 121

Tacitus, 127; and Roman Empire, 122; *The Histories*, 30–1, 119; writings of, 117–19
Thucydides, 44, 65, 73, 76, 119, 165, 180; and Aristotle, 70; and Herodotus, 58, 67, 163; and Hobbes, Thomas, 66; and Plato, 66, 78; and Powell, Colin, 63; background of, 63; debate with Alcibiades, 73; depiction of Athens and Sparta, 26, 71; *History of the Peloponnesian War*, 21–4, 26, 29, 63–4, 67, 71–2, 74–5, 114, 164, 197; praised by Nietzsche, Friedrich, 66; opposition to Herodotus, 58; Sicilian Expedition, 113; view of war, 63
de Tocqueville, Alexis: debt to Montesquieu, Jean-Jacques, 171; view of French Revolution (1789–99), 185

277

INDEX

Tolstoy, Leo, 94, 106, 185; *War and Peace*, 188
Trojan War, 29, 209; and Shakespeare, William, 111, 114; *The Illiad*, 114
Trotsky, Leon: criticisms of Kant, Immanuel, 35
Truman, Harry S., 137
Tzu, Sun: *The Art of War*, 141, 143

United Kingdom (UK): and First World War (1914–18), 212; and Second World War (1939–45), 199, 230; Royal Air Force (RAF), 230–1
United Nations (UN), 150
United States of America (USA), 71, 124, 157, 162; 9/11 Attacks, 121, 137, 190, 227; and Cold War, 121, 166; and Vietnam War (1959–75), 123, 166; Civil War of (1861–65), 126, 201, 210; entry into First World War (1917), 136; entry into Second World War, 94; Invasion of Afghanistan (2001), 224; Invasion of Iraq (2003), 65, 70, 74, 126, 137; Joint Chiefs of Staff, 246; military of, 123, 225, 229, 257; warfare of, 35 178; 'War on Terror', 121, 126, 165, 191, 226, 257; West Point Military Academy, 125

Vietnam War (1959–75), 75, 174–5; and USA, 123, 166; Chinese influence of, 178; Easter Offensive (1972), 177, 228–9; end of, 166; influences on films, 96–7; Siege of Khe Sanh (1967), 176; Tet Offensive (1968), 225; Viet Minh, 228
Voltaire: and Pascal, Blaise, 38; criticisms of Rousseau, Jean-Jacques, 5; *Philosophical Dictionary* (1764), 5–6

Weber, Max: view on warfare, 13, 227
Wilson, Woodrow, 35, 137; view of war, 136

Zizek, Slovoj, 47; military-poetic complex, 100